Tickling the English

FUDGETASTIC

The Sorcerer

Jersey Gilbert & Sullivan Society

Sat 24 May 2008 8.00pm

£16.00

History of
ORT REGENT

1 8 0 6

Naked in Hotel
Team down Team

munity

de la war
pavilion

Café Bar & Restaurant

Monday 3rd November
Dara o' Briain

To Start

Houses with no curtains

For Mains

Tickling the English

DARA O BRIAIN

MICHAEL JOSEPH
an imprint of
PENGUIN BOOKS

MICHAEL JOSEPH

Published by the Penguin Group
Penguin Books Ltd, 80 Strand, London WC2R ORL, England
Penguin Group (USA) Inc., 375 Hudson Street, New York, New York 10014, USA
Penguin Group (Canada), 90 Eglinton Avenue East, Suite 700, Toronto, Ontario, Canada M4P 2Y3
(a division of Pearson Penguin Canada Inc.)
Penguin Ireland, 25 St Stephen's Green, Dublin 2, Ireland (a division of Penguin Books Ltd)
Penguin Group (Australia), 250 Camberwell Road,Camberwell, Victoria 3124, Australia
(a division of Pearson Australia Group Pty Ltd)
Penguin Books India Pvt Ltd, 11 Community Centre, Panchsheel Park, New Delhi – 110 017, India
Penguin Group (NZ), 67 Apollo Drive, Rosedale, North Shore 0632, New Zealand
(a division of Pearson New Zealand Ltd)
Penguin Books (South Africa) (Pty) Ltd, 24 Sturdee Avenue, Rosebank, Johannesburg 2196, South Africa

Penguin Books Ltd, Registered Offices: 80 Strand, London WC2R ORL, England

www.penguin.com

First published 2009
1

Quotes reproduced from: *A Natural Curiosity* (copyright © Margaret Drabble, 1989) by permission
of United Agents (*www.unitedagents.co.uk*) on behalf of Dame Margaret Drabble; *The Geography of Bliss* by
Eric Weiner, published by Black Swan and reprinted by permission of the Random House Group Ltd;
The Architecture of Happiness, published by Penguin Books (copyright © Alain de Botton, 2006), by
permission of United Agents; and *Empire* (copyright © Niall Ferguson, 2008).

Every effort has been made to trace copyright holders and to obtain their permission for the
use of copyright material. The publisher apologizes for any errors or omissions and would be grateful
to be notified of any corrections that should be incorporated in future editions of this book.

Set in 13.5/16 pt Monotype Garamond
Typeset by Rowland Phototypesetting Ltd, Bury St Edmunds, Suffolk
Printed in Great Britain by Clays Ltd, St Ives plc

A CIP catalogue record for this book is available from the British Library

ISBN: 978-0-718-15437-0

www.greenpenguin.co.uk

This book is dedicated to all the letters of the alphabet, but in particular, to big S and little o.

Chapter 1:
What's Up with This Place?

It was about one in the morning. I was in the passenger seat of a rented car on the M4. The car was being driven by a man called Damon. We were heading back to London after I'd done a gig at a theatre called the Playhouse in Weston-super-Mare.

The night had been a huge success, thanks mainly to the audience, who were chatty and interactive. In particular, there was a man called Chris who had an answer for everything.

He told us how his appendix 'went away'. He told us about the game he plays with his step-son where he lays a hammock on the ground and attaches one end of it to his car, the other to a tree. Then he accelerates away, tautening up the hammock and firing his step-son into the air.

And when we thought we had heard all we could from Chris, he told us that he had been on the game-show *3-2-1* in the seventies, won a cruise, brought his family but that his daughter had contracted a form of TB which had been eradicated in the US for many years so they had to spend the entire cruise in the cabin.

All in all, it was a very funny night.

So, we're driving home contentedly and one of us decides to put on the radio. It was late, so the phone-ins were in full flow on every station and the one we settled on was getting heated.

The topic was a new international survey that placed England in the top ten countries to live in, worldwide. In Ireland, I remembered these surveys appearing intermittently, and a good result was always regarded as a bit of a pat on the back.

'Next on the line is Susan from Dorking. What do you want to add, Susan?' asks Dave, the host of the radio phone-in.

'Well, David, I just want to say that this is clearly a joke. I mean, look around you. Look around you. This country is going to the dogs.'

'What do you mean, Susan?' says Dave, deftly drawing Susan out.

'Well, the schools. And the crime. And the NHS. It's all going to the dogs.'

'Let's move on,' says Dave, moving on. 'Next up is Mike from Kettering. Mike, what do you think of this, then? One of the best places in the world to live?'

'I think they must be thinking of somewhere else, Dave. They clearly haven't walked around the England I know. Kids are running rampage, twenty-four-hour drinking, teenage mums. It's a bloody mess, Dave. A bloody mess.'

Dave took the next call.

'It's Kevin from Gloucester. What do you think, Kevin, are we living in one of the top ten countries in the world?'

'They're having a bloody laugh, Dave, that's what I think. A bloody laugh.'

And so the callers continued. Voice after voice decried the survey as inaccurate, misleading and poorly researched; England was a terrible country to live in. The evidence was insurmountable: failing institutions, rising crime, disastrous public-building projects. Citizens were depressed and angry and in constant danger. If the knife crime didn't get you, the MRSA would.

Not one of the callers could say that they had lived in any other country, but all of them could say, hand on heart, that England didn't deserve to be in any top ten. The place was a mess.

Now, obviously, it's a little dubious to base a snapshot of the nation on the sort of people who phone in to radio stations late at night. Until that moment, though, I would have based it on the people I had just spent two hours laughing with in a theatre in Weston-super-Mare.

In just one evening, I'd encountered a people who were clearly good-humoured, charming and spontaneous, but also, it appeared, terribly, terribly brave, given the appalling conditions they find themselves living in. And they handled this bravery in a stoic way, only under the most intense pressure resorting to phoning in to radio stations to counter any reasonable assertion that things aren't really that bad here.

How could the people of England be so happy while, at the same time, reserving the right to be so desperately unhappy?

Next time I tour this country, I said to myself, I'm going to try and find out what's up with that.

So that's what I did.

Chapter 2:
The Show

I always thought there was something funny about England.

When I was a child in Ireland, we would watch *That's Life!* on the BBC on a Sunday night, and see the locals roar with laughter at funny-shaped vegetables or dogs that said the word 'sausages'. I'll be honest: we laughed too.

And then Esther Rantzen's tone would darken, and the show would suddenly become very serious. Without warning, we would be plunged into the miserable lives of children growing up in damp public housing, or watching parents who filled their children's bottles with fruit juice and rotted their teeth, shamed or, the one I'll always remember, hearing the heart-wrenching story of an elderly couple duped out of their life savings by a travelling con-man.

On that particular occasion, Esther's chorus read out the testimony of the old couple and the authorities, and we all shook our heads at the cowardly nature of the crime. Then Esther showed us a photo-fit of the con-man.

'Maybe you've seen him,' she said, staring straight down the lens. 'Maybe he approached you, maybe you saw him at a petrol station, a pub or a restaurant. Look around you. Maybe he's sitting in the room with you right now.'

I looked around me. The only people in the room were my parents and my sister. I tried to imagine any chain of events that would lead to a complete stranger being wedged on to the couch with us. And, furthermore, what would cause us to decide to sit down, a family and this stray we'd taken in, to watch *That's Life!*.

Was this how people lived in England? Did random people often drop by on a Sunday night to watch your telly? Did you all live communally? Were there only a few televisions?

It made England seem like the most foreign place imaginable, a place where groups of strangers clustered together round the flickering light, like the survivors in a disaster movie. Even as they watched, in one of these huddled communities, a con-man was looking at his own face, drawn in pencil from a pensioner's description, and he was doing a long, fake yawn, going 'Is that the time?' and getting ready to run. England was strange.

Of course, a healthy strangeness isn't a bad thing if you want to be a world centre for comedy.

There are three places in the English-speaking world where stand-ups gather. They are Los Angeles, New York and London. Two of those are filled predominantly with US comedians. The third is the only one to have funny people from all over the world living there: Irish, Canadians, Scots, Americans, New Zealanders, a couple of Germans and the odd Dutch guy, along with hundreds of English comics.

There are a number of reasons why England is a great country to be a comic. There are comedy clubs in every town in the country. They are very popular with the locals. This means that there is a living to be made for all these comedians, playing the clubs, learning the trade and travelling from town to town. This is in contrast to New York, where the fee for a gig has been $60 for about twenty years. American comics gamble on a terrible poverty-filled few years, in the hope that when telly or movie success arrives the rewards will be huge. The American comedy world is filled with stories of household names who used to sleep in their cars, waiting for their big break.

This also means that American stand-ups, particularly in LA, tend to create perfectly crafted short sets, in order to attract the attention of casting directors. Ten-minute slots are the norm, and a lot of US comics hone their act until it's the perfect calling card for a cameo sit-com role or, even better, the six-minute slot on one of the late-night chat shows.

Most Irish comics haven't even said hello after ten minutes. In fact, on this side of the Atlantic, comedians are trained by years of doing the Edinburgh Festival into writing longer shows – at least an hour – and then eventually taking those shows on tour and performing in front of enthusiastic crowds, for sixty, eighty, even a hundred-plus nights throughout the year.

The opportunity to do long tours like these are what makes it great to be a stand-up in England and, if you're looking for someone to thank for this, turn to the Victorians.

The Victorians invented leisure.

It was probably the inevitable by-product of the industrial revolution and the invention of mass transit, and could very well have happened elsewhere, but that doesn't make it any less impressive that many Victorian innovations and entertainments still form the leisure market as we know it today. The Victorians invented everything except waterparks and Quasar.

For a start, they came up with the idea of holidays. Before the nineteenth century, holiday trips of any kind were generally for rich people, who would go on a grand tour around Europe or take trips to spas such as Bath or sea-water resorts such as Brighton. In the nineteenth century, improved transport meant that, when they had time off, day trips for the working classes and longer holidays for the emerging middle classes became possible. It was an opportunity that was eagerly taken up. Within a fortnight of the opening of Britain's first public railway, between Liverpool and Manchester, in 1830, the line was used by a group of daytrippers.

We'll get to the Victorian's zeal for inventing modern sport a little later, but the revolution that led to codifying football, rugby, horse-racing and all the rest wasn't just about the players but also about the way ordinary people enjoyed sports as spectators. Before the second half of the nineteenth century, the common people expected to attend the mass sporting events they went to for free. From the 1870s onwards, enclosed racecourses and football grounds began to charge for admission. Watching sports became a consumer activity.

And so to theatres.

It's estimated that there were around ten theatres operating in London in 1800, but around a hundred and fifty were up and running just a century later. Theatres sprang up across the country in the rapidly growing towns, where previously there had been only a few dozen theatres outside the capital. By 1892, England had more than four hundred substantial theatres and music halls, as well as close to a thousand other venues, such as pleasure gardens, assembly halls and galleries, which staged entertainment.

Theatres increased their capacity by making the halls larger, and the major theatrical spectacles and pantomimes often used hundreds of extras. Animal wranglers were also needed, as the Victorians liked to pepper their entertainment with onstage cavalry charges with real horses, or lions stalking across the stage.

Of course, try to get a real lion into your show these days and you'll have Health and Safety on your back, quicker than you can say Siegfried and Roy. Plus, they'll poo all over the tour car.

In tandem with the great theatrical productions of the nineteenth century was the music-hall scene, which grew up in the first half of the century from semi-organized sing-songs in bars and gin palaces. By the second half of the century, almost every Victorian town of any size had some form of music hall, some of them seating several thousand.

Even if the scale has changed, this is the infrastructure that remains to this day. Every town in the UK has at least one theatre and, not uncommonly, it'll be an architectural beauty that dates all the way to this golden age. This is where we comedians do our tours and, ultimately, this is why England is such a great country for us.

Enjoying the history lesson?

If you already knew all of the above, I apologize. I have no idea what history is taught in English schools. I know that in Irish schools relatively little English history is taught, other than that which directly impinged on us. (And, boy, did you ever impinge . . .)

There are, therefore, vast tracts of English history which we in Ireland don't know anything about, stuff like which Houses your kings were from; your wars against the French, or Spanish, or Dutch; or Cromwell's well-hidden charming side.

All news to us Irish.

So, while we're all learning here, I'll tell you something you might not have known. Big comedy tours don't start in Victorian music halls, or modern arts centres. They start in small rooms at the back of anonymous pubs scattered around London. These are the preview gigs where a new show takes its first steps and, while there may be only sixty people in attendance, these venues are more petrifying than most of the thousand-seaters. At least by the time you do the thousand-seaters, you know the stuff works.

With the first preview dates looming, I start preparing my routine. I'm not sure how other comedians write jokes, but this is what works for me. I sit in a room at night, chained to a desk, with a bottle of wine. I have scraps of paper in front of me covered in scribbles. I'm banging down anything that even vaguely resembles a joke, or the opportunity for a joke, or a joke's first cousin. I stare at these and think how desperately unfunny they all are.

Two glasses into the wine, I am now buzzing sufficiently to forget myself and how self-conscious and contrived this whole process is. I talk to myself, and the ideas flesh out into little rants and associations. This is where the funny starts to happen. It happens when I'm not thinking about it and just making silly stuff up and chatting away to myself while banging a few funny things together. This will lead to a couple of half-jokes, maybe more.

After the fourth glass, I'm too drunk. I just sit there, happily remembering how funny I used to be, back there about two glasses ago. Then I stumble off to bed.

At night I have that dream of arriving late and unprepared for an exam. It's been fifteen years since my last academic test and, still, before each tour, with the opening night looming and the show not yet written, my subconscious pulls that feeling of panic out of a drawer, dusts it off and spools it through to remind me that the clock is ticking and that the job isn't done.

To finish the joke, you have to try it out. A joke doesn't exist until it's been said in front of a crowd. This is true no matter how famous you are, or how good your comedy nose is. You just don't know if something is funny until you hear yourself trying to sell it to a crowd. This is a vital part of the writing process because, surprisingly often, it's not good enough. And as you're saying it, a voice in your head goes, 'What the fuck were you thinking? This isn't even remotely amusing!', and a completely separate part of your brain, which had lain dormant until this moment of near-humiliation, kicks in with a twist that suddenly makes it funny and saves your hide.

Half an idea and the panic of dying: that's how you write stand-up.

The back room of The Fighting Cocks, Kingston

An audience of young and friendly regulars.

This is how I'll describe the shows throughout the book. I'll give you the venue and who I spoke to. This particular night isn't a good example, though, since I didn't talk to anyone in particular. I just read out a load of ideas scribbled on sheets of A4. The crowd don't mind; they've seen this before.

Only a few minutes earlier, in fact, when Omid Djalili was on, trying out his new material.

And just before that, when Al Murray was doing the same thing.

They don't know this yet, but in a few weeks' time they'll only just be recovering from an unexpected visit by Lenny Henry, when who should drop in but Robin Williams. The Fighting Cocks gets a lot of senior comics trying out stuff.

I'm not sure why this room gets such attention. It may be the friendly crowd, but equally it might be that the griminess of the venue (it's a serious heavy-metal bar normally) just makes the older comic feel in touch with his edgy youth. There's no showbiz polish here. The comics stand in a corridor waiting to get on. The room is only big enough to hold sixty, and you have to clamber over the first three rows to reach the stage. The lighting is rudimentary and the entire place is tropically hot. The walls are covered in self-promotional graffiti for bands with names like Tethered Fuck! and the Luger Ballerinas.

On one of the cubicles in the gents somebody has written a message in permanent marker that is both harsh and unbelievably poignant. It just says, 'Fuck you, Sophia M. You'll never find a better match.'

Oh Sophia, what were you doing? He was clearly ready to commit.

Although, he doesn't think that highly of you, if he expects you to be standing in a cubicle in the gents facing the cistern at some stage. What can you possibly be doing in that position? Still, I don't blame you. The lead singer of the Luger Ballerinas is worth the ride.

In this room, and others like it, across London, I try out my new routines for the first time.

So, what was written on those sheets of A4? Very few stand-alone jokes, for a start. My stand-up shows are usually a mixture of long stories and some audience reaction. There's only the odd one-liner. In fact, for this first preview gig, I only had one 'proper' joke: 'What happens if you pour Dettol into a Yakult?'

By the end of the writing process, that joke had become the centrepiece of a rant about scare tactics in advertising. By the end of the tour, it led to a long routine about the perils of alternative therapies and psychics. It went on quite a journey, that little Yakult gag. None of which was obvious when I read it out that first night in Kingston.

Other ideas in these first preview shows included a story about meeting a naked man in a hotel in Newcastle that needed a crisper ending than real life had provided; an observation about video-game characters which I tried a couple of times before ditching as a bad job; and a story about Tayto crisps.

The Tayto crisps story was one that always did brilliantly in Ireland, but I was worried that, to an English crowd, it might take too much explaining. Nevertheless, it had always worked at home, and funny is funny, so the Tayto story was in.

The rest of that first preview consisted of trying to get my audience-participation skills honed again. In between tours, that quickness off the cuff is the first thing to get rusty and I, more than most comedians, need to get 'match fit' before a tour.

I'm quite an improvisational comic. A lot of comics like just to perform their routines, but I see the audience as a massive untapped source of great comedy ideas. Otherwise the show is just me onstage reciting words in the same order each night and, with respect to the actors of the world, how dull would that get? If you really use an audience you can create a unique evening's entertainment which they know won't be replicated on any other night of the tour. I even toyed with the idea of calling the entire tour 'You had to be there', in honour of those moments that an audience simply wouldn't be able to explain afterwards.

Besides, with the right questions, an audience can supply you with stuff you could never have dreamed of yourself. For example, a few years ago, I had a joke about how you could use koala bears as a bicycle lock. They would naturally latch around the wheel, frame and a nearby lamp-post, fall asleep, and stay there for up to twenty-three hours. It worked perfectly well as a gag, and then I decided to hold back the punchline and instead let people guess what it was. So I'd ask, 'What jobs do koalas commonly do?' There then followed an insane guessing game during which the audience had koalas running brothels (valued for their discretion), hanging coats, and attaching themselves as ankle bracelets on high-risk prisoners.

The greatest of all was an Irish student who shouted out, 'Guides for the Blind.'

'Surely dogs can do that?' I said.

She shook her head slowly. 'Not for walking,' she explained. 'For climbing . . .'

Presumably, the dog walks the blind person to the foot of the tree, where control is handed over to the koala, who guides the blind person to the top of the tree, past clumps of branches and whatnot, until they get to the top, whereupon the koala describes the view.

I would never have thought of that myself.

For this new show, there were various points where I could step away from the script and see what the crowd had to offer. In a section about viewing a house, for example, I could get them to offer their own answers to the question 'What do you NOT want to have happened in a house

before you move in?' That always led to a barrage of suggestions about the plague, Indian graveyards and, for the
two weeks that he was topical, Josef Fritzl.

Similarly, I had some stories about crime that I wanted to
tell, so I gambled on opening that to the floor in the hope
that I could get a funny story out of some have-a-go hero
in the audience. If I threw out the question 'Has anyone
here ever interrupted a crime?' it might lead to gold. Time
would tell.

As I tried these out, I was reminded of an older
audience-reaction routine I used to do. It was a routine that,
given the nature of my current mission, shed a very interesting light on the English. I intended to use these months on
the tour to examine England's national identity. But I had no
jokes about England's national identity. There was a time in
my career, particularly when I was working the clubs, when I
had jokes about Irish national identity, or Australian, or
American, or most whatever nationality I would find sitting
in front of me. They are a useful tool when you emcee a
difficult, drunken Friday night, say, and if you're stuck you
can just bang out a gag about the German guy in the room.

Eventually, this began to get really formulaic and dull.
The jokes always traded on a sort of received wisdom.
They're a comedy staple, but they always reduce down to
clumsy stereotypes. I got so bored of them that I eventually
wrote an entire routine where I would get the crowd themselves to shout out national traits for me.

'The French are . . .' I'd say.

'Smelly!' one half of the room would shout. 'Arrogant!'
the other would shout.

'Americans are . . .'

'Stupid!' 'Loud!'

More interestingly, sometimes I'd go, 'The Dutch are . . .'

'Stoned!' would come back quickly, and then there would be a pause until, inevitably, somebody would shout out, 'Tall!'

Then I would play the national traits game.

This was a routine where, to enormous satirical effect, I entirely demolished the notion of prejudice, by simply getting audience members to pick two personality traits off the top of their heads, then we attached them to an obscure, far-away country, also chosen at random. Then I acted out the result in a hammy way. And finally we all went home and vowed never to hate again, or something.

This was how I learned, in Weston-super-Mare (when we could get a word in edgeways past Chris), that the Uzbekistani are Rich and Gormless and the Azerbaijanis are Crazy and Bouncy.

Other, random, highlights from that particular tour included:

The Bhutanese are Impatient and Argumentative (Swansea)

The people of Albania are Well-hung and Romantic (Grimsby)

The Patagonians are Glamorous and Aloof (Northampton)

Micronesians are Fractious (Salisbury)

The Bhutanese are Happy and Unwashed (Birmingham)

Peruvians are Greasy and Cantankerous (Grimsby)

The People of Equatorial Guinea are Delightful (Dublin)

And my personal favourite, from Aberystwyth:

The people of Fiji are Well-read and Promiscuous

Well, sometimes I was making a satirical point. Sometimes I was just bouncing round the stage pretending to be an Azerbaijani.

The quickest way to halt an audience in their tracks completely, though, was to shout, 'The English are . . .' and then wait for an answer. There was never a clear response.

And the funny thing is, even as a comic in the clubs, I didn't have an easy gag about the English either. There were entire continents I could narrow down to a lame stereotype (Americans, eh? They're sooo fat!), but I could never pin down the English.

Maybe you just don't have a national identity. Maybe you just don't want to admit to one. We'll see.

After a couple of months, the previews were done, the wine was drunk and all the scribbled sheets of A4 had either made the cut or been binned. I had a set list for a two-hour show. It read:

Pregnancy test/Yakult
Science
Nutrition/Gym

Interval

Naked man
Turn down team
Community/Buying a house
Crime
G-string, Brazilian
Tayto

Goodnight and go home

So let's get out on the road. Let us take the first step away from the preview nights, and into the gilded world of a proper, grown-up, large-scale tour. Let us go ... to Coventry!

Chapter 3:
Opening Weekend

This is a very poor start. I'm supposed to be easing my way into the tour, giving myself plenty of time at each of the first few venues in order to sort out sound and lighting issues for the next few months and to invest all my energy into getting the show right.

Unfortunately, I missed the train to Coventry and now I'm spending £180 on a taxi with curtains on the windows driven by a nineteen-year-old from Pakistan in a desperate race to get to the Midlands by eight o'clock.

This was not entirely my fault. I arrived at Euston station

in good time, only to find that a derailment of a goods train had shut down the entire Midlands network.

I am not going to start attacking the English rail system, by the way; it may be a national sport here, but it's a pleasure denied to me because of how bad the Irish rail system is by comparison.

For example, if you want to travel between Manchester and Birmingham, the country's second and third largest cities, there are three trains an hour, two of them direct. If you want to make the same journey between Cork and Galway, cities of the same relative status in Ireland, you take a bus for four hours. The only way to do this by train is to make a giant 'V'; you take the train to Dublin, on the other side of the country, get off in the capital and take a train back to the other coast again.

You actually have a superb train system here, with regular connections between practically all points on the map. I should know, having spent years carting my sorry arse from one end of the network to the other. Unfortunately, the myth of how terrible the trains are here has become so endemic, and so pleasing, that even as I write these last few paragraphs, I can see you all putting your fingers in your ears and going, 'La la la la, I'm not listening, I'm not listening.'

Obviously, this is because of the magical trains they have in continental Europe, which glide silently and punctually from town to town while, at the front of the Virgin Pendolino service to Stockport, a dray-horse wheezes and heaves.

I have sat on the Eurostar when they make the announcement in Kent that the train is now travelling at 186 mph; and the English people roll their eyes as if to say, 'Well, he would say that, wouldn't he?'

Anyway, I hold no grudge against Virgin trains for my delay that day. It was really my fault for letting Damon drive on without me. Damon will be my constant companion for the year. He's my tour manager, a job description that includes everything from driver to theatre liaison to nanny, there to protect me from making stupid decisions. Like today, for example, when I should have been driven to Coventry in good time rather than attending an Arsenal–Everton match. Not a particularly great Arsenal–Everton match either, and I didn't even see the last-minute equalizer because the remaining vestiges of my professionalism made me leave early, so as not to risk missing the train. I mulled over the irony of this for three hours in the back of the generously upholstered taxi *en route* to Coventry.

Some things to bear in mind the next time you make a £180 taxi trip:

A: Carry cash. They like the money upfront.
B: Don't use up all your small talk early. Particularly if you don't have much in common with the driver.

> *'Have you ever done a trip as long as this one?'*
> *'Once, to Manchester.'*
> *'Did you come straight back?'*
> *'No, actually. I spent the night with my family.'*
> *'Nice! Will you do the same tonight?'*
> *'I don't have any family in Coventry.'*
> *'Oh.'*

Everyone should know someone in Coventry. After all, it invented the concept of 'twinned cities', establishing the first such link with Stalingrad in 1944 as a mark of mutual respect between two cities that had suffered particularly badly during the war.

Similarly, they twinned later with Dresden, unified by the horrendous bombing which both cities endured. Then they twinned with Cork, because of the high number of Irish immigrants, then they twinned with Kingston in Jamaica for a similar reason. Currently, Coventry is twinned with twenty-six separate cities worldwide although, according to Coventry City Council, 'For some years, the City Council has had a policy of not adding to the number of the city's twin towns.' Oh really? Too late now, you sluts.

Coventry is also the location of the worst afternoon I ever spent on the British comedy circuit. It was about a decade ago, it was a Sunday afternoon and, on a Sunday afternoon, Coventry is closed. Myself and another comic, Barry Castognola, had arrived over from Stoke, or Manchester, or wherever we had been gigging the night before, hoping to kill the afternoon in the town centre before the gig that night. I cannot tell you how resistant Coventry was to that idea. For a start, it seemed that the entire city centre was contained within the world's tiniest ring road. And that city was just a small oasis of concrete and closed businesses. We parked, looked in vain for anything to do, returned to the ring road, tried the next exit, failed again. It got so dull we just drove round and round the ring road picking exits at random and seeing if there was any life there. All the time, in my head, the Specials were singing 'Ghost Town'.

To anyone looking to have a career in showbiz, these are the afternoons that will test you. How much do you want it? Really? Go round the Coventry internal ring road one more time and then tell me you want it.

Tour gigs don't take place in the city centre, though. They take place on the leafy and peaceful campus of the University of Warwick, which was enjoying the spring sunshine of a mild March evening when I arrived at 7.50 p.m., racing from the plush, velveteen confines of my taxi to the back-stage area and threw on my suit for the show. Ten minutes later the tour was underway.

Warwick Arts Centre

  1 CNC setter
  1 electronic engineer
  1 quantity surveyor

There were crisps on the stage, random packets of Cheese and Onion, that had been left there by audience members as a nod to my last visit here. That time, there had been a Walkers sales rep in the crowd and I had spent the first half insisting he source some of his goodies during the interval. By the time I had come back after the break there were a half-dozen packs already there, and more arrived as I con-tinued the show. It seemed that, by the end of the gig, like a snack-food version of the loaves and the fishes, the entire front row was gorging on salty treats. I love an audience that remembers a one-off joke, but it always makes me worry what they'll remember the next time.

It won't be the CNC setter, that's for sure. It was only thanks to further questioning that I found out this stood for 'Computer Numerical Control'. Big pause from me. 'Y'know . . . for car parts,' the guy explained. 'You work in a car park?' I asked.

Of course, Coventry was, historically, one of the great car-producing areas, so I should have boned up on my manufacturing-process terminology before gigging there.

'CNC' was just the tip of a very technical iceberg, though. Every time I reached into the crowd, it was another grey job that left me scratching my head. What with my own rustiness and a new show that wasn't quite clicking yet, this was fast becoming an underwhelming start to the tour. Still to come, though, was the crime section and a first direct plea to the audience:

'Has anyone here ever interrupted a crime?'

Some shuffling of feet. One hand goes up in row two.

'Hello, sir. What was the crime?'

'A man was stealing my wife's car.'

'My God. Where were you when this happened?'

'I was coming home when I saw him in the drive trying to steal the car.'

'So, what did you do?'

'I started roaring and shouting. And the thief climbed into the car and locked the doors.'

We all mulled over the possibilities of this bizarre stand-off for a while: him outside, bellowing; the thief inside, pondering his options.

'What happened then?'

'Well, I punched in the window of the car, pulled him out, dragged him into the house and tied him to a chair.'

None of us was expecting that. I'll bet the thief wasn't either. We'd gone from a funny stand-off to a *Reservoir Dogs*-type hostage situation. Sensing that this might get a little visceral for some people's tastes, I leaned into the man.

'Y'know, this is a comedy show. So, if you could, like, keep it light, that would be great. Did anything ... funny ... happen during this time?'

'Oh yes!' he said, with an open-palmed gesture that seemed to say, 'Here's the funny bit, wait till you get a load of this!' He suddenly looked like he was on *Parkinson*. I relaxed.

'I asked my wife to fetch me a meat cleaver and she came back . . . with a carving knife!'

This he delivered with a shake of his head, as if to say, 'Ohh, my dozy wife, eh! She can get nothing right!'

It was very funny but really strange and slightly scary. I found myself furiously trying to make light of it, miming him carving away at this guy's ear while quibbling with his missus, 'Look, am I cleaving? Does this look like cleaving to you? No. I am carving. Now do you see the difference?'

I went on to ask for crime stories 103 times on that tour, and nothing topped that first night. I was still telling that story the following November. I am deeply grateful to the man in row two for sharing it. But if I go out onstage in Warwick on the next tour, and the stage is littered with carving knives, I'm calling off the show.

Cambridge Corn Exchange

1 teenage boy doling out Maltesers to his friends, at his own pace

1 salesman for a 'natural' drinks company:

> *Me: Are they completely natural?*
>
> *Him: A hundred per cent.*
>
> *Me: But they're carbonated. How can that occur naturally? Have you found the world's first fizzy-water spring?*
>
> *Him: Well . . .*

1 photographer

1 member of the venue's box-office staff:

> *Me: I'm not making a penny off you, am I?*

After a much more relaxed drive the following day, myself and Damon arrived early in Cambridge, and it is a very pleasant place to kill an afternoon – or four years, I suppose. The few hours I was there I tried to join Footlights to see if it would help my career but I was, sadly, ineligible. The ubiquity of Cambridge graduates in comedy always seemed a bit of a cliché to me; it certainly doesn't apply in the stand-up comedy clubs and carries no weight on the Edinburgh Fringe, where the Footlights show doesn't get a higher billing than the Durham Medical Students' Revue, for example; which would be no billing at all.

Then again, there was a rehearsal of *Mock the Week* once where I got all the Cambridge/Footlights graduates on the panel to raise their hands, and only myself and Frankie Boyle were left out, scowling and Celtic. Similarly, Rory MacGrath and Griff Rhys Jones, the other two on our *Three Men in a Boat* adventures, are also alumni. My presence in this world is hardly an indication of the barriers coming down either, since I'm there as an ethnic, and therefore don't count.

That said, there is one academic lesson to be learned, and that is the difference between correlation and cause. The fact that there are so many people from Cambridge working in telly isn't necessarily a sign of conspiracy; it's just the natural result of streamlining children from the age of three and having them pushed towards a small collection of universities. I'll probably mention your crazy education system later, so I'll leave it for now; just to say, if you *are* going to have an iniquitous and elitist educational system, well done you for making it sooo pretty!

Cambridge is a treat to walk around, all lovely, stone *aulae maximae* and long-scarved cyclists whizzing past. It's like the

futuristic theme park Westworld, but instead of robots playing gunfighters or Roman gladiators, they play professors of
medieval history.

Oxford is exactly the same of course, which I love saying
because it's bound to drive some pedant insane. 'How dare
you!' they'll write. 'Our river bends to the left. Our charter is
sixty years older. It's completely different.' No, wait, Oxford
is different. They have a house there with a shark sticking
out of the roof. Oxford wins.

Oxford also wins because of its theatre, which is gilt-
edged and proper, unlike Cambridge's, which is modern and
converted and was originally used for the exchange of corn.

Plus, the last time I visited Oxford, I had a man in the
front row who described himself as a food scientist. When
I asked him if there was anything even slightly interesting
about this, he paused, smiled and then said, 'Well ... I did
invent the Solero.'

The roof came off the place.

'What?' said I, as the applause died down. 'The entire
brand?'

'No, no, no. Just the tropical flavour.'

'That's really impressive. Did you do that all yourself?'

'Well, no. But I led the team.'

Let me put that phrase in context for you: 'I led the team.'
Edmund Hillary led a team. Ernest Shackleton led a team.
Wolverine leads a team. But none of them, for all their
strengths, developed the Tropical Solero.

Throughout this chat, this man's wife was sat beside him,
arms crossed and eyes to the heavens with a look that
seemed to say, '... And here we go again with the fucking
Solero story.'

Nothing was as neatly hilarious as that on my visit to

Cambridge although, notably, a young man did approach me in a bar after the show and asked for a hug. There was no good reason not to hug him, so I did, to the delight of his friends. When he unclasped, he looked up at me with genuine delight in his face, and said, 'Thank you. I've waited a long time for this.' Then he and his friends left, and I turned to Damon with a bemused look. He just shrugged and ordered another couple of pints.

Preston Guild Hall

1 probation officer
1 young man with his arm in a cast
1 greengrocer from Blackpool:
   'What?! There are people in Blackpool who eat fruit? I
   presumed it was an entirely candyfloss-and-chips-based economy.
   Who goes to Blackpool to eat vegetables?'
1 man who trains insurance people

Preston doesn't get quite the same amount of fawning coverage as Cambridge, but it does have a Corn Exchange as well, although it's a bar now, rather than a theatre, and more famous anyway for the four striking cotton workers shot there in 1842, as I read in my guidebook while Damon drove. This shooting occurred after they had been read the riot act, which is one of those phrases that has been smoothed over by common usage but whose literal meaning retains a surprising amount of force. When facing a riot, a mayor or justice of the peace would stand up in front of an angry mob and read out the 1714 Riot Act:

Our Sovereign Lord the King chargeth and commandeth all persons, being assembled, immediately to disperse themselves, and peaceably to depart to their habitations, or to their lawful business, upon the pains contained in the act made in the first year of King George, for preventing tumults and riotous assemblies. God Save the King.

At which point you had an hour to clear out before they started shooting; and when they started shooting, the Riot Act indemnified them against any death or injury caused to the rioters. The Riot Act was only repealed in 1973, although it had fallen into disuse by that time, and rioting itself was no longer punishable by death.

A version of it is still on the statute books in Australia and Canada, incidentally, albeit in a more modern idiom. The Canadian form hasn't been read in fifty years, which is just as well, as they only give thirty minutes to disperse. Busy people, the Canadians, they can't be hanging round waiting for you to get your rioting done. They want to get that water cannon back to the hire shop before six o'clock.

So here I am on the road from Cambridge to Preston, and enjoying the culture shock of travelling from cloistered academia to grey industrialization. And warming to the task of defending Preston.

Yes, Oxford and Cambridge are justly proud of their tally of laureates, but can they boast that they were the home of the UK's first Kentucky Fried Chicken? No they cannot. But Preston can, because it is Preston: City of Firsts!

In 1816, it was the first city in England outside London to be lit by gas. The Preston bypass was the first stretch of motorway in the country; and it was also the first place that traffic cones were used. Preston Football Club was one of the founding members of the Football League and the first winner of the league, and Deepdale, the club's home ground, is the oldest continuously used football league ground in the world.

Deepdale is also home to the National Football Museum, where I spent a large chunk of the afternoon, marvelling at the sheer brass neck of whoever had collected the memorabilia inside. Blagging cool stuff for a museum was far more straightforward back in the day, when the British Museum could just steal whatever caught their eye and convince themselves that the locals wouldn't understand it as much. These days you have to ask permission. At least I hope you do; although the idea of a team of tomb raiders with Lancashire accents breaking into old footballers' homes and stealing their medals is quite appealing.

The depth of exhibits is quite astonishing and 95 per cent of them could be prefixed with the words 'the actual'. There are the actual balls from the 1930 and 1966 World Cup finals, the actual replacement Jules Rimet trophy (after the original was stolen) and, most impressively, the actual jersey worn by Diego Maradona in the 1986 'Hand of God' match. The thrill of seeing that jersey in a case in front of you can only be a fraction of the emotion that Diego must have felt when he received a letter from an English football museum requesting it. He must have turned to whoever was standing near and gone, 'No way! You're shitting me, right? This is a gag, isn't it?' To the best of my knowledge, there is no glass case in Hastings containing the arrow that killed Harold.

If the presence of Diego's shirt is an impressive act of humility, there are plenty of other victories for the English to bask in here. The greatest quote in the entire museum

is one attributed to Sir Neville Henderson, British Ambassador to Germany, when offering his binoculars to the man
sitting next to him during England's 6–3 rout of the host
nation in Berlin in 1938.

'What marvellous goals,' Sir Neville is reported to have
said. 'You really should take a closer look at them.'

The man sitting next to him was Hermann Göring.

The museum should lay to rest one old chestnut, though.
The English didn't invent football. They codified it, which
is a different thing altogether, and a less emotive thing to
shout about when you next fail to qualify for the World
Cup. You didn't invent football because you didn't invent
the ball, or kicking, or fields. We should only be grateful that
the Victorians didn't gather together in a room and write the
first rules for the use of the wheel, or fire, so that you can
claim credit for that as well.

Villages have been dragging, pulling, kicking and running
against each other for millennia; you just happened to be the
ones with an empire when the upper class took an interest.
It was Cambridge University who initiated the first rules, in
1848; a further fifteen years passed until the formation
of the FA, and even then the game was sufficiently unrecognizable from the modern game that one of the delegates,
Blackheath, lost a vote to retain shin-kicking and promptly
left to turn their schism into rugby instead.

Don't get me wrong: you're great at the codifying. In a
burst of rule-making, Victorian England laid the modern
format for almost all the major sports we still enjoy.
Football, rugby, cricket, hockey and tennis – all codified by
the English in the nineteenth century. So pernicious was the
English influence that, in 1887, the Irish took the same
inter-village kick-bollock-scramble that was football and

codified a slightly but sufficiently different game, Gaelic football, so that proper Gaels didn't have to play English sports.

And how did the rest of the world compete with this? The Australians wrote the first Aussie Rules code in 1858, the Canadians did the same for Ice Hockey in 1877 and the Americans came up with Basketball and Volleyball in 1891 and 1895. All that the entire continent of Europe came up with in the nineteenth century was Olympic Handball, and that's just some weird, lame thing that won't sell tickets at the 2012 Games. It's a relatively poor return for the rest of the globe.

So the English are the undoubted champions at writing up a rule book. And, backed up by the machinery of Empire, handing the rule books out. This is often taken to prove your oft-stated love of fair play. My arse. You just liked telling people what to do; or you just liked telling them that they were doing it wrong, even though they'd been doing it that way for millennia.

And I'm sorry if that sounds harsh, but I'm telling you this for your own good. A hundred and twenty years later, whenever an English team is beaten, the line bemoaning 'this, in a sport we invented' still gets trotted out. You've got to snap out of this. It's like you want to pour vinegar into the wound. It's a bit like having Maradona's jersey in the middle of the national football museum. Had to pile on a fresh layer of pathos, didn't you? Couldn't just enjoy a nice day out at the football museum. Had to have a little bit of disappointment in the middle of it. I'll have to keep an eye on this English tendency to look on the dark side.

*

The theatre in Preston sits on top of a shopping centre – a deserted shopping centre by the time my crowd started coming in, which added to the slightly surreal mood surrounding the place. This wasn't helped by the battery pack on my radio microphone slowly dying, which led to remarkable whooshing ocean noises coming out of the PA system throughout the first half. I had to stop the gig repeatedly, for fear the audience might get too relaxed from the new-age vibe we'd created and doze off.

Luckily, the probation officer was there to get everyone nice and stressed.

'Have you ever lost anyone?' I asked.

'We lost someone today.'

'I'm sorry? There's a prisoner on the loose, today?'

'Well, it's more of a parole violation, really.'

'What the fuck are you doing here then? Why aren't you off shutting down airports, or blocking ports? What's the nearest airport?'

'Blackpool or Manchester.'

'I think we can eliminate Blackpool airport. If he's fleeing the country, I don't think he'll gamble on catching that one flight a day to the Isle of Man. What kind of criminal is he anyway?'

'A burglar.'

There is nothing more relaxing to an audience than finding out a burglar is on the run the very night they're sitting in a theatre on top of a shopping centre in Preston. A thousand people suddenly started mentally listing all the windows and doors in their homes, and trying to remember whether they'd locked them. To distract them, I turned to the boy with the cast on his arm.

'How did you get that then?'

'I'm being bullied at school.'

Bang goes your national reputation for fair play. I offered him up an inspirational speech.

'I knew a boy once, round about your age. A nice kid, but quiet. Bookish. Wasn't one of the cool kids, do you know what I mean?'

I stared at the boy, and we shared a poignant moment.

'Do you know what became of that young man?'

The boy looked at me and said, 'No.'

And I looked at him and said, inspirationally, 'Yeah, neither do I. We lost touch after school.'

Our sound problems made the show run over by at least thirty minutes and, after this marathon effort, I felt I should apologize to the stage manager after the curtain had come down.

'It's almost eleven. Sorry about that, that's a bit of a marathon. Once I'm out there, you just can't stop me talking, I suppose,' I offered, in a semi-humble way.

'Oh, don't worry about it,' he said. 'We had Ken Dodd in last week and we didn't finish until 1 a.m.'

'Jesus! How bad were the sound problems that night?'

'Oh, there were no problems. Ken does a five-hour show. *Every* show. Five hours.'

And he left me, digesting this information, and feeling a little less smug about my 'marathon' show.

One weekend into the tour, and the random nature of our travels was already giving me headspins. Tours don't get booked thematically. If you're lucky, the venues are at least close to each other. Usually, though, you joke about the crazy loops and random criss-crossing you have to make while moving around the country.

'Where are we this week? Oh, we're doing the Golden Triangle. You know, Bristol, Grimsby and Woking.'

At least the show was bedding down, I reasoned, as I did yet another post-mortem with Damon in a hotel bar in Preston. Routines had been moved, stories trimmed and the odd new gag added.

At the end of the weekend, it seemed to be coming together. I was happy with the show, and mellow with a whiskey in my hand, until Damon offered an opinion, in his other job, as late-night voice of reason.

'That Tayto story still isn't working, by the way.'

'Fuck you.'

Chapter 4:
Tickling the Cities

Our next gigs were all in the country's major cities. In any travel book about England, this would be the spine of the trip. A classy writer would hold these jewels back or, at the very least, sprinkle these famous names throughout the text. My itinerary gets them all out of the way in the first full week. In a way, this is no bad thing. What can I tell you about these places that you didn't already know? The comedy shorthand has already been written on England's big cities:

Newcastle: funny accents, don't wear coats.

Liverpool: funny accents, sentimental.

Manchester: like to hang around independent record stores in parka jackets.

Birmingham: probably Asian, or a lap-dancer.

These prejudices are relatively harmless, I suppose, depending on how you handle the Asian lap-dancer one. And if there is one thing I've learned about the English, it's that you're usually loath to give up a comedy prejudice. Germans putting their towels on all the sun-loungers? Never experienced it myself, but perhaps if you got up earlier, there might be chairs left. Can't see how it's the Germans' fault, really.

The comedy shorthands aren't much use anyway, if you don't have a lot of jokes about going out with no coat, which I don't. In fact, I don't tailor my show at all according to which city I'm in. It's not like there are even really that many huge differences to play on.

When it comes to telling them jokes, the cities aren't as different from each other as they are collectively different from the smaller towns and, most markedly, the southern suburbs. I've always found that big cities are just easy to talk to; the crowd has a strong sense of themselves and, at some subconscious level, when they answer a question from the stage, they speak on behalf of the city. It's amazing how much a crowd raises its game when their collective reputation is at stake.

It could be that cities are more cosmopolitan, more outspoken, more brash. Or it might be as simple as having a famous local football team. I will probably never mention the football team, particularly since there's usually more than one and I don't want to be in the middle of that civil war; but having a local team just means that the entire town is used to being represented and, by corollary, willing to represent.

Before I elevate this observation into some sort of general law, though, we've got four towns of repute to test it out in. First up, the Geordies.

Newcastle City Hall

    1 man who teaches pharmacists
    1 sixteen-year-old son of a man who teaches pharmacists
    1 student of modern history
    1 heating engineer

I've spent a lot of time in Newcastle, like I have in all these big cities. When you're a circuit comedian, you do a lot of weekends away, killing afternoons in the large towns waiting for that evening's show. I probably know the locations of chip shops and cineplexes in every major town in the UK. I know Newcastle well enough that it has even part-furnished my house, by way of a chair I stole from a certain Newcastle comedy club. I wrapped it in a black bin-bag to transport it, but the train was busy, so I sat on it all the way back to London.

Despite this history and even despite the modern benefits of satellite navigation, Damon and I got quite lost on the way to the show and ended up having to ask directions to the theatre from a member of my own soon-to-be crowd. Even then, we made the mistake of entering the wrong door at the front of the City Hall and found ourselves in a municipal swimming baths instead. Either that or the mayor likes his office clean. The tang of chlorine was wafting into my room all through the show, giving a pungent undertow to the entire event. The room was distraction enough, an assembly room in the Methodist tradition, bare boards, a balcony running along the sides and a giant pipe-organ at the back of the stage. Like I said about Cambridge, there are rooms in which to exchange corn . . .

Equally, there are rooms built for Protestants to preach to you about sin, in which centuries later Irish comedians will tell you jokes, and there is an uneasy intersection between the two. You can never quite forget that there's a giant pipe-organ just over your shoulder. Particularly with your nose burning from the faint toxic fumes of the cleaning fluid.

Newcastle has an interesting take on identity. I'm not sure to what extent the average Geordie would recognize himself in any list of defining characteristics given for Englishness; and yet they were once at the front line, defending the nation from Cromwell's Scottish allies in 1664. The city's motto translates as 'Triumph through brave defence', and was given by Charles I after the city held firm against the Scots.

The city's history as a border fortress goes back to when Newcastle was founded as a Roman fort, just south of Hadrian's Wall. Repeated defences against attacks from the north were staged, including one at the end of the thirteenth century in which severe damage from William Wallace's troops was sustained. As recompense, the town was presented with one quarter of Braveheart's mutilated body after he was hung, drawn and quartered in London in 1305. It was then hung over the town sewer.

While it might not have been needed as a frontier town since the Act of Union, Newcastle retains a distance from the England it was protecting. I once saw a Geordie comic, John Fothergill, respond to a London heckler with, 'Watch it, you. My ancestors were on a battlement for hundreds of years, protecting this country from marauding Scots, while your grandparents were at court . . . speaking French.'

There is even a linguistic school which claims that the absence of that Norman influence has meant that, in the north-east, they speak a language that is far closer to the original Anglo-Saxon than that spoken by their southern cousins. Their accent remains, along with the Scousers' and the cockneys', the most distinctive and addictive of all the English regional dialects. By addictive, I mean that, midway through a conversation with a Geordie, I will start to speak Geordie, even though I know how irritating it is when somebody does the Irish accent when they're talking to me. In fact, if I'm talking to a Geordie there's every chance we'll have just swapped accents after five minutes and will finish the conversation like cartoon versions of each other:

Him: Ah, bejaney.

Me: Wy-aye-aye.

And so on.

The Geordie accent is too tempting even for international diplomacy. In 1977, US President Jimmy Carter visited Newcastle and enjoyed what must be the greatest single moment in modern Anglo-American relations, and possibly the greatest moment in history generally. Having been made a Freeman of Newcastle and having received the Keys to the City in a formal ceremony, he turned to the crowd of eight thousand and shouted, 'Howay, the lads.'

Onstage, I fight the urge to do the voice. This is a good general rule, by the way. When speaking to people with an accent (particularly Irish) don't do the voice (particularly Irish). This is because, simply, you can't do it. This is worth bearing in mind at all times. You can't do the voice. Are you an internationally renowned mimic? No. You can't do the voice. It's probably the phrase I most often utter in England. Usually barked rather than uttered, to be honest, as the person I talk to suddenly goes into some hideous Toora-loora voice in order to flesh out a story about some Irish person he met on holiday. 'Don't do the voice!' I shout. 'The story won't be better if you do the voice.'

In Newcastle, I understand the urge to do the voice, and I resist. Instead, I focus on what we are talking about: what the rudest thing is to say to a burglar. This is because, in response to the crime question (Have you ever interrupted a crime?), a lady in the audience didn't want to tell me what she said to an intruder.

'It's too rude,' she blushed.

I pointed out that, earlier on in the show, I had used the ageless phrase 'Do you mind if I pull out and jizz on your tits?'

(This seems cheap and tawdry out of context but, honestly, the routine in its entirety makes a very serious sociological point.)

The lady admitted that her phrase wasn't quite that rude – it was 'Get the fuck out of my house' – and we spent some time discussing what the rudest thing to say to a burglar was. It was generally felt that when a stranger enters your home without your permission, frankly, all bets are off on the taste and decency front, and they have no right to be offended by any coarse language. In fact, we further agreed that the perfect thing to drive a burglar out of your house would be to shout, 'Do you mind if I pull out and jizz on your tits?'

What the crowd that night will probably better remember, though, is the heating engineer who, when asked to recommend a type of heater, said, 'Bison.' I had a fit of the giggles onstage describing an old woman in her flat in winter, warming her hands on a buffalo and, the bit that tipped me over the edge, hanging her drying on his antlers. It's a small room, with just space for the old lady, a small telly and a 400lb wild cow. Of course, now I could Google 'Bison' and find the full range of radiators, convection heaters and the like. But this wasn't just whimsy. I once taught physics to agriculture students in university, and one of the exam questions I'll never forget started: 'If the surface area of a cow is $4m^2$ and the cow releases heat at a rate of . . .' so, you know, it could work.

After the show, we went out, because it was a Friday and going out in Newcastle is one of the thirty-five things 'not to miss' in this country, according to *The Rough Guide to England*. There were crowds; some had coats, some did not; we had some drinks; I went to a chip shop I know; and had started to stumble back to the hotel at about three o'clock. On the way, I saw a young man accost a group of people in front of me, chat briefly and then peel away angrily. He moved on to another group, and the same thing happened. He eventually got to me.

'I'm sorry, mate, can you help me?' he said in an Irish accent.

'Hello, champ,' I said, doing the voice, because I am Irish and therefore permitted. 'What're you in town for?'

'I'm over to see the match tomorrow, but I can't find my hotel.'

This guy was hammered, by the way. Hammered. More than any of the locals, I'll admit.

'I'm trying to get to my hotel, but I can't find it,' he mumbled again.

'Well, what's the name?'

'I don't know. But I've got the key.'

'Excellent. Show me the key then.'

He showed me the key. It was a plain credit-card-sized piece of plastic, white on both sides, with just the word 'Vingcard' written on it. It was a hotel room key all right, but the only information was the address of the Vingcard corporate headquarters in Arizona, and I doubt they have a help line for just this situation.

'I'm sorry, mate. I think you're in trouble, there's no information on this.'

'But this is the key! Where's my hotel?'

'This is a generic key. It doesn't give your hotel name ...'

'Ah fuck off. Why don't you all fuck off?' he roared, and then wheeled away to grab another group of people and get the same bad news from them.

For all I know he's still in Newcastle, wandering round, looking for the Vingcard hotel.

Manchester Lowry Theatre (2 nights)

1 dentist
1 thirteen-year-old boy with a newspaper round
1 finish operator
1 benefit fraud officer
1 project manager:
    'What's the project?'

> *'I'm building a firing range in Cheshire.'*
>
> *'What, a field with a target at the end? That's a hell of a project.'*

1 property developer

1 man called Brendan who bought the ticket on eBay

My wife travelled up to meet me in Manchester, and we checked into our hotel together. As we stood in the lobby, she looked around with a confused expression.

'What's wrong?' I said.

'This hotel is really familiar.'

'Have you stayed here before?'

'No, but it still looks familiar. Wait.' She grinned, as it came to her: 'This is where Leanne Battersby came when she was a prostitute.'

Welcome to *Coronation Street* country.

The hotel in question is a boutique hotel across from Granada Studios. It's almost as famous now for the massive Christmas party the Manchester United players hosted there a couple of years ago. There are lots of places in Manchester to spot footballers: 'This is the fancy new development that Ronaldo bought his penthouse in, this is the department store Rio Ferdinand was shopping in the day he forgot his drug test' – that sort of thing. Not that I'm judging those tourists who like this kind of thing. I worked in Granada Studios once and ended up sneaking into the Rovers Return and stealing a bag of nuts. We moved house not much later and, when we were unpacking, they got thrown out, because neither of us realized they were the magic nuts. They just looked like an ordinary bag of peanuts. Next time, I'll steal the sign from the outside of the corner shop. Or one of Jack Duckworth's pigeons. Or Betty.

It would make a good crime story at least. We were crying out for one of them on the first night at the Manchester Lowry Theatre. I wasn't in the best of form, and some of the new stories just weren't working as well as they should. It all seemed to be 15 per cent slower than it should be. All through the show, this was frustrating me. The Lowry is one of the best theatres in the country, probably the best modern-build theatre.

I'll come back to this a lot, but here's the potted history of theatre architecture: slopey hill; amphitheatres; standing room only, no roof; here's the roof, stick an arch over the stage, bring the seats close; Victorians introduce velvety chairs and painted ceilings and everything is perfect, just perfect (Buxton Opera House, Leeds City varieties, Bath Theatre Royal); somebody invents microphones and theatre designers start moving the seats back – nobody consults with the comedians; theatres are designed for utility and large-scale shows – comedian now yelling to an audience who are sitting a mile away (Liverpool Philharmonic, Bristol Colston Halls); some complete arse decides that orchestras are king and we need to build concert halls, audience now *miles* away and seated in the sky in a white, white room, impossible to light without seeing every face in the room – comedian starts to cry (Belfast Waterfront, Cardiff St David's, Glasgow Royal Concert Hall); some complete fucker decides to go completely multi-function and create the 'black box' – comedian now 'democratically' on the same level as the crowd, has to spend entire show not looking at their crotches (Warwick Arts Centre, Windsor Arts Centre, a million new arts centres round the country).

Theatres are like Concorde. We had the perfect design for a while and everything since has gone backwards. Not for the touring show of *Les Mis*, of course. But for standing in a room and telling jokes, as a rule of thumb, everything pre-1900 is as perfect as it ever got.

The Lowry is a modern build, but still manages to be intimate, which is a rare feat. It may be more to do with the locals than the architecture, I suppose. I once did a show here where, during the interval, the entire front row, none of whom had met each other before, swapped their seats round just to confuse me. When I came back out, ready to pick up the thread of chats I'd already started, everyone was sitting in a different place, grinning up at me.

After tonight's disappointing performance then, I took the show apart, ditched the bits that weren't working and tried some new configurations. This happens a lot during the first couple of weeks of a tour. It's not dissimilar to being a motorbike enthusiast, I suppose, and stripping the machine down in the front room to give it a tune-up. Sometimes you just need to do the same jokes but in a different order. There was an Edinburgh Festival once where I was a full two weeks in before I realized that I was doing the show the wrong way round. One quick flip and *bang!* Much bigger laughs.

The following night in Manchester was a return to form. For a start, the dentist got caught bluffing:

Me: What's in fillings these days?

Dentist: Composite.

Me: What's that?

Dentist: Errr . . . composite.

Me: A composite of what, bluffer? Composite isn't a thing. It's a mixture of things. So, what is it? Fennel and grout? Zucchini and feathers? Bubble wrap and cornflakes?

He couldn't recall. I had to look it up during the interval. (It's fudge and tarmacadam.)

But the winner was the finish operator. Of course, you say, a finish operator will always be the most exciting person in the room. And you'd be being sarcastic and it doesn't suit you. This man genuinely had the best job I met on this tour. He made the thin metal strips that go into ten-pound notes. Go on, take out a tenner and hold it up to the light. You see that dark line? I met the man who made that.

Liverpool Philharmonic

1 teenager who wants to be a barrister
1 credit controller
1 graphic designer

Liverpool deserves a funnier room than this. The Philharmonic is plush and grand and expertly run and, if I had the orchestra with me, I'd adore it. It's just that people in the massive balcony can't see anyone in the stalls, rendering audience chat sort of pointless. Can you imagine what a waste it is not to be able to talk to people in Liverpool? I'm not saying it's all gold up there, but they aren't shy. Liverpudlians always tell me how Irish their city is, and indeed I can spot a fair few traits we might have given them. Religious competition, talkativeness, a sentimental streak and a tendency to separatism. Scousers share an Irish sense of uniqueness; an unshakeable belief that it is a unique birthright to have been born on the Mersey. This is always going to be a unifying force; if only because the rest of the population are pushed away, shaking their heads and wondering what makes them so special. I've had Scousers repeatedly tell me that X/Y/Z is uniquely great in this city (the people/the spirit/the comedy/the music, for example) and, in fact, it's bollox of the highest order. X/Y/Z is usually just as good down the road in Manchester or Birmingham. What I love about writing that, though, is that, just like in Ireland, there's going to be some Scousers who'll read that piece of non-criticism (basically, 'other towns have nice people too') and be irritated that I haven't given the city its due.

It's a ludicrous piece of indoctrination, both for the Scousers and the Irish. And it works.

Identity can be a self-fulfilling prophecy. You tell people that they are unique, or beloved for their warmth, or defined by the tightness of their community, and they'll live up to it. Just look at the difference between English football supporters and Irish football supporters at a World Cup. Before they've even left the house, one group is regarded as surly and belligerent; the other as fun-loving and friendly. We Irish constantly tell ourselves that we're the greatest fans in the world. Chances are, we're not (my money's on the Dutch, or the Japanese, or the Brazilians); the point is, it's a very enjoyable stereotype to live up to. These are all fun characteristics to have. Maybe that's why English audiences never wanted to shout out their own national traits. The traits that are traditionally associated with the English are so dull and worthy – fair play, tolerance, stiff upper lip, all that malarkey – that nobody wants to adopt them.

Anyway, the town deserves a funnier room. It doesn't help that, due to some listings mix-up, half the audience were told it was a seven-thirty start and the other half were told eight. Obviously, the only thing to do here is to start at eight, but you try explaining that when the crowd catches you wandering up to the stage door with a burger in your hand at seven forty.

Here's an example of how beautiful Liverpool can be in an intimate room: the gig in question being Rawhide comedy club, in a nightclub on the Albert Dock. I had done my show and was now mingling with the crowd and having a drink when a man approached me at the bar. He was a stocky, well-built man, shaven-headed – what I would describe as a 'squaddie' type. He stood close to me, leaned in and said:

'That was very funny.'

'Thanks.'

'No, what you were saying about Northern Ireland. That was very funny.'

'Thanks.'

I had done a few gags about the North earlier, as was expected of any Irish comic in England at the time.

He leaned in closer.

'I had a couple of friends stationed in the North,' he continued, taking a beat, 'and they were killed over there.'

I've told his story a few times in the years since, and I always pause at this point, just to enjoy the silence in the room. It exactly mirrors the silence between me and this army guy at the time. I could not think of anything to say. As I always tell it, it was like there was a giant thought bubble over my head, with nothing inside it. Just a nagging feeling that no amount of inherent Irish charm was going to get me out of this one.

There was an achingly long pause, and then the man leaned in even closer.

'Yeah. They were in an army truck,' he went on, in a genuinely scary way, 'and a tree fell on them.'

Suddenly a memory came flooding back, a memory of one of the oldest jokes in Ireland about the Northern Ireland situation, a joke I hadn't heard since I was in school. I locked eyes with the man and raised one hand to interrupt him.

'Are you about to tell me,' I said, 'that the IRA planted it?'

'Yeah,' he said, leaning back and grinning happily. 'Have you heard that one before?'

Yes I have, my friend, but never in a way that made me evacuate myself.

Birmingham Hippodrome (2 nights, the second of which was 17 March, Paddy's Day)

1 man who drives a truck filled with fasteners
1 domestic-insurance salesman
1 college student studying 'dinosaurs':
    'Thank you. I know what palaeontology is. I'm not a moron.'
1 man who worked in air-conditioning (retired)
1 man who sells light bulbs, there with his entire family,
    who also sell light bulbs

The Hippodrome in Birmingham, now, that is a room. Renovated without losing its shape or intimacy, it's the perfect model for older theatres that want to modernize. Stick as many grand glass foyers out the front as you want, just leave the room in the middle the way it was.

We had two nights of chatty joy, culminating in the world's most middle-class crime story:

'A burglar broke into the house during a dinner party.'
    'What did you do?'
    'Well, we all just presumed he was another guest.'
    'The burglar sat down with you? And what, you were all too polite to ask who he was?'

'No, no. We just caught a glimpse of him in the hall, but when he didn't appear at the table somebody asked the host where he was. And then we chased upstairs to find him.'

'And where was he?'

'My friends found him in one of the bedrooms and closed the door on him.'

'What did he do?'

'He climbed out the window.'

'So he got away with the stuff he stole?'

'No, we found it all later.'

'Where?'

'He dropped it all in the courgette patch.'

The Hippodrome is right in the middle of one of the major entertainment districts in Birmingham. There's a major comedy club there, so Damon and I know all the local landmarks, even the quirkier ones. Slap bang in the middle of the nightclubs, bars and restaurants, there's Mr Egg, for example, a local egg-and-chip caff which has achieved the incredible balancing act of being sufficiently popular to survive in a cut-throat late-night food market without ever having been successful enough to encourage someone to open another Mr Egg anywhere else in the country.

Birmingham's more famous culinary export is, of course, the balti, invented here in 1977 by a Pakistani immigrant, and proof, of sorts, of how successful England is as a multi-cultural nation. You give stuff back to cultures that they didn't even know they had. A billion people in India are going, 'A balti? What's a balti?'

There's no reason for things not to be successfully exported from Birmingham. When it was known as 'the Workshop of the World', the city was the beneficiary of the country's most extensive transport network. Now that the heavy manufacturing has been replaced by services (a sentence I could write for just about any town in England, by the way. Why don't I not, and we can just presume I did? Thanks), efforts are underway to exploit this resource, with gentrification of the canal-sides, new apartment blocks and quayside restaurants. It's a very famous (and possibly completely spurious) statistic about Birmingham that it has more canals than Venice; although, whether Birmingham is gentrified or not, you'd presume that the Venetian Tourism Board have relatively few sleepless nights about this.

Birmingham tourism is largely based instead on conferences and exhibitions. The city hosts 40 per cent of the nation's conference business, which may explain the other famous statistic about the city.

Possibly because of all the conferences (we saw a lot of men in suits in the middle of town), Birmingham has the largest density of lap-dancing clubs in Western Europe. Obviously, the last thing you want in a lap-dancer is density, but you can't fault the city for choice. Walking around that night, we were never more than a few minutes away from another Legs Eleven, Spearmint Rhino or Medusa; they're all here. There was even a club on Broad Street once which offered both 'Erotic and Exotic Dancers', although you'd want to get there early and bagsy an erotic. The men who go to lap-dancing clubs would be sorely disappointed if Carmen Miranda walked in with tropical fruit on her head. Sometimes exotic just isn't enough.

It seems unfair to dump this, ahem, into the lap of the Brummies, but Britain really is quite a, well, *porny* country. Maybe that isn't too unfair on Birmingham. After all, the local football team is co-owned by David Gold, the chairman

of Ann Summers (and, according to the 2008 *Sunday Times*
Rich List, worth £450 million), and David Sullivan, owner of
Private, the UK's biggest chain of adult shops. The Rich List
put him on £500 million in 2008. That's a lot of dildos and
copies of *Readers' Wives*.

One of the old truisms about the English is that they aren't
interested in sex, and are also a bit embarrassed by it. Like
so many of the generalizations about the country, this
one clearly doesn't apply, and it's doubtful that it ever did.
Certainly, the England of Chaucer and Shakespeare seems to
have been a fairly bawdy place, and *Fanny Hill* doesn't make
eighteenth-century Britain seem like a repressed civilization.
The Victorian era gets most of the blame for turning the
English into a nation of prudes but, again, the reality was
very different. There were around eighty thousand prostitutes on the streets of Victorian London at the midpoint
of the nineteenth century, when the population of the city
was around two million. That's roughly one prostitute for
every twelve men. Obviously, not all of these women were
full-time prostitutes – many were factory workers or seam-
stresses who did a little freelance work – but the volume of
the trade hardly suggests a lack of interest in sex.

Take the phrase 'Lie back and think of England' and
the cliché that the English, or at least English women, were
uninterested in sex. It's worth noting the origin of the
phrase. According to the Oxford English Dictionary, Lady
Alice Hillingdon noted in her diary in 1912: 'I am happy
now that George calls on my bedchamber less frequently
than of old. As it is, I now endure but two calls a week, and
when I hear his steps outside my door I lie down on my bed,

close my eyes, open my legs and think of England.' Lady Hillingdon was fifty-five in 1912, but George was still getting it twice a week, and this was apparently less frequently than of old. If these were the people who weren't interested in sex, then the other English people must have been banging like rabbits.

In November 2008, an international academic study covering fourteen thousand people in forty-eight countries identified the United Kingdom as one of the most promiscuous countries in the world. The United Kingdom came eleventh out of forty-eight countries surveyed, but was ahead of every other major industrialized country, including the USA, Holland, Australia, France and Italy. Those results were certainly reflected in an *Observer* poll, which found that roughly half of all British adults had had a one-night stand and one in five had slept with someone whose name they didn't know. More specifically, 29 per cent of men had slept with a woman whose name they didn't know, but just 14 per cent of women had done the same, suggesting that women really *are* better at multitasking.

Very little about English culture today could make you think that this was a nation uninterested in sex. If anything, England now seems to be a country drenched in sexuality – the land of the *Sun*, *Nuts*, *Asian Babes*, of casual sex, dogging and teenage pregnancy.

Certainly, to me, growing up in Ireland, the place looked filthy. Your biggest-selling newspaper had tits in it, for Christ's sake. It's hard to explain how insane that looked from Ireland, or how furtive it made it as a purchase. It's even stranger to come and live here and see that the *Sun* is regularly mentioned as a vital read, and as one of the major opinion formers in the country. It has tits in it. On page three, right inside the cover. Tits. And it claims to have won or lost national elections.

Every ten years or so, some Irish entrepreneur starts up a men's magazine and, six issues later, it splutters to an embarrassed halt. Ireland's a small media market certainly, but mainly these magazines die because there isn't the appetite to tell Irish girls that this is a career choice worth taking. There is a massive industry in England, and a very mainstream one, from page-three girls to 'Highstreet Honeys' competitions to sections in *Zoo* and *Nuts* magazine claiming to get students, barmaids or girls on the streets to lift their tops; all this based on convincing young women that it is somehow 'empowering' for them to do so. There was an Irish girl recently who took up page three after gaining an excellent degree in one of the sciences in Trinity College. She parroted this line about choice, and the country just looked at her bewildered. 'You've got a degree. Don't you get it? You're going to have a long, rewarding and successful career. That means you don't have to get your tits out.'

Don't get me wrong, we like tits. We just don't think it's a brilliant thing to base your working life on. But, and you can regard this as hypocritical if you want, we'll look at yours. Google did a survey in 2006 about which nation types the word 'porn' into their search engine most. Britain came third. (Which city was number one in Britain? Sorry, Brummies, it was you again, although Manchester was just behind.) The number-one sex-seekers online, were – surprise, surprise – the Irish. We like tits. We'd just sooner it was *your* daughters and sisters and wives that were popping them out.

Chapter 5:
You're About Fifth

Let's take a brief pit-stop from the town-to-town and look at the bigger picture. This little quest started with the vocal objections of the radio-phone-in crowd to England being ranked above its station.

So, if we do a bit of research, where does England place?

Remarkably, about fifth in almost everything.

Britain has the fifth-largest economy in the world ranked by GDP, behind the USA, Japan, Germany and China. In terms of military might, Britannia no longer rules the waves but, depending on which figures you use, is ranked between second and fifth in terms of military spending. It comes third or fourth in terms of nuclear weapons stockpiled, and fifth in terms of arms exports.

It is the world's sixth most popular tourist destination. Even in areas where you'd expect domination, England is not guaranteed the top spot – it is sixth in terms of beer consumption and doesn't even always come top in tea drinking, with Turkey and Ireland occasionally topping that list. Britain comes fourth in terms of time spent in school, and has the fourth highest divorce rate in the world.

It now comes fourth in terms of the size of its English-speaking population, behind the USA, India and Nigeria. In sports, Britain struggles to stay in the top tier, even in the sports it claims to have invented. At the end of 2008, England was tenth in the FIFA world rankings, sixth in the Rugby Union world rankings, and England is ranked fifth in the world by the ICC for test cricket. Great Britain came fourth in terms of medals won at the Beijing Olympics.

Like I said, you're about fifth.

For many of the two hundred plus sovereign countries in the world, this would be regarded as quite an achievement. Not so for the English, of course. For many, and not just the ones with access to a radio, a phone and too much free time, this is seen as an inexorable slide, as proof of an unprecedented decline and, worse than that, a form of rebuke.

Little more than a hundred years ago, Britain was the dominant world power: controlling more than a third of the world's trade, a quarter of its land area, a quarter of its population (around 350 million people), and being the pre-eminent power on the world's oceans. The unprecedented scale of the empire supported an understandable belief that there was something exceptional about the British way of life.

In fact, the empire was always fired with moral purpose. In 1896, Winston Churchill described the purpose of the empire as being: 'To give peace to warring tribes, to administer justice where all was violence, to strike the chains off the slave, to draw the richness from the soil, to plant the earliest seeds of commerce and learning, to increase in whole peoples their capacity for pleasure and diminish their chances of pain . . .'

I'll spare you how funnily that reads to an Irishman.

The point remains, though, that the collapse of the empire may have felt as much of a rejection as it did a failure. The English have had to put up with the sinking realization described by the historian Niall Ferguson in *Empire: How Britain Made the Modern World*, that: 'The empire had, after all, been one of history's Bad Things.'

The story on the home front was no better.

At the mid-point of the nineteenth century, Britain produced more iron than the rest of the world put together. Britain also produced about half of the world's textiles, two-thirds of its coal, and had the highest GDP. These things just aren't true any more. Britain came eighth in the world in terms of its exports in 2007. In the same year, about four out of five workers were employed in the services sector, with just 18 per cent in manufacturing. The country now imports 50 per cent more than it exports. In my audiences, I meet very, very few people who make things.

The loss of empire, allied to the decline in Britain's manufacturing and export success, must have felt like an awful battering for those whose national sense of identity and purpose was intertwined with its success. It's not surprising that, when empire and manufacturing crumbled, some people found it extremely difficult to maintain a clear sense of what the country was for.

Of course, a country doesn't have to be 'for' anything – it can just be a place where you raise your children, which you shout for during the World Cup and where you seek a bit of personal happiness. You'd have to presume that most of the nations of the world manage to exist very pleasantly without stressing about National Purpose.

But I'm here to analyse the English, and already we have a problem. You've probably already noted that a lot of these figures I've quoted are for Britain, and not for England. How are we to filter out the malign Celtic influence?

Well, for a start, by population. England's population forms 83 per cent of Great Britain's so, therefore, we'll take all the figures to have at least 83 per cent chance of being accurate for the English alone. I think it'll be more than that, especially for the less scientific opinion polls I might quote, for the simple reason that most of the polling companies are based in London, and probably just sent somebody out on to Oxford Street with a clipboard, with little thought for weighting the sample to include the people of the Scottish Highlands.

Even if we exclude the Celts from the equation, it won't settle this whole British/English thing, though.

For one thing, what's with all the names? Is there any reason to have six different names for each slightly more inclusive configuration? Especially since none of you can remember which order they go in. Snap quiz: without looking it up, which is bigger, Great Britain or the United Kingdom?

(I'll give you a clue. The last Olympic team was called Team GB!, despite the fact that the name manages neatly to disenfranchise any Northern Ireland athletes who had spent the last fifteen years of their lives learning to pole vault.)

When it comes to titling itself, this country is like those children who write their address with '... Europe, the World, the Solar System, the Galaxy, the Universe'.

In the small time I've been here, though, there is one, less cartographic, distinction that I've seen.

'British' is an umbrella term for everyone on the island. It's inclusive and contemporary; it seems unburdened by aspirations of purity or questions of character. 'British' is the public going about their business.

'English', on the other hand, is where all the trouble lies. Most all of the literature on Englishness is swaddled in nostalgia and wish fulfilment. Every writer on England seems duty bound, for example, to include a list of those traits which they think characterize the country.

In his book on comedy and English identity, *A National Joke*, Andy Medhurst gives an excellent overview of these 'Eng-lists', dating back to a 1924 speech by former Prime Minister Stanley Baldwin:

> The corncrake on a dewy morning ... The wild anemones in the woods in April, the last load at night of hay being drawn down a lane as the twilight comes on ... and, above all, most subtle, most penetrating and most moving, the smell of wood smoke coming up in the Autumn evening ... These are the things that make England.

Now, the first thing that people should have pointed out to Baldwin was that he seemed to have left out the England of towns and factories that most of the English were actually living in. Personally, I would also have pointed out that most of the things he eulogized weren't especially exclusive to England. Not to labour the point, but the rest of the world has also been enjoying hay, Autumn, smoke and anemones for some time now; and the best place to enjoy corncrakes in the UK is actually the Outer Hebrides.

Nevertheless the pattern was set. George Orwell stepped up to fill the industrial void. For him England was:

> The clatter of clogs in the Lancashire mill towns, the to-and-fro of the lorries on the Great North Road, the queues outside the Labour Exchanges, the rattle of pin-tables in the Soho pubs, the old maids hiking to Holy Communion through the mists of the autumn morning – all these are not only fragments, but characteristic fragments, of the English scene.

Some of which was clearly intended as a rebuke to Baldwin but still feels expressionist and sentimental, like a Lowry painting being slowly read out.

And the lists keep coming.

Andrew Stephen in the *New Statesman* said, 'Hearing Mozart's Fortieth symphony bursting out live from Cheltenham Town Hall, that's what it means to be English.'

Jeremy Paxman in his book *The English* filled half a page with:

> ... village cricket and Elgar, Do-it-yourself, irony, breast obsession, gardening, fish and chips, quizzes and crosswords, country churches, Christopher Wren and Monty Python, bad hotels and good beer ...

Even Medhurst himself can't resist having a go:

> ... *Coronation Street*, the *Radio Times*, seaside piers, the Grand National, Sheringham in Norfolk on a Sunday afternoon, Mansfield in Nottinghamshire on a Friday night, 'There is a Light That Never Goes Out' by the Smiths ...

And so on.

In literature, if you go all the way back, the first person to do this was probably Shakespeare himself, in *Richard II*:

> This royal throne of kings, this sceptred isle,
> This earth of majesty, this seat of Mars,
> This other Eden, demi-paradise,
> This fortress built by Nature for herself
> Against infection and the hand of war,

This happy breed of men, this little world,
This precious stone set in the silver sea.

By the nineteenth century, Charles Dickens was joining in:

There is in the Englishman a combination of qualities, a
modesty, an independence, a responsibility, a repose, combined with an absence of anything calculated to call a blush
into the cheek of a young person, which one would seek in
vain among the Nations of the Earth.

Latterly, John Betjemen gave his take on this eternal
question:

For me, England stands for the Church of England,
eccentric incumbents, oil-lit churches, Women's Institutes,
modest village inns, arguments about cow-parsley on the
altar, the noise of mowing machines on Saturday afternoons,
local newspapers, local auctions, the poetry of Tennyson,
Crabbe, Hardy and Matthew Arnold, local talent, local
concerts, a visit to the cinema, branch-line trains, light railways, leaning on gates and looking across fields: for you it
may stand for something else . . .

Until, finally, like a breath of fresh air, Margaret Drabble
changes the tone:

England's not a bad country . . . It's just a mean, cold, ugly,
divided, tired, clapped-out, post-imperial, post-industrial
slag heap covered in polystyrene hamburger cartons.

All these lists. All these bloody lists. The more of them you read, the more depressing and unfriendly the place appears. The more you're told definitively what England is, the more barriers seem to slam in front of you.

They're a shibboleth; a secret handshake between insiders. And if you're not from here, and don't like cricket and warm beer, you don't belong.

By contrast, no one makes a list of what defines Britishness. If you're here, on the island, you're in.

Englishness has membership requirements, and expected standards of behaviour. And all these little entrance requirements add up to something far lesser.

'Englishness' is basically a golf club.

It's a small, provincial golf club, no jeans on the tee, and no ladies in the bar, please.

All the people who wail about English identity and complain that it is constantly being eroded are like the membership secretaries of this golf club, with their insistence on a dress requirement and etiquette and teeing-off times.

And, like all golf clubs, they massively overestimate the clamour outside of people trying to get in.

As long as they keep these ridiculous lists going, the rest of the island will stick with being British.

This is part of the great personality split across this entire island. Not Celt and Anglo-Saxon, not North and South. There is a more fundamental schism, one greater battle between the two sides of the psyche.

On the one hand, we have the Pragmatics. This is the majority of the country, which gets stuff done. The NHS, the BBC, a strong multicultural society; all the institutions and achievements that mark out a successful modern nation.

On the other hand, we have the Romantics. These are the vocal minority who think things just aren't as great as they used to be; the nostalgia peddlers; the hell-in-a-handbasket merchants. The NHS, the BBC, the disaster of multi-culturalism; all the evidence of a society in decline.

Sometimes, the entire country's views on certain topics fall completely into one camp or the other.

For example, Irish people, being in most cases only a generation or two away from the farm, tend to regard animals in a fairly practical way. They're there to be eaten, petted or, occasionally, ridden round a track for cash.

England, which is a largely urban, industrialized nation, pining for an illusory rural past, treats the animal king-dom with an astonishing amount of sentiment. Just look how many of the classic animal stories are primarily con-cerned with the idea of a natural idyll under threat from modernization: *Black Beauty*, *The Wind in the Willows*, *Winnie the Pooh*, *Tarka the Otter*, *Watership Down*, even *Born Free*.

George Orwell was smart enough to place his fable about communism on a farm, since he knew the English reader would instinctively side against his own species. It's the same reason that the dog is the real brains of the Wallace and Gromit operation. Gromit is also the public face of the Kennel Club's 'Good Citizen Dog Scheme', the largest dog-training scheme in the United Kingdom. The scheme's aim is to 'promote responsible dog ownership and enhance our relationship with our pets'. It says a lot that the Kennel Club suggests that one of the main questions the course will answer is 'How do you learn to live with your new dog?'

There's no suggestion that a dog-training course might teach the bloody dog to live with you.

Charles Darwin didn't cause an uproar just because he killed God; he also pointed out that all of nature, right down to the beautiful pastoral symphony of birdsong was a vicious do-or-die struggle for existence. It's no wonder the Victorians were aghast: four legs good, two legs bad.

(Unless you're a fox, of course. Reynard is the great loser in the English fairytale of the countryside. His PR has been so bad that having him torn apart by a pack of dogs has been sold as victory for heritage and romance. Poor old things. No wonder they've moved into the city. When city dwellers have to clear vermin, they don't get dressed up in red velvet jackets, fill their hip flasks and make a day out of it. No one in London goes, 'Darling, there's a mouse in the kitchen. Fetch my tuxedo.')

Consider also the English ability to emphasize the tragedy for animals even amidst horrendous human events – the horrified reaction to the IRA's bombing of the Horse Guards in 1982, or the hoax bombing of the Grand National in 1997, as if somehow targeting horses was a new low, rather than of relatively limited importance given the human damage inflicted. When one of the horses that survived the Horse Guards bombing died in June 2004, he got his own story on the BBC and this tribute from his commanding officer: '[Yeti was] the epitome of a grand old gentleman, increasingly frail but never losing his zest for life and never, ever forgetting his manners.' It's as if the English have projected on to their animals the values they fear are disappearing from their own society.

The RSPCA is one of the largest charities in England and was the first charity of its kind in the world. It was founded in 1824 by a group which included anti-slavery campaigner William Wilberforce, and became 'Royal' when

Queen Victoria lent her authority to it in 1840. There is again here the odd juxtaposition that at the same time that England was involved in widespread barbarism in the name of Empire (Irish readers won't need to be reminded what our priorities were in the 1840s), she was also taking time out to tell people to be nicer to animals.

These days, the RSPCA raises around £100 million a year, and the Royal Society for the Protection of Birds (RSPB) brings in about the same. In comparison, Help the Aged and Age Concern both raise about £80 million each annually. And the RSPCA and RSPB are just two of the hundreds of animal-welfare charities in existence. The Charity Choice website in the UK has records for 633 animal charities, compared to 362 for the aged, 211 for the blind, and 374 for mental health. In 2006, animal charities raised 5 per cent of the total money donated to charities in the UK, the same percentage as the combined disability charities, and a little more than half of the total brought in by the entire field of child and youth charities.

You love animals. You fund, feed, mourn and happily over-anthropomorphize animals. They are an excellent example of the Romantic side of the English personality.

Religion, on the other hand, falls into the Pragmatic. It's not like you haven't had turmoil; the destruction of the monasteries, Queen Mary burning three hundred Protestant martyrs, Guy Fawkes, Cromwell and the Penal Laws. These days, though, religion plays next to no real role in English life.

In an EU survey in 2006, less than half of the people surveyed in the United Kingdom said religion was important in their life, and that figure would have been even lower if it hadn't included Northern Ireland, parts of Scotland,

and the Hindi, Sikh and Muslim communities. Twice as many people said leisure time was important in their life. The English just don't do God. Excessive religious fervour is worrying to them. This is one of the main reasons the Muslim reaction to *The Satanic Verses* shocked the United Kingdom, and why they find it so hard to understand the Northern Ireland question.

Perhaps Henry VIII sums up the English attitude to religion fairly well: he was happy enough with Catholicism until he hit the practical snag that it meant he couldn't divorce. So he invented a new religion, essentially the same as Catholicism, but with him in charge. His personal religious practices and beliefs changed hardly at all.

There is a lot of this pragmatism in the British approach to religion. In 2008, the leader of the Conservative Party, David Cameron, refused to condemn parents who pretended to be religious in order to get into better performing local faith schools. 'I think it's good for parents who want the best for their kids,' said Cameron. 'I don't blame anyone who tries to get their children into a good school. I believe in active citizens.'

Even if 'active' means 'bluffing a vicar'.

I may be a long-time-lapsed Catholic, but I still find it a bit strange to be watching the fireworks on Guy Fawkes night, something that's rarely noted elsewhere. It may be an anti-Catholic holiday, but that's no reason to deny the kids a bonfire and some sparklers. Technically, a Catholic can't become monarch of Britain, but even the Royals don't seem that bothered any more. Prince Charles once said that, when he became king, he hoped to become a 'Defender of Faith' rather than 'Defender of the Faith'. Does the monarchy need an Obama moment? Does anyone care?

Besides, there might not be that much faith for Charles to defend. Almost 8.6 million people in Great Britain, or 15 per cent of the population, said that they had no religion at all in the 2001 census. A further 4.4 million, or 8 per cent, chose not to fill out that question. It says a lot about the country that they had this option: the question specifying religion was the only voluntary one on the census, a clear signal that officialdom, although quite happy to ask you any number of other personal questions, knew to stop short of demanding a window into your soul.

(By way of comparison, in the 2006 Irish census, 94 per cent of the nation said they had a religion, with just 4.4 per cent saying they had no religion and 1.7 per cent refusing to answer. And this is the most secular generation in Ireland since Catholicism arrived.)

Mind you, in the 2001 census, 390,000 people (0.7 per cent of the population) put their religion down as Jedi. This means that there are more nerds in the United Kingdom than there are Sikhs, although obviously the Sikhs would win in a fight. In some ways, this is a silly story, but in another sense there is something intrinsically English about it. Freedom of religion is so taken for granted that it can be the subject of an elaborate practical joke (the vote was a response to an online campaign). The fact that the census enumerators ended up counting the number who wrote down Jedi also suggests a very real commitment to giving other people's religious beliefs respect, even if both you and they know that it's really a bit ridiculous. The results of this campaign were revealed in a press release from the Office of National Statistics entitled '390,000 Jedis There Are'.

In Scotland, only 14,038 people declared their religion as

Jedi but, worryingly, another 14 described themselves as 'Sith'. These people must be watched.

In his book *Hope and Glory*, the historian Peter Clarke takes issue with the idea that the history of Britain in the last century is one of decline. Instead, he says, the country's journey in the twentieth century was replacing a misguided idea of greatness with a more rational and humane one. The British, in other words, would forsake their empire and become instead a great society.

Possibly, the price of a great society is being about fifth. Sometimes greatness lies in humility. After all, the greatest list of all time wasn't from one of your poets.

'England, birthplace of giants,' it began. 'Lord Nelson, Lord Beaverbrook, Sir Winston Churchill, Sir Anthony Eden, Clement Attlee, Henry Cooper, Lady Diana.'

These were the words of Bjorge Lillelien, Norwegian football commentator, on the occasion of their defeat of the England team in a qualifier in Oslo in 1981. He continued:

'We have beaten them all. We have beaten them all. Maggie Thatcher, can you hear me? Your boys took a hell of a beating! Your boys took a hell of a beating.'

See? Some people would be thrilled to be fifth.

Chapter 6:
Only When I Laugh

Yeovil Octagon Theatre

1 man from the audit commission
1 head teacher of a primary school:
    'Ever tempted to give the kids a really solid kick up the arse?'
    'No.'
1 man who works in Tesco
1 retired naval lawyer

Yeovil is a peaceful town, set amidst the bucolic Somerset countryside, a serenity only interrupted by the sudden roar of helicopters overhead from the nearby Westland factory. I'm telling you, it's like the last days of Saigon here sometimes.

The last time I was here, I noticed that one shop had a large ring of security guards around it. I asked who was so important that they needed all the security. And, thrilled by the answer, I went and did the show. A week later, my agent received this brilliant email:

From: Simon Frackiewicz
Date: Mon 20 November 2006 18:44:01
Subject: Dara O Briain

Hi [Dara's Agent],

I was hoping to pass a message of thanks to Dara following his recent stand-up show in Yeovil, Somerset. Whilst on his pre-show walkabout, he happened to pass by my company, Robert Frith Optometrists, where the local football team, Yeovil Town, was having a photoshoot to publicize our becoming their official opticians.

Unfortunately, I was unable to attend his show myself, however I later learned from a number of my staff and patients that this is something Dara picked up on and mentioned several times during his show.

Being a small town, such publicity is of great value, and I simply wished to pass on my gratitude for having increased the awareness of our independent opticians.

In the event that Dara should find himself in the West Country again,
I would be delighted to offer him a complimentary eye examination
by way of thanks.

With kind regards,
Simon Frackiewicz

I was not turning down an offer like that. This time we drove down early in order to meet Simon at his shop in the plaza.

I was under no illusions that I needed glasses. About a year previously, I had convinced myself that it was time for spectacles when a distant road sign looked blurry one day.

'Ah well,' I thought, 'I've had a good innings. At least I'll look distinguished.'

I walked into a Specsavers and, while I waited for the consultation, I tried on a forest of eyewear. I was really getting into it too. I had a pair all picked out. I was quite looking forward to the new, distinguished me.

Then the optician, who had lenses an inch thick, invited me into a room to run the tests. It turned out I had nearly perfect vision. Good news for me, of course, but the optician didn't seem very happy. To the half blind, it must have seemed like I was mocking him. He practically spat the results out at me. You'd think I'd gone to have a prosthetic arm fitted before going, 'Oh wait, what's this in my sleeve?! Sorry!' I was the first person to be thrown out of Specsavers for having Münchausen's syndrome.

Yeovil town centre was deserted. Only the optometrist was open, and Simon was there to greet us. A younger man than I expected, he was clearly not from the West Country.

'No, I've lived in a lot of places, although, interestingly Yeovil is the first place I've lived that wasn't in that book *Crap Towns.*'

'Where else have you lived?'

'Croydon, Liverpool, Reading, Islington . . .'

And then he paused, and looked relieved for having found his way eventually to Yeovil.

Then we did an unnecessary eye-test. For a nerd like myself, it was just fun to play with the machines. I had wanted to ask a lot of questions in Specsavers, but had been discouraged by the increasingly tense vibes coming from the myopic and jealous optician. Excitingly, I discovered that things had moved on in the world of eye-testing. That chart, for example, with all the letters, is now randomly generated by a computer so that people can't memorize the bottom rows. They've also got rid of all the easy letters; it's now just a cloud of E's, H's, M's and W's.

'What else is new?' I asked Simon.

'We can also take a photo of the inside surface of the eye,' he offered. 'It's called Digital Fundus photography.'

'Why would I want to see that?'

'Well, we use it to check for possible loss of sight because of diabetes, or to monitor glaucoma or tumours.'

I nodded sagely.

'Sometimes you can tell other problems though. If you know where to look, you can get an indication of high cholesterol. Or systemic hypertension. High blood pressure. Just from looking at the blood vessels in the eyeball. You can tell there might be a problem if they look wriggly.'

And he showed me an eyeball with big, thick, happy veins, and then, by contrast, an eyeball where the veins were narrow and struggling.

'Wow. That must be awkward news to break. They only came in for some glasses.'

'Yes. Well, I try not to be the one to break the news. It shouldn't come from me. This' – he says, pointing at the eyeball on the screen – 'is only an indicator. I usually just recommend that they go and see a doctor as soon as possible.'

I sat behind a complex machine, rested my chin and forehead on a support, and the flash went off a couple of times.

I returned blinking to my seat.

'We'll just get this up on the screen then,' said Simon, and suddenly here's a picture of my eyeball, all red and unearthly and with blood vessels, I couldn't help noticing, as narrow as spider's legs.

'So how does that look?' I asked.

There was a really long pause as Simon weighed up the best answer.

'You should probably check with your GP.'

Eastbourne Congress Theatre

2 lawyers

1 carer

1 student of film, television and radio

1 clarinet teacher:

> '*To what ages?*'
>
> '*From eight to seventy-five years old.*'
>
> '*When are they going to let that seventy-five-year-old leave school? He must really creep out the eight-year-olds. I bet they always pick him last at play time.*'

A pleasant visit to the south coast, only briefly marred by the difficulties of getting a pizza delivered to the theatre. There's usually only a small window to get some dinner, between the soundcheck and the curtain coming up and, if we aren't near any shops, this involves phoning out and then directing the delivery boy to the back entrance in a way that sounds disturbingly like grooming:

'No! Come to the back of the theatre!'

'I'm not sure about this.'

'It's perfectly safe. Just bring the food all the way round the back of the building and wait there. By the skip. I'll be along in a minute.'

'Can I not just bring the food to the front?'

'NO! I'm sorry ... I didn't mean to sound angry. Please come. I'll give you more money.'

Amidst the usual mixture in the audience was the light and shade of uncovering the lawyers (a solicitor and barrister together – this is like finding sheep farmers and cattle farmers at the same hoe-down; but they all get booed like panto villains by a noisy crowd) and then a full-time carer. There really is no line of attack on a full-time carer – unless, of course, you want to look like a complete prick in front of your crowd. Once they'd spotted this loophole, though, the entire room was at it.

Anyone ever interrupt a crime?

'I once saved a woman who was having an overdose,' said one man.

'Impressive. What did you do?'

'I brought her home and put her into the lounge.'

'I'm sorry. Did you just say "lounge"?'

'Yes. I brought her into the lounge.'

Well, firstly, who has a lounge? And, secondly, who brings home junkies and puts them in a lounge?

Surely a lounge is just too twee for the sudden arrival of a twitcher. A lounge is for maiden aunts and smoking jackets and string quartets.

Although, to be fair, I've always wondered what use a chaise longue is. Too slopey for a chair, too hard for a bed. But, now that I think about it, just right for the propping up of tripped-out junkies before you slam a hypodermic filled with adrenaline into their breastplate. That's one way to bring the cello recital to a crescendo.

I asked the man's wife about this event and she said, 'I know nothing of this.'

'Well, I'm not surprised,' said I, 'you were off your head on heroin at the time.'

The most notable thing about the show was returning after the interval to a stage covered in flyers for Petula Clark, all of which had 'Save the DGH!' written on the back. The entire audience seemed to be supporting the campaign to preserve the local District General Hospital, and not have it move somewhere else. It's not a campaign I felt I should get too involved in, partly because Petula Clark seemed to have the celebrity angle covered, but mainly because they gave no indication of where the DGH was going to end up.

Britain is rightly proud of the NHS. It stands as an example to the world of how to socialize medical care. One of the intermittent pleasures of living here is seeing an injured American after treatment, waiting for a bill, until you explain to them how it works. Honestly, it gives you quite the glow. It's almost worth injuring an American just to see their bewildered and happy face at the end of the process.

Of course, it's an organizational mess. It's the world's third largest employer, after (and I think this is wonderful company to be in) the Chinese army and the Indian state railway. How well managed do you think the Indian state railways are? Do you think they wanted all those people sitting on the roof? I'm guessing the Chinese army has a really strict disciplinary structure but, other than how to deal with absenteeism, I'm not sure how many lessons there are to learn from it. So the NHS has very few organizational peers on whose experience it can draw.

From the outside, it seems to exist in a continuous flux, endlessly attempting to transform itself according to altered government policy and novel administrative philosophies. The same departments are renamed and reorganized. Hospitals become trusts, GPs become one-stop clinics, clinics become super-clinics, doctor training gets longer and then shorter, power is divested and re-invested, quotas are imposed and lifted. District general hospitals get moved. Possibly to somewhere that really needs a hospital, possibly not.

There's no correct answer, of course. All this constant reorganizing feels sometimes like getting a small boy to distribute the raisins in Christmas-cake mix, and then watching him get his head wrecked by the challenge of mixing them just right. Mix it again! No, wait, there's more on the left side now. Mix it again!

Amidst the swirl of conflicting results and studies, and tortured metaphors, let's look at just one piece of data which, to me, sums up everything you need to know about the English and their attitude towards health. The life expectancy is the silver bullet here.

Life expectancy in Britain is about seventy-nine years. This is bang on the average for industrialized countries. It's a little lower than some, obviously, like Finland, or Macau, or Jersey but, here's the real stunner: it's forty years higher than it was two centuries ago.

In two hundred years, medicine has doubled our time on the planet. For all the talk of childhood obesity, or MRSA, or cancer remission rates, this country has, demonstrably, never been healthier. NEVER BEEN HEALTHIER.

You can't imagine how much fun it is to present that fact to an English audience. It's like when you throw a ball for a dog, but you don't actually throw the ball and just palm it. And the dog stares in the direction the ball should have gone and looks confused, then looks back at you and then to where the ball should be. It's a glorious piece of cognitive dissonance. An English crowd isn't built to accept good news like that.

England is the only country in the world that would welcome the news of the longest life expectancy in human history with the headline 'Pensions Timebomb!'

(This was even more fun before the credit crunch, when you could, with justification, say 'Never healthier ... and never richer'. That really wrecked their heads.

'But there are poor people ...'

'Of course, but are they poor like the medieval poor? Who's living in mud now? Where are your Dickensian slums?'

'But there's poverty ...?'

'Yes, and there are still people who need help. But poverty comes with free education and universal healthcare now. Can you not even give yourselves credit for that?'

No, clearly not.)

So they point to Finland and say how much better the healthcare is there.

A couple of points to bear in mind about life expectancy. You should only worry about a differential if there is any way you would ever move to Finland, Jersey or Macau and, frankly, what with selling one house, buying another and changing all your money into kroner or whatever, it would be a lot less effort to just cut down on your cheese intake. Complaining about the marginally better cancer remission rates in Sweden is exactly the kind of behaviour that will stress you into an earlier grave anyway.

There is no bad news in the average health tables which you couldn't counteract with a few lifestyle changes.

Luckily, for the English, we all have to die, and thus, something has to kill us. The numbers have to add up to 100 per cent. If we cure one disease, something else has to fill in the gap.

If they cured cancer in the morning, the English papers would lead with 'Heart Disease on the Rise!' Very few nations are so obsessed with their own unhealthiness as the English. In a recent EU study of twenty-eight European countries that I came across, one in twelve people (8 per cent) from the United Kingdom said that they would generally describe their health as 'bad'. This put the UK in the top ten for perceived 'bad' health, with only Portugal, of the western European countries, having a higher proportion. By comparison, only 3 per cent of people in Ireland said they had bad health. In the same survey, slightly more than one in three people in the UK (34 per cent) said that they had a long-standing illness or health problem. This puts the UK fifth in Europe, behind Estonia, Lithuania, Finland

and Hungary. By comparison again, only 19 per cent of Irish people said the same thing.

Poor things, lie down, you must be feeling weak. You're not actually weak, of course. The life expectancy is *longer* in the UK than it is in Ireland, longer by 0.8 of a year. I hope that, after I die, you spend the following ten months telling yourselves what a surprise it was that I went first, since you've been the sick one all this time.

Here's another interesting thing to note:

Almost one in four English claims to have suffered from an allergy of some kind. This is compared to one in sixteen Irish people. A survey of British GPs in 2006 revealed that three-quarters of the doctors surveyed believed that their patients' food intolerances were entirely in their minds. Another poll of patients found that one in five people had found out about food intolerances from a celebrity inter-view in a magazine or on television.

Or we could just take the word of the GP I met in Belfast who told me:

'The main problem with the NHS is the 99 per cent of the patients who aren't sick.'

Bath Theatre Royal

1 children's nurse
1 civil engineer
1 project manager for a mobile-phone company
1 photographer:
> *'What do you shoot?'*
> *'It's mainly nuns and pigs.'*

So where can they go, these not-sick people? Well, they used to go to Bath.

In 1676, Thomas Guidott, an Oxford-educated doctor, published 'A Discourse of Bathe, and the Hot Waters There. Also, Some Enquiries into the Nature of the Water'. (Today it would be called *Aqua Magic: Five Steps to a Fabulous You.*) He maintained that large numbers of people had been cured of a wide variety of ailments by taking the mineral waters at Bath, both through drinking the water and bathing in it. His follow-up book, *The Register of Bath*, detailed hundreds of further miracle cures, including lameness and sterility. By a lucky coincidence, Dr Guidott actually ran a medical practice in Bath, and was one of the chief beneficiaries when the ideas in his book became fashionable.

Another Bath resident, Dr William Oliver, published *Practical Dissertation on Bath Water* in 1707. A large number of similar works by other mineral-spring-adjacent medical researchers emerged at around the same time. The aristocracy rushed to take the waters at Bath, with Queen Anne making frequent visits to the spa town. Catherine of Braganza, the wife of King Charles II, popularized the mineral springs at Tunbridge Wells. It's obvious to us now that, outside of the placebo effect, there was no medicinal benefit to any of this. Indeed, in July 1665, the diarist Samuel Pepys noted the negative effect the waters had on an acquaintance: 'It seems her drinking of the water at Tunbridge did almost kill her before she could with most violent physique get it out of her body again.' What the craze for mineral spas, and the later craze for seawater bathing, did demonstrate was the English elite's capacity for hypochondria (Daniel Defoe described Bath as 'the resort of the sound, rather than the sick'), their enthusiasm for new health fads, and their ability to exert a profound influence on the way people thought about their own health. That never went away. Three centuries later, Princess Diana did wonders for the colonic-irrigation industry while, in May 2006, Prince Charles gave a speech to the World Health Assembly in Geneva arguing for increased use of homeopathy and other alternative therapies.

Sixty years on from the birth of universal medical care, there are more than fifty thousand practitioners of complementary or alternative medicine in the United Kingdom but only fifty-eight thousand GPs. The annual alternative-medicine spend is thought to be at least £2 billion and possibly up to £5 billion. Around six million Britons use complementary or alternative therapies each year. On this basis, given the massive advances in medical understanding since the eighteenth century, it's possible that a certain medical gullibility may be an unexpected national characteristic in itself.

Medicine versus quackery is one of the long-running battles for the soul of this country. Is Britain the land of William Harvey, Alexander Fleming, Joseph Lister and Florence Nightingale, or the land of drinking spa water, aromatherapy and homeopathy? This divide is obvious, even within the healthcare system. The Royal London Homoeopathic Hospital has been funded by the NHS since 1948, and the NHS has been spending up to £500 million a year on alternative therapies in recent years. However, in November 2008, the government's chief scientific adviser, John Beddington, told MPs that he could see no scientific evidence that homeopathy worked and he would look into its funding through the NHS.

There are those who take a benign view of homeopathy,

who speak of the positive benefits of simply giving patients time and attention. Fine, but it's still just water and sugar cubes pretending to be medicine.

The tooth fairy is nice; it brings a lot of joy and comfort to a large section of the population at a time of medical distress; but I wouldn't spend £500 million of public money on it.

It would be a small victory for the Harvey and Fleming side of the national character if the NHS could shake itself free of this nonsense. One of the central theses of Peter Clarke's history of modern Britain, *Hope and Glory*, is that the British people traded in their empire abroad for a new empire at home – I suppose you could even call it an empire of health and welfare. In all the criticism of the National Health Service, the English sometimes forget the extraordinary fact that they have created an institution at their heart that says, 'If you are sick, we will look after you.' Flawed as it is, there is still something dignified and impressive about the NHS. Indeed, I defy any English person to watch the section on the National Health in Michael Moore's film *Sicko* and not get a lump in their throat. Of course, being English, they will probably then rush to get the lump checked at the GP's, then put some arnica on it to be on the safe side.

Later in the year, at the very end of the tour, I had the blood vessels in my eyeballs checked again, albeit indirectly, by having a blood test with my GP. The results were a wake-up call to cut down on my cholesterol and do some exercise; a few months later I was able to repeat the test and find out that I was out of the danger zone. All this was handled briskly and efficiently by the doctors and nurses in the clinic;

when I was there later for my child's MMR shots, they made a point of checking how my own health was again and offering encouragement.

This was a great experience both for me and for the food-delivery boys of Eastbourne. With the cheese removed from my diet, there was no place for pizza. And no longer must they be ordered to wait, frightened, by the back of the theatre, wondering what will happen to them when the mysterious Irish man appears, hungry, with cash.

Chapter 7:
All This Clean Living Had
to End Sometime

Canterbury Marlowe Theatre

Dave, chief executive of a derivative software company:
   'Couldn't do something original, could you?' (Nobody got that joke.)
1 bed-and-breakfast owner – 6 guests tonight
1 paladin
2 wizards
2 geomancers
4 orcs

Canterbury is an inordinately pretty town, almost entirely populated by visiting French schoolchildren.

This prettiness was almost its undoing in 1942, when it got bombed by the Luftwaffe despite having no military significance. It was chosen, alongside York, Bath, Norwich and Exeter, from a German travel guide, the *Baedeker Tourist Guide to Britain*; reportedly, Nazi propaganda officer Baron Gustav Braun von Sturm said, 'We shall go out and bomb every building in Britain marked with three stars in the Baedeker Guide.'

Which is unfortunate, because the Canterbury Tourist Board was initially quite proud of the good review. They even had banners printed: 'Canterbury: three stars in Baedeker!' The campaign has never been revived.

I've played the Marlowe Hall once before and I learned an important lesson there.

In the front row that night was Bob, who designed university courses for a living. At one stage I asked, 'Where is the last place you bought a bed?' (someone got asked this every night, it was part of a routine). In answer, Bob pointed vaguely off into the distance, as if all beds in Canterbury came from a mysterious valley just yonder ...

When asked to name this bed-producing wonderland, Bob just said, 'Planet Thanet,' which, and I cannot stress this enough, TOOK THE ROOF OFF THE PLACE. They stamped and roared and clapped. Clearly Bob had said the funniest thing ever heard in Canterbury. I didn't understand what he was on about and just repeated it – 'Planet Thanet?' – to more huge acclaim, feet stamping and laughter, and so we had a five-minute chat about this wondrous far-off planet and its mattress-mining alien population. All to insane laughter. Eventually, I had to tell the crowd, 'I literally don't have a clue what we're talking about here,' which got another cheer.

I found out later from people gathered at the stage door that Thanet is a nearby district and the people living there are regarded as slightly different by the inhabitants of Canterbury. Hence Planet Thanet. Comedy, eh? You spend your entire life learning how to craft punchy and hilarious material, when the better skill is simply to spot a much-loved local joke and just shut up and let the crowd enjoy telling it to each other.

So, I have a history with this town. And not just onstage. I once spent a weekend here for an ITV documentary with some Live Action Role-Players, or LARPers, or, commonly, 'people who dress up as Hobbits for the weekend'. During the course of my stay, they taught me magic (spells on scraps of paper) and combat (foam swords with a carbon-fibre core) and made me wear rubber, pointy ears. I had to create an elfin character with elfin traits to go with the elfin ears. I even gave him an elfin-sounding name, Morgan Fairchild, which none of the Orcs recognized, because who remembers *Falcon Crest*? I was also coached in the history and customs of the world I was entering, the name of which I can't remember, but it sounded a little like, but not exactly, Middle Earth.

And then we went to a scout camp just outside Canterbury and ran around having adventures. We fought battles and cast spells, and defended plywood castles and attacked MDF keeps and followed a carefully constructed narrative which had been specially written for the weekend. And when we got thirsty, there was a pub, in a large plush tent, run by a lovely couple who spent their weekends selling people mead and ale at LARP events and Civil War re-enactments. This couple even went as far as to contact the organizers of each weekend in advance to find out the plotline and invent characters for themselves that would fit into the story. Although, to be fair, their characters were invariably inn-keepers.

Everyone stayed meticulously in character all day, and were duly sullen, or uncommunicative, or aggressive, until midnight, at which point the story was put on pause and we all instantly reverted to being normal people getting pissed in a beer tent, in silly clothes.

At the end of the weekend, I then had to perform a stand-up show to them, about them.

I think the LARPers presumed that this was the point at which I would unleash my scorn.

The default position, it seems, when dealing with people with unusual hobbies is to be arch and superior. All week-end, they had been friendly to me, but there had been an undercurrent of worry that I would turn on them at the end and start slagging them off. This is what had happened when some reporter from *Richard and Judy* came down; 'God, look at this lot,' was the tone. They've let us come along and film them – but how tragic are they?

This is a common stance among junior reporters trying to look cool on the telly, of course.

People with obscure passions are essentially fodder. And it's best to appear to be poking them with the far end of a shitty stick in case any of their 'not cool' rubs off, and they can smell it off you when you get back to Soho. There is an army of people like this in telly, who care about nothing outside what they're told to care about by *Heat* and *Closer* magazine, and who dream of being 'Entertainment Corre- spondents', despite it being the dumbest, most regurgative, most pointless job in the universe.

When I was eighteen, I studied maths in college, which I loved, but I ran away from my classmates the minute we were out of lectures and hung out with the 'cooler' kids instead. I was deeply self-conscious about looking nerdy and unattractive; painfully so, on reflection, and probably quite rudely too, to the rest of my class. I don't think I was one iota more successful with women because of this; still, I persisted in denying myself the chance to enjoy a heartfelt passion because I didn't have the self-belief to be independ- ent. I was the trainee Entertainment Correspondent. My LARPing friends in Canterbury learned this confidence, years before I had.

So, this smug scorn is no national trait, by the way, as much as a by-product of the global explosion in celebrity culture. It does weaken the argument, however, for some unique English regard for eccentrics.

By the end of the LARP weekend I had really come to admire this lot. They were funny and friendly, and despite what the man from *Richard and Judy* would like to think, they didn't really think they were orcs or trolls. The whole week- end was just a giant board game brought alive by their enthusiasm and imagination. They had a hobby that was no more an irrational waste of time than following football teams or bands or *Coronation Street* and for which they only got grief, but they carried on because they found joy in it. When it came to their private comedy show, I did it in character. Morgan Fairchild did the one and only show of his/her stand-up career.

And when I returned to Canterbury on this tour, a pair of rubber pointy ears had been thrown up on the stage for me and I wore them with pride.

Cheltenham Town Hall

1 Sainsbury's branch manager from Cardiff
1 aircraft engineer
1 secondary-school student
1 quality-assurance manager

The Café Rouge was booked out in Cheltenham tonight.

This is the massive knock-on effect of a tour like mine. This is the huge economic benefit to local traders. Oh sure, there may be traffic congestion, public drinking and occasional crowd violence, particularly when the audience spills out of the theatre and on to the streets, joked up and ready to fight, but, to a local mid-level restaurant like Café Rouge in Cheltenham, the benefits of being booked out between six and seven thirty on a Tuesday night are immeasurable.

I didn't even know you could book a table at Café Rouge. It's one of those perfectly adequate chain restaurants, like Pizza Express and Est Est Est, which are on every high-street in the UK, where you know exactly what you're going to get, and that includes a table. I'm not saying that these places can't be full; I just don't expect them to be booked out. It sounds like a low-quality phone prank – ringing up Café Rouge to make a booking:

'Hello, I'd like to reserve a table for next Friday please.'
   'I'm sorry, you'd like to . . . what?'

'I'd like to reserve a table for two, for next Friday.'

'This is Café Rouge. You just come along. You can't book.'

'Why not?'

'Because ... because ... because I don't know where I'd write it down. It'll be a completely different set of staff by Friday, and it's not like we have a board or a book for this ...'

I was wrong, though. You can book Café Rouge, at least in Cheltenham, at least in the hour before my show. There was no table there, no table in Pizza Express, no table in Ask. In each of them, my future audience members watched me walk in, enquire, get turned down and shuffle out again.

In the end, I had chips in the dressing room.

Cheltenham proved to be a lot more hospitable after the show. After a couple of dry weeks of driving straight home immediately, Damon and I were overnighting, and fuelled with talk of England's twenty-four-hour drinking culture, we headed out into the night.

Now, I know that there is a long history of Irish people getting drunk in Cheltenham. The National Hunt festival held in March each year can attract upwards of forty thousand punters from across the Irish Sea and has come to be regarded as a particularly Gaelic week. So much so, it has led a lot of people in the UK to overestimate just how much of a shite Irish people give about horse-racing.

'Big week for you,' I remember a taxi-driver saying to me once in London, when he heard my accent.

'Oh really? Why do you say that?' I replied, buying time while I wondered how this guy knew about my upcoming root-canal, my VAT deadline and my plans to sit around for a couple of days playing *Gears of War 2*.

'Cheltenham, of course. I'm surprised you can tear yourself away from it.'

'Oh, it's not really that big a deal for me actually.'

'Of course it is. You're Irish, aren't you?'

'Yes, but we're not all into horse-racing.'

'Of course, you are. All the Irish love Cheltenham.'

'Well, actually, most of us don't really . . .'

'Yes, you do. All Irish people do. Cheltenham. Big week for the Irish.'

I'm not exaggerating, he almost started a fight with me over this. He just refused to accept the idea of an Irishman in London who didn't care about horse-racing. I tried offering evidence, other than myself, by phoning other Irish people who testify to no love of the turf. I even tried logic.

Homer is a man, I said. All men are mortal. Therefore, cabbie, Homer is mortal.

But, Cheltenham is full of horse-racing fans. Cheltenham is also full of Irish people. I accept this. That does not add up, however, to All Irish people are horse-racing fans.

It does add up, in my book anyway, to All Irish people who are horse-racing fans are IN Cheltenham, leaving the other 3.9 million, who couldn't give a shite about horse-racing, well alone. So, shut up and drive or I'll get another cab.

That logic seemed to work.

Anyway, my Cheltenham gig didn't fall during the National Hunt festival and so I wasn't getting pissed with the Irish, I was getting pissed with the English. And, as much as in Ireland, drinking has a central place in English society.

The nature of English drinking has always been a subject of debate in the country, with a certain aspirational tendency to presume that, with just the right tweak in the licensing laws, a sudden eruption of cafés will occur and it'll be just a couple of glasses of Chardonnay before the match. With the perfect piece of legislation, you'll all go Mediterranean.

This is never going to happen. Your drinking is more about binges and serious drunkenness, which is more in keeping with the Germanic and Nordic (and Irish) attitude to alcohol. This might be further evidence that those Mediterranean Romans did little to civilize British society, and that the Angles, Saxons and Vikings were a bad influence on the growing nation during its troubled adolescence.

Or it might just be that you're a northern country and this is the way northern countries drink. People don't drink as heavily in warmer climates because it's hotter there, and hot and drunk don't mix. And they drink wine in hotter climates because that's where grapes grow; in northern climates we grow grain.

It's become the norm for English people to think that they are drinking at unprecedentedly high levels. This is partly because the *Daily Mail* keeps telling them that they are or, at least, that feral, out-of-control young people are, and partly because they are indeed drinking considerably more than their parents or grandparents did. But, in reality, as Peter Haydon, author of *An Inebriated History of Britain*, has pointed out, modern Britons 'are rather poor drinkers compared with our ancestors'. (He also notes that Elizabeth I could drink stronger ale than any of the men at her court, which was seen as an entirely admirable trait in a queen. It's difficult to see Elizabeth II pulling the same stunt.)

The fact is that England has a long and distinguished history of heavy drinking.

Before there was a plentiful supply of clean water, beer

and ale were staple, healthy parts of the English diet for hundreds of years. Monks in the Middle Ages, for example, had an allocation of around ten pints of 'small beer' – a weaker beer made with leftover mash – every day. In the sixteenth century, it's estimated that average beer consumption in England was around 850 pints of beer per person per year. Although drunkenness became a crime under Elizabeth I, heavy alcohol consumption remained the norm. At its peak in the eighteenth century, the Royal Navy's grog ration was half a pint of 50 per cent proof rum mixed with 4 pints of water, served twice a day – more than enough to keep the sailors quietly buzzed all day long. Like many heavy drinkers, it wasn't until Britain switched over to shorts that the trouble started. Gin, in particular, swept through British society – it was said that you could get 'drunk for a penny and dead drunk for two'. By the last years of the seventeenth century, it was estimated that consumption stood at twenty-four pints of gin a year for every man, woman and child in England. In eighteenth-century London, where two pints of 'mother's ruin' were consumed per person per week, gin was cheaper than milk.

I'm not sure which part of that last sentence is more striking. Is it 'two pints, per person, per week'? Or 'gin was cheaper than milk'?

To you, this whole gin-epidemic episode might be old news. But, as I've mentioned before, we aren't taught a lot of English history in Irish schools. So you can understand my glee at discovering the gin epidemic. We get a lot of grief, the Irish, about being heavy drinkers, but You ... had a Gin Epidemic. Oh sure, we like a pint now and again but ... You had an Epidemic ... of Gin.

This is like finding out that your disciplinarian stepfather actually has a teenage police record for possession of marijuana.

And it wasn't a passing thing either. It wasn't 'That Summer we all went a Bit Mad on the G&Ts.' You remember that year? It was just one barbecue after another.

No, it was a thirty-year bender, from 1720 to 1751, at best estimates. An entire generation, clinking glasses, because the previous monopoly on distillation had been broken in an effort to reduce imports of French brandy, the French being out of favour, and replace it with the Dutch drink made popular since the arrival of your first Dutch king, William of Orange. Over the next thirty years, the price of gin plummeted as the supply increased. Mass drunkenness followed. New laws were introduced in 1729 and 1736 to curb the trade, which only succeeded in creating prohibition and the sale of gin under 'medicinal guise'. It was sold in bottles with the instructions 'Take 2–3 spoonfuls of this 4–5 times a day or as often as the fit takes you.' When traders were taken to court, they actually submitted the defence that their business was legal as the unpopular 1736 law had given the people colic.

It wasn't until the Tippling Act of 1751, which attempted to license the trade and draw it into respectability, that the consumption of gin began to fall, although it helped that you entered the (almost completely impossible to explain) Seven Years War in 1756 and all the drinkers had to go and fight.

It was as part of the campaign for the 1751 act that Hogarth produced his famous illustration 'Gin Lane' which chronicled the many social ills of the foreign drink. It was accompanied by a sister print, 'Beer Street', which demonstrated the hearty, healthy drunkenness of the patriotic beer-drinker by contrast. John Bull himself held a tankard of ale, after all. And it was cheaper, industrially produced beer and stout that took gin's place.

Despite attempts throughout the nineteenth century by the temperance and abstinence movements to reduce alcohol consumption, the English continued to drink pro-digious amounts of beer and spirits. In 1900, they were still drinking about 250 pints of beer and close to 7 litres of spirits per person per year on average. And that average includes children and the 10 per cent of the adult population who were abstinent, so the actual drinkers were getting through a good deal more than that.

This golden age of English drinking was brought to an end by the Great War. Lloyd George said that the country was 'fighting Germans, Austrians and Drink, and as far as I can see the greatest of these foes is Drink'. Restrictions on pub opening hours followed, as did a weakening of beer and an extraordinary law that banned the buying of rounds. Consumption levels plummeted and stayed at low levels for almost fifty years.

In recent decades, the UK has tried bravely to get back to the good old days. In 1956, which was close to the low point of the century in terms of British drinking, each Briton over the age of fourteen drank an average of 180 pints of beer, 2 one-litre bottles of spirits, 3 bottles of wine and 4 cans of cider – about 5 litres of pure alcohol – each.

These figures have continued to grow. By 1965, average consumption had grown to 6 litres of pure alcohol, by 1975 to 8.8 litres, by 1985 to 9 litres, by 1995 to 9.3 litres and a genuinely impressive 11.4 litres in 2005.

Much of this is because of the greater number of women drinking since the 1950s; and, since the amount of beer drunk has stayed pretty static since that time, a further portion of the increase is due to the massive increase in the amount of wine consumed. British households now spend more on wine per year than they do on beer and spirits combined.

So the evidence for the *Daily Mail*-style social apocalypse-mongers is mixed. It looks bad next to the mid-fifties, but then the *Daily Mail* tries to make everything look bad next to the fifties. The mid-fifties often pop up when the English Romantics get all nostalgic, like some glorious template of a simpler time. In this, though, their view isn't just rose-tinted. There was less drinking, less than half in fact. It's just that today's grandparents weren't the norm, the standard from which people had slid; in the bigger picture, they were the statistical blip. They just weren't putting the effort in.

As for the current generation, we'll return to myself and Damon's excellent work in the field. Do you want to know what we learned on our trawl through Cheltenham? For a start, if you want street violence, public drunkenness and the grimier side of British drinking, a Regency spa town isn't the place to find it.

Well-to-do young people, the scions of middle-class Gloucestershire, tumbled out of boutique vodka bars nestled in arcades. If there were superpubs, we didn't see them. The streets were relatively quiet, even by eleven. We found a chintzy vodka bar, and even managed to grab the only table. All around us at eye-level were the crotches of Cheltenham because, as the government push to have more 'continental' licensing hours, the publicans go the opposite direction and encourage people to do their drinking standing up. This is called 'vertical drinking' in the industry. It works the same as taking all the seats out of shopping centres. Keep you moving, keep you consuming. If you can't rest your glass anywhere, you will drink more.

The vodka bar shut at twelve. We were pointed to a row of clubs in a Regency arcade across from the theatre and blagged our way into the one on the end, Sub-tone, which ranged across three floors and was thronged with punters. And, like descending into hell, we worked our way down; from the piano bar, singing 'Sweet Caroline', possibly repeatedly, my memory blurs, we eventually found ourselves in the basement nightclub, still compos mentis, but now dancing. Dancing, like the thirtysomething white men we were. They played 'Jump Around' by House of Pain, which is practically the Irish national anthem, and I jumped around. I jumped up, jumped up and got down.

England introduced twenty-four-hour drinking in 2005. The idea behind this was that it was time to allow the English drinker to make a mature choice about when and how much to drink.

Twenty-four-hour drinking ended before 3 a.m. in Cheltenham. In many parts of England, it ends before midnight. It has led to no great revolution in English lifestyle; in fact, for those of us who work at night, England is still a terrible place to drink. If you don't fancy a city-centre superpub, or dancing, there's nowhere to go. Most of us are sitting somewhere in the gap between the legislator's ideal of Mediterranean restraint and the grim reality of drinks manufacturers pouring lemonade-flavoured raspers down the throats of teenagers as quickly as possible.

In February of 2008, a Home Office review of the all-day-drinking laws showed that drinking and violence had remained at roughly similar levels since the laws had changed, although the peak time for violent incidents had moved forward by an hour, suggesting that the kind of people who like a drunken scrap *had* altered their behaviour; they were having a couple more drinks before punching you in the face on the way home.

That dreaded binge drinking had been happening all around us on that night out, certainly by official standards, since the official definition of 'binge' is four pints or more in a single session for men and three pints or more for women. Incidentally, what does it say about all of us, that every time I tell people the official definition of a binge they go, 'That's not much, is it?'

But no, that's not much. It's practically a self-fulfilling prophecy, pretending to be a statistic.

In Irish terms, that would make a 'binge' about half a 'session' and about a third of being on the 'complete rip'.

By government standards, about six million Brits binge drink at least once each week. And if they came home after four pints, they'd probably be quite shocked if someone shouted 'Binge drinker!' at them.

I certainly would have felt aggrieved by the branding. We got back to the hotel by 3.30 a.m. that night. We'd only been out for four hours, in a truncated night that could have gone on just a little bit longer. Luckily for us, the hotel bar was still open.

Chapter 8:
I am the Sorcerer!

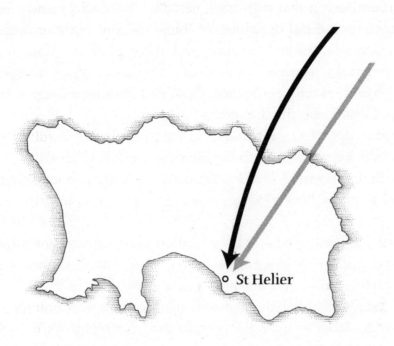

o St Helier

There's a certain childlike thrill to landing on an island. A proper island, that is, one you can see in its entirety as the plane comes in to land. There's a fairytale quality to it. It's just not normal. Of course, usually when people land on an island small enough to take in with a glance, they're on holiday and mundane life is on hold. It's more than just that happy association, though. It's not just a Pavlovian response to a couple of visible coastlines, or the memory of Hervé Villechaize, a dwarf in a white suit, shouting, 'The plane! The plane!'

When there's this much coast and this little land, your brain tells you, No! Normal life cannot work here. Something must have been sacrificed. They don't have the room here for all the stuff we have clogging up the mainland, so they must have prioritized. The islanders have taken this clean slate, and rebuilt from first principles. What have they shown that we really need? What will make a community work in such a small space?

And you start wondering what they can survive without. An MRI machine? A piano factory? A waterpark?

I lived on the Holloway Road in North London for a couple of years when I moved over from Ireland. At the rougher end of Islington, the Holloway Road is like London's version of the famous Afghanistan trade routes. Everything was available there if you knew who to ask. You want silk, spices, illegal DVDs, a black taxi, shop mannequins, S&M gear; it's all somewhere on the Holloway Road. My favourite was always the small shop at the northern end of the street which claimed to be 'London's Premier Golf Trophy Shop'. All it sold were hundreds of huge, gaudy, multi-level trophies with little silver golfers on the top.

The islanders will survive without a Golf Trophy shop.

It's not just infrastructure, though. Given a chance to rebuild society away from the mainland, what laws would you change? What freedoms would you grant? The possibilities for re-invention are endless. Islands are a place to hide, somewhere to begin again, to regress, a place for the lawless. Welcome to the last wild frontier. Welcome to Jersey.

The arrival in Jersey was a little too drizzly to sustain this much magic. It was a grey day, and the stone walls, green fields and rain made it feel much more like the west coast of Ireland than fifteen miles from France. As the taxi sped out of the airport, accelerated to thirty-nine and a half miles per hour and then held there, in deference to the absurdly strict motoring laws, it felt like commuting through County Galway on a wet October Sunday.

On the St Helier waterfront there was an old Ferris wheel, or at least the shell of an old Ferris wheel, with only a couple of remaining carriages dangling in the rain. It looked like every nightmare of a deserted and run-down beach resort, out of season and out of favour.

'The Jersey Eye could do with a lick of paint,' joked Damon. There was a long silence from the driver. We just presumed he was sad to see it fall into disrepair. He probably had his first kiss on it or something.

Luckily, this grim day wasn't my very first impression of the island. I had been in Jersey once before, the summer previous, when I had come over to address a conference of accountants. That arrival had been far more glorious, not least because Jersey's most famous resident, Alan Whicker, had been sitting on the plane beside me. Looking exactly as dapper as you would hope, his blazer and tie marked him out as someone who had made an effort for the journey, single-handedly raising the flight from Stansted out of the mundane and into the glorious age of travel that he always embodied. I felt like John Candy on *Planes, Trains and Automobiles* next to him. I introduced myself, of course.

'Hello, Mr Whicker. My name is Dara O Briain. I work sometimes with the BBC doing travel documentaries. I just wanted to say how much I admire your work.'

He smiled back.

'Hello. Yes. I've seen your work. Well done.'

Now, let's be clear about one thing. Alan Whicker had no idea who I was. Alan Whicker has not seen my work. Alan does not catch a lot of Dave, or type 'Mock the Week' into Google to find clips online. I was just a large stranger on a plane, leaning into his field of vision and claiming to be a part of his world. He's just a very classy man, and that's what very classy men say. I left, skipping, and he could carry on his day, elegantly.

If that was one lesson in how to conduct showbusiness, a far harsher one was to follow.

I was doing the after-dinner speech in a hotel ballroom in St Helier. In an unusual piece of double booking, there were actually two accountants' dinners that night in that hotel. I was speaking at one, and at the other, bizarrely, the address was being given by Nick Leeson, the man who broke Barings Bank. Quite why you'd invite an arsonist to address the firemen's dinner I don't know. It makes a perverse sort of sense, I suppose, but I was pretty sure that my accountants were going to have the more memorable show. And they did, although not because of me.

The coffees were being served when I was introduced to the stage. A man in a gold chain of office read a brief biography and told the ballroom that they were all very happy to have me here and could you please welcome onstage . . .

And I bounded on to a round of applause that was on the polite side of enthusiastic. Nothing wrong with that, it's an accountants' annual dinner in a ballroom. It's not a rock and roll crowd.

I warmed them up with some quite excellent jokes about Jersey's recently introduced General Sales Tax, jokes which, having told once, I will clearly never need to tell again. In fact, I'm guessing that my opening with jokes about Jersey's newly introduced General Sales Tax will make you, the reader, either go, 'Wow, Dara, how professional are you!' or, more likely, 'Wow, Dara, you really are some manner of whore.'

I don't care. Them GST gags were gold. Pretty soon, the venue was kicking, accountant-style. There was almost definitely laughter, some momentum and energy and, just occasionally, a brief smattering of applause when a good punchline was unleashed. The roof was not coming off the joint, I would not be carried out shoulder high and my face would not be appearing on any currency. But I was definitely getting away with it. Take that, Leeson, I thought, you hack.

Then the woman collapsed and the gig turned weird.

The first sign of this was the sudden sound of chairs moving in one corner of the room. All the people on one table had seen the woman slump to the floor and were now scurrying around trying to help.

The number of people who can realistically offer any help in this situation won't ever be more than two or three, but the tables in this hotel ballroom seated ten and that left half a dozen accountants desperately trying to look as concerned as possible. And what help could they offer? Some use *they* would be to the woman's husband:

'Help, help, my wife has collapsed!'

'Does she need her accounts done?'

'Why, actually, yes. It was the stress of not having her VAT in on time that caused her to collapse.'

'Well, unfortunately, we're not those kind of accountants. She should have collapsed in the other ballroom.'

So there's a collapsed woman, her by-now frantic other half and, swirling around, a collection of accountants offering all manner of advice and trying to look useful. Lift her up, hold her flat, give her something to drink, stick a pencil in her mouth, revive her, don't revive her – and now the rest of the room is beginning to notice. As each table turns towards the human drama unfolding at table thirteen, my audience is beginning to drain away and still I'm telling my little jokes.

This is a showbusiness dilemma. A man might be sharing the final moments with his wife and, while he bends over her to hear her precious last words, her message of love after the life they've spent together, I'm still cracking out the gags onstage. But, equally, a tipsy middle-aged woman may have slipped off her chair while falling asleep at yet another of her husband's dull works dinners. When she opens her eyes, the whole room is suddenly staring at her while the after-dinner speaker is tapping his watch and clearing his throat impatiently. The embarrassment would be legendary. The gravity of the first situation has to be balanced by the likelihood of the second. Whichever path I take, I have to commit to it entirely. I either stop the show completely, or carry on without mentioning it at all. There is no middle ground, no throwaway quip to lighten the mood before carrying on: 'Hey, I thought I was the one dying here! But anyway . . .'

Luckily, while one part of my brain carries on telling jokes and the other furiously weighs up the probabilities, the situation is taken out of my hands. One of the organizers very noticeably walks into the space between the top tables and the stage, on to the dancefloor basically, and makes the twirly hand-over-hand signal, which is internationally recognized as 'Keep it going'. Except in basketball, where it means 'Foul. Travelling.' I went with Keep it going.

Now we have the second dilemma. What material best covers a medical emergency? I can't pretend I'm unaware of the situation, which is showing no sign of calming down. But I have to soldier on, making sure that whatever story I start telling, it won't include any punchline that might suddenly seem horrendously inappropriate. I sometimes finish shows with a routine about the dangers of being eaten by a shark. We might skip that entire bit tonight. And it wouldn't hurt, either, if whatever line I did finish on, just also happened to be the funniest joke in the world. But this isn't like dying onstage. The audience aren't turning against me. In fact, they realize that it's really difficult for me precisely because it's so awkward for them. They desperately want to see what's happening over on table thirteen, but propriety demands that they also have to pretend that nothing is happening. I'm pretending to do a gig, and they're pretending to listen to it. And it works. I deliver a gag – I cannot recall what it is – and they start to laugh, louder than before. I tell another story, and they laugh at that as well. All is well. We are getting through this together.

And then there's a huge clatter of tables moving and chairs scraping the floor as hotel staff push a stretcher right through the middle of the crowd.

I just went, 'Thank you and good night!' and walked off the stage.

Jersey Fort Regent

1 fifteen-year-old who wants to be a vet, here with his
   mum, a teacher
1 teacher of IT for thirty years:
   'They laughed at you at first, didn't they? Back in the seventies,
   with your wooden computer.
   "Just you wait," you said.'
1 lawyer down from London to see the show
1 man with a weird laugh
4 accountants

I opened with the story of the woman collapsing from
my previous visit. It seemed like a nice experience to share,
especially since there were two couples in the audience who
had been at that fateful accountants' dinner. It's always useful to have someone to corroborate the stories; not least to
reassure the crowd that nobody died on the night. (Nobody
died; she had just fainted and came to with the help of a
glass of water.) Not that I was stuck for opening lines.

We could start with the venue. Fort Regent looms
solidly over St Helier. Built in the early 1800s as a response
to the French invasion of 1781, it is a proper military
keep with dense, high walls and set at a strategic location
facing France. The absence of any other subsequent French
invasion could be taken as proof of its success as a deterrent, although Napoleon may have had other priorities
by that stage. It was de-militarized in 1927, in good time for
the German invasion of 1940. The occupying forces used
the fort until Liberation Day, 9 May 1945, when Jerseyman
Major Hugh le Brocq demanded their surrender and hoisted

the Union Flag over the fort at 4 p.m. Liberation Day is still celebrated, and falls the day after VE day, indicating that there were a full twenty-four hours during which the people of Jersey were politely coughing and checking their watches and waiting for the Germans to get the hint and leave.

In the absence of any impending invasions, the fort passed into civil use and over the years became an iconic leisure facility on the island, housing a swimming pool, a mini-golf course and cable cars. These days, it is a proper leisure centre in the modern sense, i.e., a gym, filled with exercise equipment and sports facilities. It is the world's most secure gymnasium. It certainly has the best-equipped backstage area in showbiz, particularly suitable if your rider demanded sixty weight machines, forty elliptical trainers and three squash courts. It's at moments like these that I wish I had an entourage.

Instead, I have Damon and, to kill time before the show, he and I went to play pool instead. The informal layout caught us out, though. We never realized that, somewhere between the dressing rooms and the pool tables, we crossed some invisible line called 'backstage'. Mid-frame, we suddenly found ourselves greeting the first wave of punters coming in.

'I hope you're good, I came out in this weather for you,' said the first.

'I'm missing the Eurovision for this,' said the next.

We knocked the pool on the head and retreated to the gym. They're a feisty lot, the Crappos.

Oh yeah, they have their own nicknames. You can call them Jersey 'Beans', which comes from the historical popularity of a bean casserole, but also, and slightly more awkwardly, you can call them 'Crappos'. It's from the French '*crapaud*', meaning toad. It's a Jersey *v.* Guernsey thing, but accepted benignly. Visitors are nervous of embracing this, naturally, but the islanders are well used to it, leading me to this line:

'Listen, I was told what to call you ... it sounds rude to me but I was told you don't mind ... so here goes. Hello, Cunts!'

That got a big laugh.

You know the way that if you bring two similarly polarized magnets close together, they repel each other? And the closer they get, the stronger you can feel that repulsion. Now fill an island with English people and put it fifteen miles away from France. You can feel the Englishness radiate through the place. I'm not saying that, secretly, the people of Jersey are French and it's the similarity that drives them apart, so maybe magnets were a terrible analogy. Allergies! That's better. You know the way it's easy to forget that you have a terrible allergy to dogs, say, until you're forced to move house and live right next door to a kennels. Except that, in this analogy, the French are dogs, so, again, it's a bad one.

All I'm saying is that Jersey just feels unbelievably English. In fact, like the most English place on the planet. Oh sure, all the road names are in French (or Jèrriais, the local dialect), but it's not exactly coming down with baguettes. The locals would point out that Jersey, like the other Channel islands, is a crown dependency and not part of the UK. They would note the 2007 agreement with the UK Lord Chancellor which affirmed, among other things, that Jersey has a separate international identity to the UK, and that the UK will not act on behalf of Jersey internationally without prior consultation. They would probably even point to a survey in 2000 in which 68 per cent of islanders supported independence.

But it couldn't feel more English if it was just off the M25. Jersey is the home counties on a raft. It's the world's most scrupulously polite border town. It's like Tijuana with an excellent neighbourhood-watch scheme.

This shouldn't sound cold or dismissive. That gig in Fort Regent was easily one of the best of the tour and the audience were chatty and enthusiastic and more than happy to laugh at themselves. It was also littered with moments of unexpected topicality.

I have one joke about how, in Ireland, everyone knows what parish they live in while, in London, I have absolutely no clue, because, as I say in the show, 'I haven't caught the priest marking out the boundary with his smell glands.' I then mime a Catholic priest rubbing his scent on a fence post to alert other priests that they've moved into a new parish. Basically, I'm making a terribly clever joke about territory and the pervasive umbrella of the Church, unavoidable in Ireland. Then it just descends into me miming feral priests stealing food from bins and acting out the discussions among neighbours about how to deal with them:

'Spray them with a hose. It's the only language they understand. Apart from Latin. They also understand Latin.'

In Jersey, I get about two words into this 'bit' when I hit the unforeseen speedbump of the words 'I don't know what parish I live in.' Jersey is broken into twelve parishes and, if you live on the island, you will know exactly what parish you live in. For a start, each parish has its own police force. If you speed in Jersey, these are the people you answer to, often in person, in a local town hall. This was explained to me by an Irish woman drawn to the island by the financial trade whom I met after the gig.

'We're all stockbrokers, and we buy nice cars and then we can't go over 40 mph. And sometimes you do, and if you get caught, you have to drag your arse all the way back to the same parish to apologize to the elders.'

And then she said a lot of rude things about the local police force that I can't corroborate.

Don't get me wrong, the Irish love a committee. And the French are known for a tangle of local bureaucracy. But thirteen police forces for an island of eighty-eight thousand people? Just give everyone a badge and be done with it. They can all patrol their own field and set their own speed limits, and we'll just go accelerating and decelerating randomly round the island.

The massive parallel to England, though, is that small portion of the population who think that what they have is at all times in danger of being destroyed, and mainly by modernizers, or foreigners. BBC Jersey reported during the year on the proposition that the island could be connected to France by bridge, with the Sweden-to-Denmark Öresund bridge touted as the model. A quick scan of the comments on the website shows a healthy debate, but often punctuated with gloriously apocalyptic visions of the future from the type of people who seem to mix up the word 'immigrants' with 'zombie army'. Like this guy:

Peter: Let's talk about the millions of immigrants just wanting to get our jobs for less money, our life ruined by thousands of cars landing here. What about our life? Our pubs? Entering a pub and just can't be there 'cause there are too many people around. HELL ON EARTH!!!! BRIDGE? HELL BRIDGE! NO WAY!

I know, I know, all those immigrants, with their low-paid jobs and cars but yet still sitting in pubs all day – how do they find the time? Nothing tops HELL BRIDGE! for a nightmarish turn of phrase, although this came close:

> **Amy:** I don't think that the bridge is a good idea, don't just think about how much it might cost think what could happen may-be if one of the French brought over a dog who had rabies and it got passed around or something

Don't keep that rabid dog all to yourself, François! Pass it around, we all want a go on it.

But surely even the protectionist fringe can see some upsides:

> **Richard:** I think the only benefit is that I could go over the bridge at will and pick up some nice French cheese and freshly baked bread – Yum Yum!!

See what I mean? No baguette shops. There isn't a single French-bread shop on the island. The smell must float over with the breeze every morning and drive them insane. One half-decent *boulangerie* and they could save themselves the cost of a bridge.

So it's the usual English mix of self-styled Defenders of the Way Things Are to normal punters getting on with life. The latter are more fun to drink with and all of them seemed to be gathered around St Helier's Royal Yacht Hotel when I emerged after the show. Jersey kicks off at the weekend, I can report, and the young and moneyed throw their cash, and themselves, around with some abandon. With the perfect excuse not to drive home for once, Damon and I were happy to join them. We started in the quayside bar but, as the rounds kept coming, we forced our way deeper into the revellers, towards the music. The drinks continued to flow.

Eventually, I had to step away from the dancefloor, and I was in the nightclub toilets, enjoying a moment of quiet concentration, when the man at the next urinal turned to me and said: 'Oh, it's yourself!'

(This existential conundrum is a common form of address for the Irish. It's a welcoming form of greeting which deftly avoids any possible social death from mislaying a name: 'Is it yourself?' is both familiar, and impossible to say no to.)

He, himself, was William McDevitt, an Irishman working in Jersey and brother to a girl who was in my class in primary school. He knew that I had been performing on the island, but Munster had played a Heineken Cup rugby match that afternoon and that had been his priority. After Munster won, though, he and his friends, fired with a renewed patriotism, decided I should get their, by now quite sozzled, support.

'So we presented ourselves at the theatre and asked for four tickets. And we got the last four seats.'

'Excellent,' said I. 'What stage was I at when you got in?'

'Not so fast,' said William. 'As we were being led through to the theatre, I had a look at the tickets, and the name of the show was "The Sorceror".'

'"The Sorceror"? Why would my show be called "The Sorceror"?'

'Y'know, I just presumed that's what you call yourself these days.'

And he showed me the ticket. The words 'The Sorceror' were written in huge letters. And, underneath it, only slightly smaller, 'Jersey Gilbert and Sullivan Society'.

'So when did you realize . . .?'

'We were led through the theatre to the only empty seats in the place, and when we sat down and looked up, some woman was onstage in a petticoat. And she started to sing. And we all went, "This is the wrong fucking show," and just stood up and walked out again.'

'That's very funny.'

'Maybe for you, but the woman in the box office wouldn't give us a refund. I spent £64 on you today.'

And then we left the bathroom, went back to the night-club and I tried to buy him £64 of drink as an apology.

We left Jersey feeling a little ropier the following morning. As we drove past the St Helier waterfront, we saw the Ferris wheel, the same as yesterday but with at least four extra carriages bolted on to it. What had been our symbol of decay was actually in the middle of being built.

'That Jersey Eye is taking shape, isn't it?' said Damon.

'It certainly is. It'll be ready for the summer,' beamed the taxi driver.

And we sped past, the needle never going past forty.

Chapter 9:
Tickling the 'Burbs'

Back on the mainland, we enter the southern suburbs. I'm taking a very broad and loose definition of 'suburbs' here, to include new and dormitory towns and anywhere, basically, where a large proportion of the crowd will rise the following morning and get the train into the centre of London for work. This covers a vast swathe of the south-east, whose own identity and independence is swallowed up by the gravitational pull of the giant mass of London nearby. From Tunbridge Wells to Maidenhead, from Watford to Chichester, these towns are anywhere up to fifty or sixty miles away from the capital, and often the audience I get aren't even from these towns but from the pretty villages surrounding. These are the places that people move to when London wears them down and they want some bucolic approximation of country life in which to raise their families, albeit one with a regular rail service to London Bridge.

Three things make these gigs difficult. The first is the newly formulated Dara's First Law of Identity. The greater the sense of local identity, the more audiences talk. When we visited the cities, we mentioned the corollary to Dara's First Law: the presence of a noted local football team makes for a chatty crowd. Here in the suburbs this is particularly noticeable. Any idea how Tunbridge Wells FC are doing? No, neither do I, and neither do the people of Tunbridge Wells. They are more famous for some eighteenth-century baths, and your average spa doesn't inspire that much loyalty. As I've said about the cities, even if you're not a football fan, you'll have heard your town mentioned enough times within a competitive context to be used to the idea of it being represented; and, by extension, you will sub-consciously represent it when you're talking to me.

Here, in the south, we can also postulate Dara's Second Law: the more modern the jobs, the less the crowd care. There is a hard and fast rule about the 'what do you do for a living?' question: it works if the audience have any clue what the job involves. Which is great if it's a policeman, baker or astronaut. The crowd has an automatic emotional response, and curiosity, about those kinds of jobs. Ideally, everyone I speak to would have the sort of job you've read about, aged seven, in a brightly illustrated Richard Scarry book called *Things We Make and Do.*

Less helpful is electronic engineer, insurance fund manager or IT consultant; and the suburbs are full of IT consultants.

The final thing that adds to the challenge of making people laugh is prosperity. What the hell, let's make it Dara's Third Law: rich people don't laugh much. They smile contentedly, they're happy to be there, they chortle a bit, but you can't shake that sense that they're indulging you. 'Well done, funny chap,' they're saying, 'that is an amusing story you're telling. You've done well; but then so have I, haven't I? Look at my lovely wife. We live in a big house. Eldest is in Cambridge now. Life is good.'

There was an entire night in **Chichester**, for example, where a crowd that consisted mainly of architects and property developers smiled benignly but contentedly, and where the only extreme reaction was during the routine where I take an axe to homeopathy, and the crowd sort of shuffled in their seats as if to say, 'Well, you say that, but whenever little Rupert gets a sniffle . . .'

My favourite subset of the contented are men in senior management, or the bosses of their own companies. I find these people to be quite a compelling subspecies of their own. They've been surrounded by juniors who are obliged to laugh at their jokes for years, and the daily absence of a natural predator has left them quite out of condition, performance wise. I can spot this whenever I ask a middle-aged man in the audience, 'What do you do for a living?' and he says, 'Not much!' and looks around expecting the laugh it gets in the office. It can be quite disorientating for them to see that this kind of response is neither original, nor particularly funny.

In **Aylesbury**, we had a foreign-currency trader who

looked very happy with himself in the front row, so I spent the night quizzing him about life in the bureau de change:

'Do they bring you tea, in the little booth?'
    'Which country has the prettiest notes?'
    'Do you ever get jealous, watching all these people going off on their holidays?'

It was all quite gentle, I thought, but clearly far more vicious than the respectful joshing he got from the juniors at work. When I came out for my encore, he walked out, wife in tow.

Rock journalists write about people losing their 'edge', but I think that's a deliberately self-congratulatory term. I think that success makes people lose their curiosity. They find a comfort zone; they build a wall around themselves and they raise their children there. If all goes to plan the kids hit their teens, find it all claustrophobically dull and leave to make their mark.

The suburbs exist in order to make young people tetchy and eager to move to London. That's the circle of life, I suppose. It's like *The Lion King*, but set in Basingstoke.

High Wycombe Swan

1 former army-truck driver
1 man from N (or Penge; or Enne; or something)
1 man from a data storage company
1 teenage boy

High Wycombe is a good example of the 'burbs'. Situated about thirty miles north-west of London, it was once a thriving market town with a successful furniture industry. Now it is commuterville. It has also sold itself under the slogan 'High Wycombe – A Place to Get Excited About!'

I myself have not had the chance to get excited. In all the years I've been travelling to the Wyc, I've never seen it open.

This is not a problem unique to High Wycombe. We often arrive into towns in time for a six-thirty soundcheck. In other words, after all the shops are shut and the streets are deserted. The only signs of life are the members of my audience smiling out at me from pizza restaurants as I walk past the windows trying to get a feel for the place. For all I know, the shops never open in King's Lynn, Woking or Carlisle.

Tonight then, as usual, I wandered through the empty streets to the Wycombe Swan Theatre and therein tried to convince a nice, well-to-do crowd that there's something inherently amusing about working in data storage. They weren't convinced.

The man from Enne, or Penge, or wherever (it was difficult to hear and, after asking three times, I was in danger of boring the arse off the room; when in doubt just go with whatever you think the person said), told us that the village he lived in had four pubs and that his favourite was the Horse and Jockey.

'What's so great about the Horse and Jockey then?' I enquired.

'The guys are really great in there,' he said, clearly not intending it to sound quite as gay as it did.

Nevertheless, I was looking for any comedy angle at this stage. I took the low road.

'How would you describe yourself then, as a horse, or a jockey?'

No answer.

During the crime story, as if to underline the refined tone of the area, somebody claimed to have stopped some under-age drinking. This got booing from the youth of Wycombe, but stood as a helpful reminder that this is a part of the world that takes law and order seriously.

For example, High Wycombe has an extraordinary tradition of weighing its mayor at the start of their year-long term and then again at the end to see if they have put on weight by living it large at the ratepayers' expense. The weigh-in is done in public and, if the mayor has filled out a little, the town crier announces it by shouting, 'And some more!' to the crowd. Then they take the mayor round the back and beat the shit out of him.

I had my own little run-in with taste and decency in High Wycombe once, but from an unlikely source. My first tour of the UK was as support to legendary American comic Emo Phillips. Emo had been a bit of a hero to me, and I eagerly accepted the invite to travel the country with him for a couple of months. Almost instantly though, it transpired that, as a hard-drinking, single, twentysomething Irish comic, I had little in common with the clean-living, married, fiftysomething Californian that I had been paired up with. It was like a bad buddy movie. We struggled to find anything to talk about in transit and wherever we overnighted I bolted out the door in search of the local nightlife as soon as I decently could. By the end of the tour, I felt guilty about my contribution to this personality clash and, just before the final show, in High Wycombe, I pre-sented Emo with a gift, an anthology of work from the Irish humorous writer Flann O'Brien. Emo looked quite taken aback.

'I'm sorry,' he said, examining the volume, 'I didn't get you anything.'

'That's all right,' said I. 'It was your tour and I really appreciated the chance to work on it. It's just a small thank-you.'

I left him in his dressing room and was heading to the stage when Emo ran out to catch me.

'Listen,' he said, and there was a pregnant pause, 'you should curse less onstage.' And then he smiled and turned back to his dressing room.

Would this be a better story if I said that, From that moment on, etc., etc.?

Well, sorry. I went on stage that night and ripped the skies a new one, such was my generosity with the f-bomb, the c-word and, just for the night, the newly coined g-word, q-word and x-word.

After that performance, I'm surprised the good people of High Wycombe let me back in again.

St Albans Arena

1 man from the Foreign Office
1 investment salesman
1 carpenter and joiner
1 man who runs a cleaning company

Even though the Americans still tend to think of the suburbs as their invention, modern suburbia really began in London at the end of the eighteenth century, when increased wealth allowed a new class of wealthy Londoners to consider moving out to the pleasant rural areas to the south of the city.

Nowadays, even though the suburbs are scorned for their meticulously pruned hedges and tense, petty neighbourly disputes, they are the heart of the nation. England is a suburban nation. By any reckoning, more than half the population lives in some kind of suburb, and this figure goes as high as 70 per cent in some experts' estimation. Roughly a third of English households live in semi-detached houses, according to the 2001 census, making it the most popular type of home.

There is also a subtle difference between dormitory or satellite suburbs in the UK and those in the USA. Because England is so much older, and so much smaller, many of these places weren't green-field sites. The towns I visit are more 'Expanded Towns' rather than 'New Towns' in the conventional sense, and many of them had distinct identities and histories before they became swallowed up.

St Albans, for example, is a fairly posh dormitory town of about 120,000 people about twenty miles north of London. Most of the interesting things about St Albans happened a long time ago, and the town doesn't seem that likely to repeat them any time soon. The first British saint – the eponymous St Alban – was martyred here by beheading in the third century; the St Albans School includes Adrian IV, the only British Pope, among its past pupils.

The first version of the most English of all documents – the Magna Carta – was drafted in St Albans Abbey. Ye Olde Fighting Cocks, just down the road from the abbey, has a strong claim to be the oldest pub in Britain.

Currently, though, about one in five of the population commutes to London each day. The property agency, Savills, describes it as the 'über-commuter town' and, in April 2009, the *Guardian* reported that residents of St Albans pay the most tax per capita of any town or city in the UK – about £10,000 each, more than double the national average (Hull was the lowest town on the list).

You can also tell a lot about St Albans by the fact that the council ran a massive campaign to get St Albans selected as the most expensive Monopoly property on the new version of the board game launched in 2007. The top squares were decided by a national internet vote and, following the campaign, in which the town's mayor appeared on radio to battle with rival mayors, St Albans replaced Mayfair as the top square, having taken 10 per cent of the million plus votes in the competition. A spokesperson for Liverpool, which ended up as the cheapest square, said, 'I suppose you can spend a lot of time on this sort of thing in a place where nothing much else is going on.' That is what we in the comedy industry call a zinger.

My gig in St Albans was one of two halves. In the first, I struggled to lift the energy at all. The man from the Foreign Office was certainly able to confirm that his job was a lot less interesting when the only bit of empire remaining was Gibraltar, which is basically a monkey safari off Spain.

The man selling investment products took the time after each question to confer with all of his friends, as if all his public pronouncements had to be cleared with a committee.

The man who ran a cleaning company just stared at me like I was filthy.

'I'm fucking hating this gig,' I said to Damon at the interval. 'I can't wait to get out of here.'

'Yeah ... well, the thing is ...' Damon started, awkwardly, 'I wasn't going to tell you, but *The Times* is in.'

I have a rule about not knowing when we have reviewers in. It dates back from the small rooms in Edinburgh, where you'd scan the forty people in attendance furiously, looking for the one with a notepad. And then you'd spend the rest of the hour directing the entire show at that one person in a desperate attempt to bump yourself up a star on the ratings. It was a route to madness.

In the larger theatres, there's no danger of seeing the man with a notepad, so this embargo is a bit pointless and Damon was right to spill the beans. I absolutely tore up the second half, thus proving that those three laws I wrote about earlier should really only be viewed as a guideline, and that I should put some more effort in.

When the review was printed a couple of days later, I scoured it to see if the *Times* comedy reviewer Dominic Maxwell had spotted this sudden upsurge in energy. And even though it wasn't mentioned explicitly, he did note that I could sometimes be a little more 'inclusive', including this exchange:

> 'Have I come out with the wrong face?' [O Briain] asks, as audience members are slow to answer his questions. 'Am I like a bear sniffing you f***ers for fresh meat?' Well, quite: sometimes it does look like he's out to mock the weak.

And if I thought I had dodged that bullet, well, there was a sting in the tail.

> The show tails off when O Briain oversells a story about crisps, palpably trying to force finale-levels of funniness out of an amusing anecdote. Following which, his usually endearing habit of providing footnotes for his own material –

the crisps routine goes down very differently in Ireland, he tells us – just clogs up the ending.

It was only telling me what I already knew – that Tayto story had to go.

Croydon Fairfield Halls

1 coffee-machine-repair engineer
1 father of a twelve-, fourteen- and seventeen-year-old
1 student of television and journalism
1 quite hostile teacher

Historically, of course, people lived where they worked – rural people lived near their land and urban people lived close to their workplace, often in a flat over their shop or business. Until large-scale mass transport, the suburbs were only there for the very, very rich, who had large estates outside of the town, or the very poor, who couldn't afford to live within the walls. One of the definitions of 'suburb' in the 1668 edition of the *Oxford English Dictionary* was 'a place of inferior, debased and especially licentious habits of life'.

Is it unfair to bring this up when talking about Croydon? Maybe. But the town doesn't really sit in this company in many ways. It's a lot closer to the centre of London, and it certainly doesn't strike you as quite as settled and middle class as the others. It also looks like Frankfurt, for some reason. Every other town along the South Circular looks like every London village: houses, houses, houses, then suddenly a broadway of banks, pubs, fried-chicken shops and a Boots, then houses, houses, houses until the next village. That's the way London is. Until you hit Croydon, and suddenly it's a boulevard with tower blocks on either side. It looks like one of these cities built so that the people could travel underground to avoid terrible weather; like the summers in Atlanta or those harsh Montreal winters. Croydon, of course, gets the same drizzly nothing as the rest of the country. A visionary architect must have kept saying, 'Just give me one town and I will change the way you view urban planning for ever!' So they gave him Croydon and he didn't. He's probably working in a bakery now.

It was a different kind of tough crowd that night. One man sat side on to the stage with a scowl on his face.

'Are you enjoying the show, sir?'

'Not really. My wife wanted to come.'

Any attempts to draw him into some happy banter fell on deaf ears, lending the night a tense air.

After the show, I was due to have a drink with the builder who was working on my house, who lived locally and had asked to come along. While we chatted, Damon noticed an event taking place in the room next door.

'You should come see this, this is great!' he reported back.

In the conference room of the Croydon Fairfield Halls, uniquely among theatres in the UK, there was a boxing ring. Before the show, I had noted how many shaven-headed men had turned up for my show with gym bags. 'This is not my usual crowd,' I had said to Damon. It turned out they weren't my crowd at all. We sneaked in just in time for the top of the bill, and I stood with Damon, my builder and his wife, watching two heavyweights slug it out.

More theatres should offer this service. Two large men, pounding each other round the ring, while a comedian looks

Tickling the English

on, bobbing and weaving in sympathy, a pint in his hand. And, in his mind's eye, the difficult audience member keeps failing to connect, no matter how many haymakers he throws, until with one left hook from the funnyman, *bam!* and he's being counted out: 1, 2, 3 ...

... and all the time the comic just keeps dancing.

Basingstoke Anvil Theatre

1 man who sells telephone systems
1 karate teacher
1 cargo manager

To end this week among a typical slice of England, we reach Basingstoke on 23 April, St George's Day.

Basingstoke was once a prosperous market town, which developed into an industrial centre when the railway arrived in 1839. However, being almost fifty miles south-west of London, it avoided initial growth as a commuter town. After the Second World War, it was then used as a destination for the development of public housing in the 'London Overspill' plan and also took off as a dormitory town for the wealthier class of commuters. It's a generally wealthy place, with some big local employers, high per capita living standards and low unemployment. It's 97 per cent white and has very high levels of owner-occupiers compared to England as a whole. Unsurprisingly, Basingstoke has been a solidly Conservative area since the 1920s. This, then, would seem like the perfect place to enjoy such an important day.

St George is the patron saint of England. He is also the patron saint of Portugal, Greece, Georgia, Lithuania,

Ethiopia, Palestine and the Spanish region of Catalonia, so he must have a terribly conflicted time during the European Championships. There is some debate about his identity, however there probably was a real St George – an officer in the Roman army who lived in what is now modern-day Turkey and was beheaded because he refused to renounce his Christianity. He was martyred, supposedly, on 23 April AD303. His body was buried in Palestine, where his mother is thought to have come from originally. As a Christian martyr, George was revered in the Eastern Church, which explains why he's the patron of Georgia, Greece and Palestine.

Just to confuse things, he's also retrospectively considered by Muslims as having died 'in a state of Islam', just as Jesus and the Jewish prophets are considered holy men. He's seen as a martyr to monotheism and, in parts of the Middle East, he has become entwined with the Islamic figure El Khidr, to whom mosques are dedicated in Jerusalem and Beirut.

Even the Christian church where St George's remains are supposedly buried is venerated by Muslims. In 1995, travel writer William Dalrymple asked the local priest if he received many Muslim visitors, to which he replied, 'We get hundreds! Almost as many as the Christian pilgrims. Often, when I come in here, I find Muslims all over the floor, in the aisles, up and down.'

Why St George is the patron of England takes a little more explaining. It wasn't until the Crusades that George became a major figure in the English imagination. The St George's Cross – a red cross on a white background – was actually the flag of the City of Genoa, but was flown by English ships in the Mediterranean from 1190 onwards as

England enjoyed the protection of the Genoese fleet. This means that the Muslims like George, but are a little less taken with the flag and, given its role in a major religious war, I'm not sure I blame them.

The crusaders tended to wear the design, and returning crusaders also brought the whole dragon myth with them to England. Edward III made St George the official patron of England and, in the Middle Ages, St George's Day was a popular holiday like Christmas or Easter.

As England expanded and became the United Kingdom and then the British Empire, the Union Jack replaced the St George's Cross in most places and celebrating the feast day also became less common. In the early 1960s, St George's Day was actually demoted to being a minor memorial in the Catholic Church.

In the last few years, there has been a campaign to re-launch St George's Day, in an effort to find a few non-sporting occasions for self-celebration. It was part of the Romantic, nostalgic side of the English personality, and also an expression of that bizarre section of England I mentioned at the beginning of the book that likes to perceive itself the victim of a terrible injustice. How can the Celts have their day? Why has everyone heard of Paddy's Day and not of Brave St George? Where are our parades?

There are a couple of simple reasons why St Patrick's Day is a massive global success story and St George's Day is not. Obviously, there's the drinking, the parades and the enormous Irish diaspora, which clung to the festival as a celebration of home and, as they became more successful in their new lands, developed it into the cavalcade of Guinness and green that it is today. To a huge extent, it was the foreign Irish that made Paddy's Day into the brand you recognize today. In the last decade or so, we've had to expand it unrecognizably in Dublin from a parade on the day, into an entire weekend of festivities, and all of this just to keep up with the Americans. They would come over and wonder why it was a smaller party in Dublin than it was in New York.

England can have none of this. You drink as much as we do, but we've already seen you don't really approve of it, and you certainly would never sell yourselves internationally on a reputation for drinking. You have a diaspora, of sorts, in the sense that you have ex-pats all over the world. This is fundamentally different to Ireland, however, in that your diaspora is mainly in Provence, where they moved to of their own accord. In the tragic tale of Irish emigration, very rarely was anyone overheard on the coffin ships saying, 'Well, we've just always wanted to run a small hotel in the Dordogne. The kids have reached that age, so we said, what the hell, let's go for it.'

It also doesn't help that St George never even set foot in England. There are no historical sites to venerate, because he was never here. This is similar to the never-ending English devotion to the hymn 'Jerusalem', despite it being a long feedline to a very curt and obvious punchline:

And did those feet in ancient time
Walk upon England's mountains green? *No.*
And was the holy Lamb of God
On England's pleasant pastures seen? *Nope.*
And did the Countenance Divine
Shine forth upon our clouded hills? *Still a big nooo, I'm afraid.*
And was Jerusalem builded here
Among those dark Satanic mills? *No. It wasn't. Sorry about that.*
And it's 'built', by the way.

There is a far, far more fundamental reason as to why it is ludicrous to compare the two festivals. A far more obvious reason, and one which always makes St George look like a small boy trying to play a man's game.

St Patrick's Day is a religious festival. It is a very important religious festival. It is a very important religious festival in a country that basically has had only one religion for hundreds of years and a religion that is taken very seriously. It is a Holy Day of Obligation, so if you're a Catholic, you have to go to Mass. And since everyone in Ireland (give or take; up until recently) was a Catholic, that means that the entire country came to a halt. Are we beginning to see where St George might be looking like a fairly half-arsed competitor yet? Ah, but there's more.

St Patrick's Day falls in the middle of Lent, the Christian festival of penance and self-sacrifice. For forty days and for forty nights, blah blah Jesus in the desert, for our sins, blah blah, the devil tried to tempt him, blah blah, everyone has to give up sweets. And Everyone Had to Give Up Sweets. Or cigarettes. Or pints. It's almost the only thing I regret about Ireland's move towards secularism, that future generations won't have that shared experience of ditching the Mars bars for six weeks.

Obviously, it was a problem that, in the middle of this season of self-sacrifice, lay our largest national fiesta. So, an Irish solution to an Irish problem. On 17 March, you got the day off Lent. Don't ask me how that worked theologically. Presumably, Jesus walked out of the desert, just for the day, watched the parade, wore a big Guinness hat and ate as much chocolate as he wanted. And then the following day, back into the desert. Either way, for decades and decades and decades, St Patrick's Day was the oasis of fun in a generally grim month and a half.

Now, tell me how St George's Day is supposed to compete with that? No amount of photo opportunities with Boris Johnson and some Morris dancers can compete with the power of an autocratic Church with a 95 per cent monopoly, combined with the sugar rush of the sudden infusion of six bars of Cadbury's Dairy Milk.

St George's Day can't get close. For a start, it isn't even a national holiday. Even if you wanted people to celebrate it, they have to go to work.

It has no context, no history and no purpose. It smacks of wishful thinking by a right-minded committee that thinks you can just parachute these things into place, as long as you get the logo right and, probably, they've got a team of consultants working on that right now. £400k later and they'll show you a letterhead of George and a grinning dragon doing a thumbs-up.

There was already an attempt to do this with a 'British Day' in 2007. Communities Secretary Ruth Kelly MP and Immigration Minister Liam Byrne MP, publicly launched the idea and came up with ways of celebrating Britain Day after a year of canvassing public opinion. A twenty-seven-point list of recommendations was circulated which should just have been photocopied directly from the back of the envelope it was written on. The ideas were vague and random:

3. By using TV to inform about British history; a speech by the Queen; TV link-ups around country.
5. By encouraging young people to visit or help older people; celebrate voluntary work.

Until, inevitably, and with a certain blunt honesty:

13. Through drinking . . .

And before the list was even finished you could feel the straws being clutched at. It just became a collection of random, positive words:

20. By appreciating the country; weather; enjoyment.

The British Day plan was quietly dropped.

The fact is, you can't reverse-engineer something like Paddy's Day. And you probably don't want to. Are you ready to put aside your ambivalent attitude to religion in general, and instead force the entire country to convert to Catholicism and then give the Church hierarchy unfettered access to the reins of power? We know you don't want it and, frankly, I didn't move to England to sit through that again.

Face it, England is the victim of its own success. You can't gobble up other nations, absorb them into your flag, and then whine that your original flag doesn't get the attention it deserves. All this crying over the St George's flag is like a fat girl who ate everyone's cake wailing that she can't fit into her party dress any more. This is what you wanted with the empire; suck it up.

Moreover, it might be worth asking if there isn't a bigger price to pay for the kind of cultural success Paddy's Day has achieved.

There isn't an Irish person alive who hasn't cringed at the sight of Guinness hats and leprechauns being bandied about like That's Who We Are.

Every year, we see the footage of drunken American kids wearing 'Kiss Me, I'm Irish' T-shirts and getting hammered in our honour. Even at home, the day has always been a bit of an underage drinking festival. I appreciate the craic as much as anyone; I just dislike the entire nation being reduced to a caricature.

All those campaigning furiously for a St George's festival might be wise to ask themselves if they want to see England narrowed down to a man in a cartoon dragon costume running down Fifth Avenue. 'Tally Ho!' they'll shout, in a Dick Van Dyke English accent. 'Tally Ho!'

The show in Basingstoke passed without any mention of George at all. In fact, we had forgotten what day it was until, on the drive home, we had to swerve to miss a solitary, stumbling drunk wrapped in a St George's cross.

As he wandered home late and emotional, this celebrant seemed to have sufficiently enjoyed himself without any committee help. He didn't look like he was pining for a parade. He didn't seem like he needed someone to step in and organize a party for him. A pedestrian crossing, maybe, but as for the rest of the day, he seemed to have navigated that perfectly well on his own.

Chapter 10:
From London to London (in a week)

After the blur of motorways, we have a few days of commuting like a normal person. We land in London, at the Hammersmith Apollo, not ten minutes from my home and probably the most crucial week of the tour.

For one thing, it's the biggest room of the tour. Three nights here in front of over ten thousand punters would be a big deal anyway, even without the extra weight: this is where we record the tour DVD.

The night you record the DVD is always among the most important and, sadly, least enjoyable of the whole escapade.

For a start, it's burdened with pressure. This is the snapshot of a year's work; the one iteration of an ever-changing show that gets trapped in amber and presented to the world as an item of record. 'This was my show,' it says. 'This is what I talked about every night up and down the country. If you didn't come along to see it live, this is what you missed.'

And it's not, of course. The show changes every night, depending on who's in and what happens. And the best you can hope for is that on the single night that you've hired six cameras and sound and light and an outside broadcast van and put on a nice suit, well, the best you can hope for is that that isn't the night where all the seats at the front have been block-booked by an electronic-engineering company. This is not the night for the crowd to break all three of Dara's Rules.

The exam dream you have before the tour is replaced by the more vivid panic of standing in front of a crowd going what do you do? – what do you do? – what do you do? And every smiling face replies, 'I work in IT.' 'I, too, work in IT.' 'Well, actually, I also work in IT, but in an even more obscure niche than the previous two.'

And at the end, when the filming stops, you find out that row two is filled with astronauts, firemen and undersea welders, all sitting there shrugging and going, 'Why didn't he talk to us?'

God, the times I pine for an underwater welder onstage.

But this neurosis is for the end of the week. First, Monday night in the Apollo with no cameras, then a quick spin around the country, then back home to Hammersmith for Friday and the big day on Saturday.

London Hammersmith Apollo

1 service locator
1 business adviser
1 proctologist

Monday is a romp.

I was not expecting this. For the last couple of years, comedians have been colonizing this legendary rock venue through the BBC *Live at the Apollo* series, which has become an increasingly important landmark gig for a rising comic, plus a rare chance to do more with that Edinburgh show you'd written than carve it into tiny portions to hand out to panel shows.

It's a great show to do but, Jesus, a cold crowd sometimes. The punters get the tickets for free because it's a TV show, they have no clue who's going to be on, the room is really brightly lit, so that everyone is 15 per cent more self-conscious than they should be and, if they don't know you, it can feel vast out there.

I remember the first time I appeared on *Live at the Apollo*. Before you come on, you have to stand behind a giant sign at the back of the stage that spells 'Apollo' in light bulbs which, like all set dressing, looks great from a distance but, up close, is just a load of light bulbs. At least when it moves, though, it's genuinely done mechanically. Most of the time, walls that slide and doors that open on telly shows are done by hand so, as you wait to go on, nervously running through the lines, muttering, 'Don't fuck up the first joke, don't fuck up the first joke,' there's a bloke standing next to you with Allen keys and gaffer tape hanging off his belt muttering,

'Don't fuck up opening the door, don't fuck up opening the door.'

On *Have I Got News for You?*, for example, the backdrops spin into position as the show starts. What you don't hear at home is the footsteps of the props guys racing from backdrop to backdrop, trying to get them turned in time.

The second time I appeared on *Live at the Apollo*, I was hosting the show, rather than appearing as a guest. This meant that I would warm up the crowd, welcome on the guest comic and then, when they had finished, wrap up the show. This went to plan perfectly almost all of the way to the end. The idea was that I would say 'Goodnight!' in my showbiz way, and then turn and walk slowly back towards the giant sign, as it rose and a plume of dry ice rolled out to greet me. The credits would roll under this long walk, with the audience's cheers bringing me home. I would then turn and smile my final goodbye to the crowd, the sign would descend and the show end.

Sadly, no one told the crowd.

I said, 'That's all from us. Thank you! And goodnight!' and turned.

At which point the entire room got up out of their seats and started leaving. Which is fair enough – they thought it was the end of the show. As I walked back into the set, I could hear the thud-thud-thud of thousands of velvety theatre seats flipping upright.

The cameras were still rolling though, so I had to keep my steady and majestic pace.

Behind me, conversations were starting, people were rustling with coats and turning their phones back on.

The Apollo stage is vast. Still I am walking, the loneliest man in the room, still keeping this show going while three and a half thousand people are filing out. The sign begins to rise, smoke billows out, I reach the back of the stage and turn. And I salute a half-empty room, fake smile on my face, acknowledging an applause which ended about thirty seconds earlier.

A few stragglers notice me and just stare, some quizzically, but most in a sad way, thinking, 'Poor guy, just can't let it go. It's over, Dara, it's over . . .'

So, with those as my most recent memories of the Apollo, I walked out dreading a big cold room, and it was a romp. We met a 'service locator', which, behind the fancy title, was a man who sources cables underground for construction companies. It's a surprisingly straightforward task given the right meters and detectors apparently; but still a job that has the potential to look a bit magical. Obviously, you find the cable first, then you hide the meters and detectors in the giant sleeves of your wizard's robe. Then you take out a coat hanger and divine.

You do some incanting first, of course. You can't do divining without a bit of incantation. It just doesn't work without the incanting. Anything that sounds, you know, sort of . . . Sumerian. Repeated over and over until you collapse, drained, pointing down at the tarmac and with your last breath, 'Your . . . cable . . . is . . . here.'

This is exactly how stage psychics work, by the way.

Our service locator didn't seem that interested in adding a touch of occult mystery to his day job but was thrilled when, later, during the inevitable Fritzl family mention by the crowd – we were in that fortnight when the story was everywhere – I mentioned that a man with his ability to sniff out things underground might have been quite the help to the Austrians.

As for the proctologist, I don't have to tell you that having someone in the audience who examines arses would probably get a laugh or two. Any comedian can make some-thing of that. But finding a proctologist with a broken wrist? I thank you. And, before you ask, a light bulb.

London should be fun, being my home town.

This is a minor embarrassment, by the way. I released a DVD in 2008 that contained a show in London and a show in Dublin, and I opened both with the words, 'It's great to be home.' This made me look like Richard Nixon.

It is more than possible, though, to be both Not British, and a Londoner.

This is my claim on Londoner status. Not long after I'd emigrated, I was doing a comedy-circuit gig in a room above a pub in Tufnell Park in North London. I was looking round the room, preparing my rag-bag of international put-downs, noting how many New Zealanders, how many Dutch, how many Americans were in the room, and it was suddenly obvious that I was missing an entire ethnic group, possibly the largest in the city.

This group, to which I also belonged, consisted of the massive group of people who came to London because this was London, one of the great cities of the world. We had come between the ages of twenty-five and thirty-five; we had come from all over the world (and all over the UK); and we had come because this was the world centre of our industry, because this was where opportunity existed and this was where the exciting stuff was happening. This was our common nationality, and where we used to come from was just backstory. We were Londoners now. That was our ethnic group.

Great cities have a gravitational pull. For me, there are basically four of them, New York, Paris, Tokyo and London, and they exist to distort the space around them. They draw the population in, usually young and ambitious and willing to endure shitty houseshares in the city's endless warren of sub-divided three-storey Georgian houses.

England plays host to London, much like it plays host to the Premier League. It used to be yours, and now it belongs to the world. And you can whine about the day-to-day hassles and the foreign faces or you can relax and enjoy the fact that you have something genuinely world-class and iconic on your doorstep.

You want proof of London's international iconic status? In any Hollywood science-fiction movie, when they show that montage of all the alien attacks from around the world, London always gets flattened first. I've lost count of the amount of times I've seen Big Ben flooded, zapped or struck by a meteor. That's how you measure global brand-reach.

How well the capital fits into England is another matter.

The great English trait of Romantic nostalgia is curiously absent in London. It's possibly because of the transient nature of the population. Maybe if there is nostalgia in the hearts of the people of London, it is for somewhere other than London. That might explain the rush away from the city for some at a certain age. Maybe nostalgia is too simplistic an emotion to attach to anything as massive and messy as a city of eight million people, although that hasn't stopped New Yorkers or Parisians.

If the English were to be glibly summed up as pragmatic but a bit moany, though, then this is the perfect capital city for them. The city is massive, and Londoners negotiate daily a ludicrously complicated transport system, by underground, overground, bus and boat. This gives them endless opportunities to complain, but it also forces them to perform route calculations of astonishing complexity, usually without even looking up, for fear they might make eye-contact, or show weakness or share a human moment with a fellow commuter, which is not the way things are done in London.

My favourite-ever joke (of my own) is about Londoners and their gift for re-routing. It was about the response to the bomb attacks on 7 July 2005. This is the joke:

> The media reacted as if the attacks would, or should, be greeted like 9/11 had been in New York. Of course, the attack was nothing like 9/11, and besides ... this is London. They've had the Blitz and then there was the IRA ... In fact, the response in London to the attacks was much more:
> 'There's been a bomb on the Piccadilly Line!'
> (Long thoughtful pause and then, like a problem being solved ...)
> 'Well, I can get the Victoria Line ...'

(You might need to see me deliver that one, actually. It's all in the way you say 'Victoooria Line ...')

The joke always worked fairly well outside the city, but phenomenally well in the London clubs, even the weekend after the attacks. I remember reading pieces in the national press about 'How long before Londoners can laugh again?' As it turned out, the following weekend.

You want a really, really dark sense of humour? *Time Out*, the London listings magazine, printed a letter during the Jean Charles de Menezes investigation from an anonymous man who asked if it was wrong, when reading about the wrongful death of the Brazilian shot in Stockwell tube station, to have realized that the route de Menezes was taking would shave ten minutes off his, the reader's, commute.

Londoners: Not sentimental.

Portsmouth Kings Theatre

1 managing director of an architectural IT company
1 IT infrastructure manager
1 repairman for catering equipment
1 voiceover artist
An old man named Stanley

The fickle wishes of the tour give us a few nights away from London before returning for the big shows at the weekend. Portsmouth first, although, strictly, it's Southsea, on the outskirts of the city, which is all nightclubs and chip shops and bars and this beautiful, proper theatre.

The street also has both a Kwiki Mini Mart and a New Kwiki Mart, which hints at a long-running and wonderfully low-stakes feud.

Whenever I've gigged in Portsmouth it has been along this drag, and it took *Three Men in a Boat* to get me into the centre of the city proper and to one of the most striking architectural sights of the British coast, the Spinnaker Tower.

More than twice the height of Nelson's Column and built in the shape of a giant sail stretching towards the English Channel, the Spinnaker Tower appeals because it combines the majesty of its design with the humanity of having a broken external glass lift, ever since the opening day, when it malfunctioned halfway up and a load of dignitaries were trapped. Engineers had to take the internal lift all the way up to the viewing platform, and then abseil down.

This is the perfect blend for the English. Now the locals can admire the stunning views across the Solent and the dominating shape on the skyline; at the same time they can tut and roll their eyes at how inept it all is. 'Oh, it might be pretty, but does it work?'

It's like Terminal 5 and the O2 centre in Greenwich (formerly the Millennium Dome, of course). Both of them are fine, fine buildings. It's hard to think of a sleeker airport in Europe, and the O2 is a model of how to feed, water and entertain twenty thousand people without the need for burger vans and rain-gear. Sadly, both will never recover from start-up problems which will forever leave them as easy punchlines for bad newspaper columnists.

It's one of the more unusual English national traits I've discovered. You're not scared of the *grands projets*; you seem to regard it as unnecessary, however, to test them before the big opening. Maybe you think it's hubristic to do things well, that the odd broken luggage carousel shows that you haven't lost the run of yourselves amidst the vastness of this construction. You need something to complain about. You want that imperfection. It's the dropped stitch that separates you from the divine.

'I am Ozymandias, king of kings! I would like to apologize for the late running of these trains!'

Nottingham Royal Concert Hall

1 trainee lawyer
1 IT trainer
1 man who makes fireplaces:
   'Out of what?'
   'Wood.'
   'That's tempting fate, isn't it?'
1 wildlife photographer

Nottingham is an attractive market town, built around the largest town square in the country. Boots the Chemist started here, as a chemist, before some genius realized that if they just sold sandwiches as well, they could probably open at least three branches on every street in the country.

Nottingham makes much of Robin Hood, including the magnificent Robin Hood Experience, a good-hearted 1970s tourist attraction which showcases the best of 1970s animatronic archers and recorded medieval-crowd noise. They'll polish it up some day, and it'll lose all its low-tech magic.

They don't make as much of the founder of the city, the Saxon chieftain Snot. In fact, the city's original name was 'Snotingaham' – literally, 'the homestead of Snot's people'. If anyone wants to campaign to restore the name, I'm on board.

Nottingham is also very popular for stag weekends, serviced not just by the pubs and clubs but also by the vast number of quad-biking/clay-pigeon-shooting type activities in the area. Stags are lured here by the oft-quoted stat that Snotsville (the proper name, thank you) has the country's most favourable male–female ratio. Sadly, this statistic dates back to the city's textile industry during the war. Right now, that would give it the nation's most favourable eighty-five-year-old male–female ratio, but still the stags keep coming, little realizing the 'grab-a-granny' weekend they have in store.

Strangest fact I learned: the world premiere of *Reservoir Dogs* was held in Nottingham.

Oh, and other strangest fact: the world record for 'number of people dressed as a zombie' was broken here, at the videogame festival Gamecity.

So Nottingham is, quietly, pretty cool.

A fun gig, too, during which we learned one exciting wildlife fact: ducks don't do sultry.

Iain Smollett was the wildlife photographer. And while the UK is certainly better than Ireland for wildlife, it's no Kenya. (Ireland has no wildlife worth speaking of. If there was a wildlife-tour company in Ireland, it'd be called 'Chance of a Fox' or 'The Odd Hedgehog'.)

'So, Iain, what do you shoot?'

'It's mainly ducks.'

'Is it possible to get much out of a duck?'

'What do you mean?'

'Do they have much emotional range?'

'Oh yes. They're quite varied. Territorial, or nurturing, or ...'

'Could you make them sexy? Can you make a duck glance over his shoulder in that coy, slightly saucy way? I mean, if you call yourself a photographer ...'

So Iain showed me a photograph of a duck glancing over its shoulder, he claimed, in a sultry way. Do you want me to describe it to you? It doesn't merit a thousand words. It's a duck. It's a duck, looking slightly to the left. If this is as sultry as it gets for the duck world, it's a wonder they breed at all.

Sheffield City Hall

George – who rolls steel
1 T-shirt designer
1 plumber
1 accountant
1 IT contractor

And so the gigs roll along happily, keeping my confidence high for the big DVD show at the weekend. Next up is a trip back to Yorkshire, usually home to the most talkative people in the country. Gigs in the past in Leeds, Selby, Bridlington, Halifax and Huddersfield have all been uniformly wonderful. Similarly, Sheffield is the home to one of the best comedy clubs in the country, The Last Laugh, a famously sweaty gig in the back room of the Lescar pub. You'd do a forty-minute set, and come off drenched and have to change in the kitchen as the punters wandered past the door. For some reason, I can still see the giant tubs of margarine, as I tried to look casual while conducting a post-mortem, shirtless and glistening, with show host Toby Foster.

This trip, I am doing my show at the City Hall, which is by no stretch of the imagination a sweaty room in the back of a pub. However, ten minutes into the show, and I am drenched again. But now it is with a cold, cold sweat. The kind you get when you realize that there are 1,950 people in the room and it just isn't working.

Let's see how this happened. I ran out to applause, mentioned a few of the other nights on the tour, hit them with the schtick about how much I was looking forward to chatting to them tonight and then said, 'Right, who's here?' and leaned in towards the front row. And, instinctively, 1,950 people seemed to back away.

Have you ever made a room clench? That's what it felt like. They puckered up. They curled into a ball. They went foetal. It was like doing a show to an alarmed hedgehog.

I managed to frighten a room full of people so badly, their natural defence mechanisms kicked in and they made a smaller target of themselves.

From the very start it was all one-word answers and nods. They were giving me absolutely nothing to work with, and all the fluid that would normally be lubricating my mouth began to drench my shirt instead.

Dying onstage is a bizarre piece of evolutionary biology. Why exactly would we have developed a response to fear that dries the mouth and thickens the tongue just when we need them most? What caveman antics required this most specific of fight-or-flight responses?

If you've never gone through it, these are the stages:

Firstly, panic. An internal panic when Plan A gets nothing, and a quick root around to find a Plan B. Secondly, a viscosity of the brain. When Plan B fails, it takes markedly longer to find Plan C. Sometimes you end up doing Plan A again. This is not good. It never works better the second time. The mouth begins to dry now, and you suddenly become very aware of how bad this looks. Normally, on stage, you're not self-conscious at all. You're too busy doing the job even to consider how ridiculous it looks. When the laughs stop, there is a very sudden realization that you might look very foolish indeed in front of these people. This is the fight-or-flight moment. Do you politely exit, with some good grace and dignity, or do you plough on and hope that something, anything, in your sorry script will gain some purchase with the crowd and turn this around?

The answer, hard-earned, is of course C: you stop what you're doing, tell the audience how shit it's going and blame them. You've done this before, it always works. The only difference is them and, frankly, you're a little disappointed. You've made the effort to come here and they haven't brought their A-game. You'll go through with this, but you expect better, starting with the next joke.

Then you go back and do Plan A again. Fuck 'em.

This night in Sheffield wasn't quite death though. I had still a show I could do, I still had at least ninety minutes of tested material that I had no difficulty getting out, and that the crowd were enjoying. I just couldn't get them to engage in any one-to-ones. All the bonus, all the gravy of the off-the-cuff, all the ad-libbing to sprinkle on top of the show, all gone.

I walked off at half-time, and Damon was already there, going, 'I know, I know ... Remember, though, you've not played the City Hall before. Maybe they just weren't expecting it to be so ... interactive.'

After the show, I was sitting, still a little shell-shocked, at the stage door, when a cheery punter passed by. 'That was great!' he said, and was genuinely surprised when I almost grabbed him by the collar.

'How the fuck was that great? You all said nothing to me! I couldn't get a word out of you!'

'Well, we didn't come to hear us. We came to hear you. That's what we're like in Sheffield. Bands get really thrown as well when we don't sing along. We come to hear *them* sing the songs though.'

That's what they're like in Sheffield. They won't make cream with you, but they love the cake.

London Hammersmith Apollo

1 security guard:
    'Where?'
    'Putney.'
    'You're a security guard for Putney? Do you stand on the bridge forcing traffic back?'
    'No, for the police in Putney.'
    'The police in Putney need security? How dangerous has it got in Putney?'
1 financial manager for Boots
1 Navy signalling guy
1 photographer (mainly interiors)
1 oil refiner
1 schoolboy
2 cobblers
10 special guests

In London the next night we were back to a world of chat. Did you know that the Signalling Corps does not use Morse code any more? I certainly didn't but was set straight by the Navy signaller who arrived ten minutes late and caught my attention. Flags they do use, but really just for the hell of it, it's all digital encryption now.

He also said that, no, he does not sing 'YMCA' when doing semaphore. He had to agree that there was something inherently camp about it, as there would be about any military activity that could be done equally well with pom-poms. Pom-poms might even be easier to see in a storm than flags. And they're more fun to make. For a professional communicator, the Navy signaller seemed as if he would have been happier left alone at this stage but, after Sheffield, I felt starved of attention and, besides, he arrived late and had a cool job.

For the DVD recording, I had been forced to do some fact-checking for legal purposes. Little things like advertising slogans and product names. You can still mention them, but have to make sure you don't spend the entire tour slagging off Tefal for selling a 'Stealth' kettle and then the night before the record find out that it was actually Kenwood. Y'know, schoolboy errors like that.

I mentioned a long time ago that the only real stand-alone joke the show contained was about Dettol and Yakult. Neither brand could be said to come out of the joke badly, but we were still put on alert when my agent received a call midway through the tour from Yakult head office.

'We hear Dara is doing a joke on his current tour about our product,' they said.

'Yes. Yes he is.'

And there was a long pause, during which my agent pondered how to tell me that the Yakult gag had been nixed, and tried to come up with another probiotic yogurt brand that would work just as well. Then the reply:

'We've never been in a show before. Could we come and see it?'

Ten tickets were happily despatched to Yakult and,

when I delivered the gag, the usual laugh was followed by a distinct and very specific cheer from Row H.

After the show, the Yakult team came round to the stage door and presented me with four trays of Yakult. Oh yeah, that's pretty sweet. 192 tubs of probiotic yogurt. I can't offer any great testimonial, however: none of them got drunk. Life on the road just doesn't suit a rigorous digestive regime and, when we got home in June, they were all still in the boot of the car.

The other, more crushing, legal requirement for a DVD recording is that a verbatim transcript is taken to be analysed for any possible slander issues and to help the edit. Then, for some cruel and perverse reason, a copy is sent to me. This is the grimmest reading. You know the way you don't recognize your own voice on tape? Try having it written out word for word.

Offstage Announcement

Ladies and gentlemen, welcome to the Hammersmith Apollo, please put your hands together and welcome on stage DARA O BRIAIN.

Dara O Briain (Onstage)

Lovely! How are you? You in good form? Good evening, good evening, good evening, good evening, good evening! Hello, how are you? Welcome, ladies and gentlemen, to the Hammersmith Apollo! Are you in good form? Very, very good. My name is DARA O BRIAIN.

And rapidly descends from there. This is some banter with the crowd to put them at their ease:

Listen, you're a really good crowd like whatever, there's some crowds where you kind of have to work and melve them together like but you're there, you're there already, right. No, hey hey please, please I don't want you to take that as; that's not meant to be some shitty showbizzy hey you're a great crowd kind of a way right. I'll just indicate that I judge you as much as you judge me so we're equal there right.

It may help at this stage if you read these in one of those Marge Gunderson from *Fargo* accents; or like the Swedish chef from *The Muppet Show*. Or whatever accent you enjoy doing to indicate that somebody is mentally deficient.

Some stuff may have been lost in translation, but that still doesn't explain 'melve'. I presume I got caught between 'meld' and 'merge'. Is melving an audience vital to the success of the show? Probably not.

And how about this gem, where I react to the news that one of the audience members works in the oil industry but, hilariously, in Reading, and how difficult it must be to strike oil in Berkshire:

> You know you're right it is just magic and maybe there is oil in Reading. Why can't we just dream? Anyway that be great if you went home afterward the gig it be great if you went home like and you're in the bath and suddenly just saw up out of the toilet and you Mary, Mary this couldn't be that would be too lucky wouldn't it. Just started shooting up out of the thing. Anyway where was I, oh yeah, yeah, yeah I was talking about the whole oh psychics at that was it right.

There's sixty pages of this stuff. It's just heartbreaking.

*

We recorded the DVD on the Saturday night, and it's been out for a while, so I can be honest now and say that there was a moment during the night when I thought that the nightmare I mentioned earlier was going to come true. With all the cameras in and the audience brightly lit, we were doing the one take we'd get of the whole show. And I thought it was going to be a bad one. Not rubbish bad. But mediocre bad.

It was during a routine I loved, about how much of a crock homeopathy is, and, just that one time, I felt I was losing them. I've looked back over it since, and even though it's a routine dear to my heart, I do think I began to look a little nerdy and preachy, which is always a winning combination.

And then, just when the energy was dipping, some woman shouted out 'Energy' from the stalls. I still have no idea why. You can tell on the DVD that I had no idea at the time and, with nothing else to do, decided to take it as the invitation to mime 'Energy' back at her. Then somebody shouted 'Stealth' and I mimed that, and the whole show changed direction. There was a huge whoosh! of energy back into the room from this off-the-cuff nonsense, and that got us all the way to the end.

And if you pause the DVD at just the right second, you can see the relief on my face.

I'll end my visit to London with a nice moment. Not from the DVD night, but the night before. In my encore, I recap the show and say a final goodbye to all the people in the front row. On the Friday night, the last of those was the Navy signalman. I had been intrigued by his revelation at the start of the show that Morse code was no longer in use by the Navy. Sufficiently intrigued, in fact, that, during the interval, I had gone online in the dressing room and found the Morse code alphabet. I spent the break slowly writing out a private message for him. At the very end of the show, while getting him a huge round of applause, I presented him with the note.

It's always tickled me that, at the end of such a huge show, two hours long, in front of 3,300 people, the final punchline actually took place hours later, when he'd got home, fished the note out and sat down and dusted off an old textbook to find a Morse code alphabet. And, letter by letter, he would have spelled out:

B.E.T.Y.O.U.D.O.N.T.A.R.R.I.V.E.L.A.T.E.
T.O.M.Y.S.H.O.W.A.G.A.I.N.

Chapter 11:
No Wood, Just Trees

It's at this point that things begin to blur. The gigs are beginning to meld into each other and the mileage is steadily increasing. Sometimes it's easy to spot a theme from the week's travel and, at other times, like this batch, it's just a random collection of towns, from East Anglia to the Midlands, and out to Wales and Northern Ireland. And then back to East Anglia again.

Moreover, the clutter is mounting in the car, unnoticed by myself and Damon, but worthy of a sharp upbraid any time we have to give anyone else a lift.

'What the fuck is this on the floor? This car is a tip.'

Discarded Lucozade bottles and sweet wrappers, sports supplements from the newspapers, half-eaten shanks of meat, all of them steadily encroaching on my leg room. The atmosphere isn't helped by the two shirts I wore in the previous night's show drying out in the back. It's always the same two shirts as well, on heavy rotation, so the stench builds up across the week. Sitting in that car is like living in a mobile bachelor pad, but for a lonely, mean old bachelor, given that all I do in the car is sleep, eat and argue with the radio. We're permanently set to BBC Radio Five Live, partly for sport, partly for the excellent Simon Mayo show on the drive to the venues, and partly so that I can wear off my adrenaline after the show tutting and complaining at the lunatics on their late-night phone-in show – the kind of people whose fault it is I am writing this book in the first place.

Actually, I have no idea how we started listening to Five Live all the time. I always presumed it was Damon's choice but, one day near the end of the tour, I noticed him switch over to Five Live when I got into the car and began to wonder if he had always thought it was my choice. At that stage, it would have been weird to ask, so it stayed.

I used to drink on the way home. I remember on a previous tour the moment at which our hire car hit 10,000 miles. 'Jesus,' I said. 'I can't believe we've driven 10,000 miles.' To which Damon sharply responded, '*We* didn't drive 10,000 miles. I drove, and you just sat in the passenger seat drinking.' It wasn't that curt rebuke that stopped the boozing; it was the waning thrill of arriving home smashed at 3 a.m. to a sleeping house.

A few years back, when the tours were smaller and didn't

merit a tour manager driving me, I used to travel by train, stay in tiny hotels and, after the gig, drink my rider. My rider at the time was eight cans of cider, and there were a few nights where I would sit in the hotel room at 1 a.m., wide awake still from the gig, glugging at a can and watching the African Nations football highlights. Great days.

There is a tendency to overplay the loneliness of life on the road. It's certainly a shock to go from the comedy clubs, where twenty minutes of jokes allows you to hang out with your comedian mates at the disco afterwards, mingling with the audience and feeling like the king of the room, to your first theatre tour, where at the end of a two-hour show, you take the applause, go to your dressing room to towel off and, when you walk out, the building is deserted. It can be strange to reconcile that the latter is reward for success at the former. (It's not just the punters who scarper either. There was one time in Middlesbrough when I took a little too long to gather up my cans and I was locked in.)

The tours now aren't lonely though. Not with me and Damon sitting quietly together on the long journeys, listening to a radio station neither of us chose.

King's Lynn Corn Exchange

Of course, if we wanted to spice things up, we could stop off and buy some pornography on the A1 on the way to King's Lynn. At the Adult Pit Stop, just past Sandy, before you get to Biggleswade. Sandy is a town, by the way, rather than the girl from *Grease* fallen on hard times and now used as a landmark for truck-stop red-light joints. The Adult Pit Stop has only been there a couple of years. Apparently, it used to be a

Bar-b-cue place before. But if there's one thing a trucker wants more than fried chicken . . .

Similarly, on the M62, there are ads for escort services. And calling prostitutes 'escorts' might fool you if it's a spot of dinner followed by 'executive stress relief', but a woman who will visit your truck? That's a prostitute.

We don't stop, of course – that would genuinely be as weird as any old couple suddenly stopping off at a sex-shop while they were on the A1. It's embarrassing enough that Damon is always up and about before me in the morning and, by the time I surface, he's ready to leave.

'Have you, err, settled the bill?'

'Of course.'

'And did that include . . . the movies?'

'Yes. What did you watch?'

'*Casino Royale.*'

'Again?'

'Fuck off.'

King's Lynn was shut when we arrived, so we watched a junior boxing club training in the car park while we sat on the banks of the river Ouse and enjoyed the mild evening.

During the show, the most popular audience member (getting a huge unsolicited cheer from the crowd) was the operations manager from a sugar factory. Clearly the people of King's Lynn appreciate the everyday miracle of beet to grain. Me, I liked the guy who did marketing to pigs. That wasn't really his job, but his description was so long and technical that I just decided to take the words 'marketing' and 'pigs' out of it and run with that idea instead. Luckily, we had met another man who installed ATMs for a living (who got no cheer from the crowd – more of a sugar place, King's Lynn) – and so the issue of how to get disposable cash to pigs was quickly solved.

All in all, a pleasant gig, even if it was in another bloody Corn Exchange. One tiny frisson: the night after me, Jim Davidson was on. When there are a number of comics touring at the same time, you tend to criss-cross the country, seeing each other's posters in the lobby and occasionally having the odd near-miss. In the past, I have left notes in the dressing room for Ross Noble and received ones from Al Murray. Stage-hands speak in awe of the latest Ken Dodd marathon. This, however, was the closest I had come to ever meeting Jim Davidson.

Frankly, I got the chills. This is because, unbeknownst to him, Jim used to feature in the show.

A couple of years ago, I had done a joke on *Have I Got News for You?* which was condemned by gay rights group OutRage! Previous targets of OutRage!, by the way, include Robert Mugabe, and then, me.

To be fair to them, it wasn't a joke I'd have gone to the wire to defend (it was something about Elton John and Billy Elliott) and the routine I did was about how, if I did try to defend it, I'd suddenly find myself on the wrong side of the comedy divide. Hence a bit with me and Jim Davidson playing golf (my generation of comics don't really do golf) which includes the lines:

Dara (*readying to tee-off*): Jesus, Jim, I'm getting awful trouble off the queers.

Jim (*standing with club*): What seems to be the problem, Dara?

Dara (*still readying to tee-off*): Ah, they can't take a joke. (*Pause, turn to Jim*) They can take a cock up their arse, but they can't take a joke, what! Eh?!

(*Jim and Dara roll around laughing before Dara strikes the golf ball 275 yards down the fairway.*)

Obviously, I'm quoting out of context, so you don't get the full satirical point but, still, you can see why Jim might not like it . . .

Cardiff St David's Hall

In Cardiff, we were on the night after Ken Dodd. This is the closest I have ever come to the legend. While I was onstage, Damon found the sheet backstage with his show timings:

Ken Dodd

First Half: on 19.03 – off 21.53
Second Half: on 22:17 – off 00:13

The man is a monster.

Leigh Delamare Services on the M4, on the way back from Cardiff

When people ask, I always name this as my favourite services, although I think it's just because I find the name memorable. There is a mystery services somewhere out there, neither I nor Damon can remember where, which had a twenty-four-hour McDonald's, which would make it my favourite services if we could ever find it again. It may have been only a dream.

My actual favourite is probably Leicester Forest East on the M1. This is really two service stations, one on either side, joined by a covered bridge filled with restaurants over the motorway. This makes it one of the few places in the world where you can enjoy fish and chips, a lamb shank, or maybe a lasagne, while through the windows, three lanes of traffic appear to be hurtling towards you at 80 miles an hour.

I'm also fond of the Sandbach services on the M6, because I once convinced a woman there that I owned the place. She looked really surprised to see me here, as if, since I host *Mock the Week*, I should be using some sort of celebrity services, just behind a velvet rope:

'Actually, I'm just checking up on the place.'

'Really?'

'Yes. Me and Frankie Boyle have invested our money from *Mock the Week* in a number of service stations. We're thinking of adding this one to our portfolio. Tell me . . . how have you found the facilities on your visit here?'

'Emm, fine, clean, I suppose.'

'Excellent. Thanks for the input.'

Life on the motorway is filled with longing. For home, of course. For a cleaner car. But also for the many unexplored delights that go zooming past your window at 70 mph.

Take, as an example, Billing Aquadrome, off the M1, junction 16. Haven't been there, desperately want to go. I don't even have a clue what goes on at Billing Aquadrome – it just sounds incredible. Water is involved in some way, but in an incredibly futuristic way. If it was just an aqua*dome*, I'd know what to expect. It's just slides and a wave-pool. It's not though. It's an aqua*drome*!

This is like a dome, but in many more dimensions, like a hyper-cube, which, as we all know, is a four-dimensional cube. In my dreams, Billing Aquadrome is like an Escher painting. Water flows in all directions at once, and up, and down. And out. And into the past and future at the same time.

I cannot fully explain how exciting Billing Aquadrome is in my imagination.

I also want to go to Gulliver's Land (M1, junction 14), the National Space Centre (M1, junction 21), the Heights of Abraham (M1, junction 28) and, most of all, Birdworld (M3, junction 4).

These are the most compelling of the road signs I see over and over again from the passenger seat as I traverse the country. Each of them appears twice on big brown signs before the exit, which we go whizzing past. On the way out, we're in too much of a hurry to stop. On the way home, these places must surely be closed. I always make the same promise to myself as we zoom by: 'Some day, I'll take the time to really see these places.'

Please let these not be my final words: 'I never went to Birdworld.'

Northampton Derngate Theatre

1 council worker
1 MD of a company that makes medical supplies
1 man who runs a bingo hall
1 sweet old lady (retired)

I can say without fear of correction that Northampton was the worst theatre in the country. Not this one, the Derngate is fine. But the one that was there before, the Deco, was the shittiest room in the land. It's a design thing. Try to imagine the worst possible configuration of a theatre. Firstly, make the stalls as small as possible – even though the stalls are the most expensive, prime seats and, also, being the seats below the stage, the easiest ones to talk to and make laugh, and thus the heart of the room.

Put all your effort into the balcony, which starts at eye-level to the act and stretches narrowly into the distance. Then put all the stage lights at the front of the balcony, again at eye-level, so that the comic is left blinded if he has the temerity to do anything as brash as look towards the crowd. This way, the comic is unable to see any audience members but aware that, even if he could see them, they wouldn't be able to see each other.

And this is the best bit. This is the bit that, even if you thought everything else was just whining, luvvie, get-a-real-job-or-stop-complaining stuff, you'll get how this bit is just evil. This is just dastardly. At the back of the room, on the far wall, way past the unseeable stalls and the blinding lights and infinitely long balcony, way to the back and high on the wall so that it is the only thing you can see, do you know what they had? A clock. A fucking bright yellow, illuminated clock.

They built a room so difficult to get laughs in that it already makes time grind to a halt. And then they put a clock in front of you, so that you know just how much longer you have to stay there.

They've torn down the Deco, and I requested the chance to piss on its rubble.

The Derngate was fine, although there was a strange moment when, during the crime stories, a nice old woman at the front made the point of clarifying that the burglars whom she had caught in her bedroom were Irish.

'I don't think that's important,' I said.

'But they were Irish.'

'I'm sorry,' said I. 'Am I in Middle England?'

'Yes!' said the crowd.

Buxton Opera House

1 casualty doctor

1 manager of a market

1 builder (injured; he fell off the second rung of a ladder. Now available for very low building jobs)

1 man who organized danger holidays for schools

The location of the mythical 'Middle England' is not something I'm going to get into here. Frankly, I think it's an internal matter and you should sort it out amongst yourselves.

If I had to make a literal recommendation, it would be Buxton in Derbyshire. This is both for its position and tenor; it's slap bang in the middle of the country and terribly middle class. It also seems to have the largest catchment area of any gig in the country. People come from all over England to see the show in Buxton. The people I spoke to had come from Yorkshire, Cheshire and Nottinghamshire. I had appeared in closer venues to all of them, but none of them seemed to mind the trip.

It helps that the Opera House is a beautiful, beautiful

theatre. It's easily one of the prettiest in the country. It's also one of the best-run, with a busy and varied schedule of festivals and touring shows. Buxton hosts, amongst other events, an opera festival, a light-opera festival, a Gilbert and Sullivan festival, a puppet festival and the Buxton Festival, which features rare opera and spoken word.

The programme is also notable for its policy not to book any clairvoyants.

There is hardly a theatre in the country that doesn't include a couple of psychics every term. For good reason too. Talking to the 'other side' shifts tickets. I remember once being terribly proud of myself the first time I sold out the Swansea Grand. Then the man on the stage door pointed out (unnecessarily, I feel) that, two days earlier, Scouse Ghost-bluffer Derek Acorah had been in, performing his second sell-out show of the week. I even have a name for how disappointing that news was. I call this 'the Swansea Bring-Down'.

Nowadays, as we tour around, we keep note of the up-and-coming post-mortem bullshit merchants as we come across them. And they always sell out.

This makes them a strange anomaly in the history of showbiz. They are the only field of the entertainment biz to remain successful despite never having delivered.

Their continued success is despite the fact that they aren't actually talking to the dead, because, not to be too obvious about this, talking to the dead is impossible. If talking to the dead was possible, then why would we never have received any useful information from the dead? Where are all the Wall Street clairvoyants, then? Why aren't the CIA using them for military intelligence? Why aren't all the historians beating a path to the doorway of Sally Morgan, telly psychic, to settle long-standing academic disputes?

Because it's all horse-shit. And I'll happily see them in court. I call as my first witness, my dead grandfather. Your challenge, psychic, is to tell me which grandfather.

I could be more gracious about this vile industry – after all, they are just for entertainment purposes and legally obliged to say so, except that they prey on the weak and the bereaved and the misguided and present them with new memories of their dead loved ones, memories that they just make up onstage.

I would play Buxton ten times a year if they'd have me. Mainly for the beautiful room, but also because they don't go for this hideous charade.

They book psychics in the **Belfast Waterfront**, but, in the credit column, they don't take them seriously. A well-known telly corpse-chatter was on the week I visited Belfast and, according to sources (the gossipy stage crew), she had a terrible show. The industry term is 'to die onstage' but that just seems like a clumsy pun here. How about 'She stank up the room'? 'She went down in flames'? 'She bombed'?

The lady in question walked the stage for an hour, getting nothing right. Apparently, the spell was broken quite quickly and, once the suspension of disbelief (this woman can talk to the dead! Oh wait . . .) was over, it just became an awkward stand-off. Seventeen hundred people watched a woman demonstrate no extra-sensory perception at all and, before long, they began to circle.

'Stacey,' one voice said (her name isn't Stacey; if you ever meet me in a bar, ask me and I'll tell you her name, but for the time being, let's leave it at Stacey). 'Stacey, what about my mother?'

'When did she die?' asked Stacey.

'Oh, she's not dead.' Laughter from the crowd.

'Stacey, what about my sister?' shouted a different voice.

'Is she dead?' Stacey checked.

'No.' More laughter.

'Is there anyone who would like me to do an actual reading?' Stacey said, getting noticeably irritated.

'Stacey,' said a third voice. 'What about my father?'

'Is he dead?'

'Yes.'

Stacey adopts the pose. She summons voices from another realm, feels a presence coming through, begins to make contact with the dear departed ...

'Oh, no, wait,' interrupts the voice. 'He's here beside me.'

Long, long laughter.

They have a pretty dark sense of humour in Belfast anyway, as Damon discovered. Spotting the nervous visiting Englishman, the stage crew would tease him by pointing at random passing strangers and, in a hushed tone, whispering, 'Do you see him?'

'Yes.'

And then they'd look both ways, lean in and slowly spell out, 'I.R.A.'

Damon would be left sneaking a glance at the perfectly innocent primary-school teacher wandering past with his shopping.

Ipswich Regent Theatre

1 organic farmer
1 database manager from Norwich ('Boo!' go the crowd)
1 man who worked in flood-danger protection:
   'Any tips?'
   'Yeah. Live on a hill.'

Just when we're almost finished with this ridiculous week, the nightmare journey. Returning from Belfast into Stansted, we started out for East Anglia. We got word from the sound crew a couple of hours ahead of us, however, that the A14 was impassable, just as similar news was coming through on Five Live travel. We pulled off the motorway at what, it later transpired, was the last possible moment, and found ourselves in countryside. Then the scramble started to find alternative routes, veering down from M to A to B on our road designations, while the sat-nav kept loudly correcting us. She couldn't see the sense in routing the trip round eighteenth-century farmhouses and duck ponds when there was a perfectly good piece of four-lane tarmacadam just to the left of us. We're supposed to get to the theatre with a couple of hours to spare. When the screen gave us an ETA which was fifteen minutes later than the time the show was supposed to start, the sat-nav got ditched, and it was just me with a map.

As the roads got narrower, and the time of the gig grew closer, my directions were getting more and more staccato. What had started as 'Why not try here?' became 'Fifty yards right turn. Now sharp left. Stop admiring the farmhouse! Make a left here!'

All this time, we're making frantic calls to the theatre to arrange another sound system and to get them to do their own soundcheck. 'Just mumble in an Irish accent, and we'll use those settings.'

Some months later, I was on Five Live and had the pleasure of sharing the experience with Nick, the travel guy. 'You know all that banter and bonhomie you have in here? Well, we were stuck in traffic, waiting for news, and it sounded like you were having cocktails.' God bless him, it wasn't his fault, but we wanted to blame somebody.

We got to the theatre with five minutes to spare. The crowd were already in, the new microphone was on stage, and nobody would ever have known the shitty, panicky day we'd had. All that crowd will remember was that I walked out with my flies undone.

Norwich Theatre Royal

It was a much shorter hop across to Norwich the following day, enlivened mainly by passing my absolute favourite road-sign in the country. It's for the nearby town of Wymondham.

It's a brown sign, meant to entice passing travellers by listing in graphic form the many delights of the town. You've seen these before, thumbnails of leisure by the side of the road. A little boat, a crossed knife and fork, a carousel.

The Wymondham sign has a picture of a church and, next to it, a duck. And the duck is the same size as the church. This is a promise that cannot possibly be fulfilled. There is no way that this small Norfolk town can be harbouring a duck the size of a cathedral. Surely the authorities would have been called in by now. How can they bake enough bread to keep the duck happy?

This piece of whimsy kept me happy all the way through the show. Then I went home, took a couple of weeks off and became a father.

Chapter 12:
I Will Always Love My English Child

There are very few times that I have used stand-up as a form of therapy, but this is definitely one of them.

In 2004, I performed a show in Edinburgh and later on tour called Dara O Briain: Migrant Worker. It was partly about the difficult beginnings of multiculturalism in Ireland and how, despite denying themselves the credit for this, the English had very successfully dealt with the issue. The show touched on how little experience the Irish had with different cultures at all.

The centrepiece was a long story about attending a Catholic/Protestant wedding and the shocking discovery that, despite years of hype, the two faiths seemed to have little or nothing to distinguish them. In fact, they actually used the same words, in the same order, all through the service. Sample joke:

> 'That's not a mixed marriage. A mixed marriage is one side of the room saying "Mazel Tov!" and the other side firing guns in the air. A mixed marriage is one side parading a giant paper dragon through the room while, on the other side, men with spears are leaping up and down, trying to win a mate. That's a mixed marriage.'

In the middle of that show, though, there was a smaller routine, less of a showpiece, but one that has probably had more profound echoes in my life.

It was the 'I Will Always Love My English Child' routine.

There is very little written about one aspect of multi-cultural societies. While there is so much discussion about how different the newcomers are to the indigenous population, I've rarely heard any talk about how much of a contrast the children of immigrants are to their parents.

That might not sound like a big deal to you, but imagine you're from Salisbury, say. Now imagine your little Salisbury children. Imagine calling to them. And now imagine them answering in a strong Nigerian accent. That's how weird it is for the immigrants. You just don't presume that your children will sound different to you.

(I pick Salisbury, because I once tried to explain there how strange it would be to have an English child, and they just looked at me, genuinely puzzled, as if to say, 'But ... all children are English.')

It doesn't help if you're familiar with the many accents here, by the way. Being able to tell different English accents apart doesn't make them less foreign. I mentioned the idea of this routine to a friend of mine, an Irishwoman living in London, while we were all out in a bar once.

'I'm doing a bit about how weird it would be to have a child with an English accent,' I said.

'I know EXACTLY what you mean!' she said. 'I don't know what I'm more afraid of, if my child goes, "Ello, Mummy, awright, yeah!" or "Mummy, Mummy, Natasha has a pony, why can't I have a pony?"'

And we fell about laughing, to the bemusement of our partners, both of whom are English.

The accent is only the most superficial manifestation of this alien culture I'm bringing a child into. Not alien to the child, of course. But most people have some element of patriotism and a sense that they and their family are all from the same somewhere. It feels unnatural to carve a schism through a family on nationality. But that's the only way to do it if you're an immigrant. I am Irish, my children will not be. That was my country, they are from somewhere else. They won't be raised Irish, in a ludicrous, artificial holding pattern, until they get the chance to go 'home'. They *are* home. I hope they'll be interested in my heritage, but I won't be demanding that they go to Irish-dancing classes. I hope they won't want to go to Morris-dancing classes, but at least it's their own.

Incidentally, none of this is informed by any fears that an Irish child would be at a disadvantage in England. Quite the opposite in fact.

The Irish do appear to receive unequal treatment within English society, but this unequal treatment is almost universally in our favour. The simple fact is that, as a group, the Irish in England have done really well. Irish people, along with the Chinese and Indians, are more likely than British people to have high GCSE marks. They are also more likely to have a degree – one in four Irish people versus one in six white British people. More than one in three Irish workers is employed in a managerial or professional job, compared to one in four British workers. It's hard not to think that, if the English are biased against the Irish, they're not very good at it.

(Some of the stereotypes do appear to be true, by the way: Six out of ten men and four out of ten women with an Irish ethnic background living in England drank in excess of the recommended daily levels on at least one day a week, according to a major survey in 1999. This was by far the highest of any ethnic group and far above the norm for the UK. And one in five Irish men was involved in the construction industry, much higher than the national average of one in eight. I'll just steer the kid away from concrete mixers. And whiskey. That's generally good parenting, though, isn't it?)

Despite these clear advantages to being a Paddy, I think the child should get to have its own nationality, rather than mine. Obviously, that's the healthy attitude to take, but the notions of passing on nationality are adhesive, and I was glad of an entire month of gigs in Edinburgh to do the routine and shake off these old ideas; to free myself to stand up in front of a crowd and say, 'I will love my English child.' And when that felt comfortable, I took the show to Ireland, where I could have some proper fun with it.

You can make an Irish crowd boo by saying something like that. Not a proper 'Boo!', like a 'Get off the stage, we hate you, boo!' But still, it taps into our sense of England being (at the very least) our panto villains. You were a lot worse than that, and for a long time, not that you realized it. G. K. Chesterton once remarked that 'the tragedy of the English conquest of Ireland in the seventeenth century is that the Irish can never forget it and the English can never remember it.'

England's role as historical nemesis has reduced down now to the moustachio-twirling vaudeville villain. If you mention England on an Irish stage, you should have a piano player trilling, 'Dant-dant-daaaahh.'

I used to tell a joke about how you could eliminate binge drinking in Ireland by simply running a poster that said, 'Binge drinking! It's very English, isn't it?'

And, in that spirit, the words 'I will love my English child' always felt faintly transgressive and empowering onstage –

like shouting, 'I'm here and I'm queer!' It is the love that dare not speak its name.

'I will look at my English child,' I told them, 'without there being an asterisk above their head that leads to a footnote saying, "But you shouldn't have invaded the country for eight hundred years."'

Of course, only a monster would ever boo a parent's love for his child, so I piled it on.

'I will love my English child, even if' – the audience looks wary – 'he scores the winning goal' – building unrest in the crowd – 'for England against Ireland' – a chorus of boos – 'in Croke Park' – the addition of the sacred home of Irish sport raising the boos to a thunderclap crescendo. I'm onstage pointing at a blameless, imaginary child while an Irish crowd roar, 'Hang him!'

Panto villains are so much fun.

With the decision made, then, my child will be raised here and draped in the flag of St George. However, it might be worth seeing what challenges come with being a young person in England.

The school system alone is a proper head-wrecker. Now, the choice you make for your child's education is always going to feel like an experiment. The problem, of course, is that each of us has only had one childhood. None of us has much evidence to go on, other than how happy we are with how we turned out, and how much we'd like to replicate that for our little ones.

Personally, I went through an all-Irish-language education, which left me bilingual and argumentative. These are both traits I would love to pass on, but there are sadly very few all-Irish-language schools in London. Therefore, with no option of trying to foist a re-creation of my upbringing,

I am free to judge the English system without baggage. You have three options: The Gamble (on the state system), The Lie (about your newfound religion or your newfound address) or The Enclave (of middle-class, fee-paying parents). Wonderful.

(I'm not going to join in the game of presuming that English schools are rubbish. Irish people love to convince themselves of the unparalleled excellence of their school system, and that all England has is Grange Hill with more knives. This is despite the fact that we have a national language, taught to us compulsorily for fourteen years, and almost no one can speak it. Every day! For fourteen years! Plus, somebody pointed out to me exactly why I shouldn't be so smug about the Irish system: 'Dara, you're a professional clown; your wife, who's English, is a surgeon. Which education system did you say was better?')

The entire language of parenting in England, especially among the middle classes, tries to imply that every single decision you make for your children is vital, utterly vital, to their later success in life. My own recollection of childhood is that it was primarily containment until I was about fourteen, and then I started to get a little more focused and stuff began to sink in. Not so in England, where every choice made from the age of three is at a junction where the path to a decent university and personal fulfilment can be missed and never picked up again.

The Irish school system is more focused on a general education than England's, meaning that students are doing seven subjects when they finish rather than three. The Irish university entrance is centralized as well, meaning that the pressure occurs right at the end of the student's education, in a national set of exams at eighteen, rather than at the start, when parents desperately push to get their beloved into the right school at four.

It can be earlier than that even. There is a noticeboard near my home which carries an ad for a local toddler group. This is essentially a soft-play area, a place for parents or nannies to get a breather while their little ones run around. Nonetheless, the ad contains the words 'Give your child the best head start in life!' Don't mess this up, parents; there's a place at Cambridge at stake.

Paradoxically, all this worrying about schooling takes place in a bizarre and negative wider context.

If there is one part of English culture which looks truly inexplicable to an Irish person, it is your attitude to your own young. For some reason, you think they're scum.

Now, obviously, I don't think that you, the reader, as an individual, loathes your own children. In all likelihood, you're probably quite fond of them. But English society, and the media in particular, absolutely fucking loathes them. On the one hand, they're violent – perennially happy-slapping ASBO magnets, skulking round estates, waggling knives around and putting the word 'innit' at the end of every sentence. On the other hand, if you can get them to go to school, the only way they can be taught is if every subject is made 'relevant', so that they're never three minutes away from a reference to *Big Brother* and *Skins*, even when they're studying physics; and the exams they do are remedial and they all get A's, which just goes to show (somehow) how stupid they are.

The public perception of young people is so bad in this country that, if I meet a teenager who isn't feral, I immediately run to the parent and grab them and go, 'How do you do it? How?'

On one of the last days of this tour, in fact, me and Damon spent a long drive north listening to a story breaking about this very phenomenon.

A survey conducted for the children's charity Barnardo's had found that more than half of British adults (54 per cent) think that children in Britain are beginning to behave like animals. Almost half of those surveyed (49 per cent) also thought that children represented a danger to adults and each other. Roughly one in three adults agreed with the sentiment that it feels like the streets are currently infested with children and, most insanely, more than four out of ten British adults now feel that something needs to be done to protect society from children.

Barnardo's had commissioned the poll as part of a campaign to combat the increasingly negative picture the British public has of its own children, but said that even they were shocked by how negative the views expressed were.

The strangest thing was that, all day long, we were sitting in the car listening to people calling radio stations to react to this survey when it was released; and the people who phoned in didn't seem to respond with surprise at the ridiculous levels of overreaction. No, the general response was to treat the survey as proof that, yes, children are be-having like animals. They didn't recognize the survey as a rebuke; they took it as evidence: everyone thinks young people are out of control, so it must be true.

The Barnardo's survey is only the latest to point out this unhealthy prejudice. For example, for one week in August 2005, the research company Ipsos MORI examined the national and local newspapers for references to children and young people. They found that 57 per cent of the stories published portrayed young people in a negative light, compared to just 12 per cent of the stories which painted a positive picture.

Of course, the perception in matters such as crime is always skewed towards fear. A study called 'Youth Crime and Youth Justice' from 2004 found that three-quarters of British people thought that the number of young offenders had gone up in recent years, despite the fact that the number had actually fallen.

This survey also found that 64 per cent of the people who had negative views on youth crime were basing their answer on media reports rather than personal experience of youth crime in their area. Barnardo's has also pointed to findings from the official British Crime Survey which suggest that the general public feels that young people commit about half of all crime, when the reality is that they're responsible for about one-eighth. Ipsos MORI reported in 2006 that British adults believed that about half of all crime committed by young people involved violence, while the real figure is around 20 per cent.

This bizarre misrepresentation is beginning to get international attention as well. In October 2008, the United Nations Committee on the Rights of the Child published a report on the status of the rights of children in the UK which expressed concern 'at the general climate of intolerance and negative public attitudes towards children, especially adolescents, which appears to exist in the UK, including in the media'. The Committee also had 120 separate recommendations on how Britain could treat its kids better, which Mark Easton, the BBC's Home Editor, accurately described as 'almost as if the social services have arrived and informed us that we aren't suitable parents'. The report's recommendations included ending the ASBO system, protecting children who appear on reality TV, and stopping the use of so-called 'mosquito sprays'. You couldn't find a more fitting metaphor for the way in which Britain views teenagers, by the way. The mosquito spray is a high-frequency sonic device which emits an annoying noise that only younger ears can hear. It's used to prevent teens from loitering in public places and was, naturally enough, invented in Britain. More than three thousand of these devices have been sold in the UK, despite claims by human-rights campaigners that they infringe on young people's civil rights. One person quoted in the media as being in favour of the use of the devices was one Chrissy Barclay, a Crime Prevention Officer for Hertsmere, who summed up a good deal of Britain's attitude to kids by saying: 'Young people have to learn that certain behaviours are not acceptable, like standing in groups and being intimidating, or gathering outside shops and off-licences.'

Or, to give such behaviours their technical name, free assembly.

I'm not saying that all of England's teenagers are saints. In 2006, the Institute for Public Policy Research pulled together the results from a wide range of European research surveys, which suggested that English teens were either top or near the top on all of the main indicators of 'bad' behaviour – sexual activity, drug-taking, drinking and violence (although Ireland was ahead of the UK on binge drinking and use of some drugs). However, they didn't invent bad behaviour.

In November 2008, Frank Field MP gave a speech at the University of Leicester on the threat of a new generation of teenage monsters. Mr Field, Labour MP for Birkenhead, suggested that the basic cause of this downward trend in

British society was 'the growing collapse in the art of good parenting'. It was a far cry from the golden age of the 1950s, which, he claimed, 'were the peak years for Britain being a peaceful and self-governing kingdom'.

Here we go again: the fifties as popular touchstone for the nostalgia peddlers. Unsurprisingly, this is nonsense.

In the 1950s, far from patting themselves on the back for how great everything was and how polite young people were, the British media and establishment were convinced that young people, especially teddy boys, were out of control and were being led by dangerous new trends and foreign music down the path to juvenile delinquency. The newspapers went from referring to the group as 'Edwardians' to 'teddy boys', then 'spivs' and 'hooligans', before moving to 'gang members' and 'gangsters', although there was no evidence of gang-type organization within the Teds, barring occasional random mob violence. There was even a whole series of exploitation films depicting the threat posed by rampant Teds to society, with titles such as *Violent Playground* and *Cosh*.

The sociologist Stanley Cohen, who popularized the term 'moral panic', has suggested that the teddy-boy hysteria was the first real British moral panic over youth culture, with Britain repeating this wild overreaction to every new manifestation of youth culture that has come along since. After that, we had the mods and rockers rioting on Brighton Beach in the 1960s, and then innumerable instances of football violence in town centres up and down the country throughout the seventies and eighties. Scary young people didn't arrive in the UK along with happy slapping.

But, given what we know about the English character, it shouldn't be that surprising to find out that they may have arrived much earlier. In his recent book, *The Gangs of Manchester*, Andrew Davies finds that the English capacity to misunderstand juvenile bad behaviour is at least 120 years old. His book deals with the late Victorian 'Scuttlers' – youth gangs that caused a media storm in Manchester from 1860 onwards. MPs called for the reintroduction of flogging in 1890 to deal with the problem. The chief expert on the problem, Alexander Devine, wrote in his 1890 work, *Scuttlers and Scuttling: Their Prevention and Cure*, that Scuttling seemed to be caused by poor parenting, lax discipline in schools, scarce facilities and entertainment for young people in Manchester's slums and the 'malign influence of sensationalist novels'. One hundred and twenty years have passed and, while bad parenting, school indiscipline and poor facilities are still very much present, England can feel proud that they triumphed over the menace to their children represented by sensationalist novels.

What seems to be the big problem here is that, as far as I can see, England has chosen to ethnicize its young. In this country, they are treated as a tribe apart and described in harsh general terms that drag them all down. Young people commit crime, young people are violent and out of control, old people are frightened of young people. Replace the word 'young' with the word 'black', or indeed 'Irish', and see how ludicrous and damaging these generalizations are.

By contrast, the Irish attitude to its youth is extraordinarily positive. They are regarded as well-educated, ambitious and confident. They are told at an early age that it is great to be Irish, that Ireland is a young country (whatever that means) and that the world is grateful to have them around.

They can't handle their drink, of course (sorry, young people of Ireland, but you're generally terrible drunks, shouty and uncoordinated; I've been watching you stumble round festivals for years now, roaring, 'How's it goin'!' and 'Legend!' at each other and falling over. You'd think with the practice you've had …). Ireland isn't a particularly violent society either, and people are more readily seen as the victims of societal ills, be it drugs or unemployment or immigration, rather than the instigators of crime.

I blame the Pope. John Paul II visited Ireland in 1979 and famously said, 'Young people of Ireland, I love you!' What could the very Catholic older generation do but agree? They couldn't contradict the Pope. And the young people have been basking in that glow ever since.

Barnardo's learned one important lesson. The feral nature of young people is just one of those things – like the failure of Terminal Five and the uselessness of the NHS – which the English people Cannot Be Talked Out Of.

In thirty years' time, a new generation of parents will be bemoaning the youth of the day, shaking their heads and wondering how society has declined so far. Among them will be my own children, cursing their lot as they struggle to eke out an existence, little suspecting that it's their father's fault. If I'd just brought them to that toddler group all those years ago. That was where I went wrong.

Chapter 13:
The Backbone of the Nation

With summer looming, we head out for one last week on the road before taking a break. In a triumph of organization, or thanks to a rare burst of good luck, this handful of gigs falls in a straight line, directly up the spine of the country. First up is Derby and, for one night only, a proper healthy meal.

This wasn't my idea, it was the idea of some producer on Gordon Ramsay's *The F-Word*. As an item on the show, they wanted Gordon to join me backstage at one of my gigs, and we would prepare a light, nutritious dinner, of the type, the story demanded, that was impossible to eat when you're a stand-up comedian touring the country.

It's not impossible to eat healthily on tour, it just requires a lot of motivation. The schedule tends to work against it. You arrive for a soundcheck at six thirty, the show starts at eight and you finish close to ten forty-five. In order to have a decent meal, I'd have to eat at 5 p.m. Or 11 p.m. Not many quality restaurants base their business plan around these timings. So it's highstreet chains and nervous pizza boys for early-bird Dara and curryhouses for the after-show wind-down.

This means that I am also not the best placed to discuss England in terms of food. Is it getting better out there? I hope so. One of the old reliable canards about the English was that they were fundamentally uninterested in food. It was never very clear whether this was because English food was terrible, or whether English food was terrible because the English weren't interested in it.

Traditionally, the food here could generally be reduced to the formula 'X and Y': roast beef and Yorkshire pudding, bangers and mash, or fish and chips. Cooking wasn't about carefully combining separate ingredients but, rather, an incredibly literal style of cooking the ingredients and then placing them on a plate side by side. It's no coincidence that England's main contribution to world cuisine has been the sandwich – a food that allows you to eat with one hand while continuing your card game with the other. At least in Ireland we made stew.

The English, as a nation, are also relatively new to dining out. As John Burnett points out in *England Eats Out: 1830 to the Present*, going out to eat for leisure purposes was largely restricted to the rich in England until after the Second

World War. Poorer people did eat outside the home, but it was generally because they had to for work, and they tended to eat very basic meals from food stalls, pubs or, later, in 'caffs'. It wasn't until the arrival of post-Second World War affluence that eating out in a proper restaurant became a regular activity for ordinary people. A certain nervousness caused by this late arrival may be the reason why there are so many English jokes and sketches about table manners. The Hungarian author George Mikes remarked in 1946 that 'On the Continent people have good food; in England people have good table manners.'

Given this late start, though, the English have taken to eating out with great enthusiasm. UK households now spend around £77 billion on food and non-alcoholic drink for consumption at home, but they spend £78 billion on eating outside the home. This means you now eat out more than the Americans or, surprisingly, the French.

The English insecurity about food has in many cases morphed into open-faced snobbery. (Have you seen *Come Dine With Me*? It would be better titled *Come Judge My Soup, You Pricks*.) This superiority could be easily applied to the country's favourite dishes. After all, no one in Bologna would recognize Spaghetti Bolognese, and Indian food in the UK is all made by Bangladeshis. Chicken tikka masala, once described as Britain's real national dish by former foreign secretary Robin Cook, was apparently invented by a Bangladeshi chef in Glasgow sometime in the 1950s – but this snobbery is missing the point. What makes the English a great nation is their pragmatism, and food is, after all, a practical consideration. They accepted that their own food wasn't that great and enthusiastically embraced the offerings of their new arrivals. The Bangladeshi, Indian, Italian and

Chinese immigrants who served up this food adapted it to the tastes of their new customers as best they could. In turn, the Brits mixed together the things they liked. We like curry and we like chips, so we'll love curry chips. We like Mars bars and we like deep-frying, and so on.

Today, there are close to ten thousand Indian restaurants in the United Kingdom, serving around 2.5 million customers a week and, if they are largely run by Bangladeshi owners, who serve adapted versions of food from the subcontinent with chips, then so what? The curry industry is worth about £1 billion annually, and British manufacturers export chicken tikka masala to India. Any other nation would just call it fusion cuisine and move on.

Tonight, in Derby, I had a celebrity chef all to myself, and all I needed to enjoy it was to get the producer to stop banging on about healthy eating. I'm a big man and, in the eyes of telly people, that reduces me down to 'Problem eater! Let's send in an expert!' I didn't want a diet expert, I wanted something nice to eat, for once. Gordon was my fast-track to a decent steak. Then the fucker turned up with prawns and rice.

For the record, Ramsay was charming and friendly and buzzed around in that way 'alpha males' characteristically do: dictating the pace, talking non-stop and telling you stuff you already knew about your own job. The more obviously driven amongst us often do that. I call it the 'Let me tell you about that' opening.

You meet an alpha male and they'll say hello and ask what you do. You'll say 'Nurse' or 'Air-traffic controller' or 'Pope'. And then the alpha male will immediately go, 'Let me tell you about nursing/aeroplanes/delivering Mass in the Vatican . . .'

Gordon had a little of that about him (at one stage he started telling me how to handle a crowd at a live cookery demonstration), but he carried it well. Besides, I'm a solo operator, he's the one with the four thousand staff to keep geeing up. I only have to keep myself motivated, and that's enough of a struggle sometimes.

'We're going to make something with chervil,' said Ramsay enthusiastically, to blank looks from me. Then he dragged me into Derby's local market and pointed at vegetables for ten minutes, while I failed to identify them:

'Cale?'

'It's a marrow.'

Then we were rushed back to the kitchen in Derby Assembly Rooms, and I watched him cook. The dish he was preparing was a Spicy Tiger Prawn Pilaf, and I heartily recommend you Google the recipe and give it a crack; I had to Google it later myself, partly because Gordon was cooking so quickly but mainly because I was constantly trying to fend off questions he'd been told to ask about my poor eating habits and lectures he wanted to give about the importance of a healthy, balanced diet. I had no interest in getting health advice from Gordon Ramsay. I just wanted something tasty for my tummy.

Despite this educational undercurrent, we had a pleasant afternoon out-cursing each other, and I parted company with the celebrity chef on good terms. He left me the best single meal I've ever had before a show and, as a bonus, confused a good-sized chunk of the audience, who'd spotted him on the way out and spent the whole gig wondering when he was going to make an appearance.

'It can't be a coincidence,' I could hear them muttering. 'He must be coming out for the encore.' Sadly for them, by the time I'd delivered my first gag, Gordon was long gone.

Derby Assembly Rooms

    1 man who works in business continuity
    1 teacher, whose wife is also a teacher
    1 man who works for the Nottingham police force as a
      'performance tester'
    1 lorry driver

The Assembly Rooms in Derby is a great comedy room, easily in the top five in the country. There is no architectural reason for this. It's a pretty ugly modern build, and it lacks the intimacy of the Victorian theatres. The town centre outside is no help either: one big concrete plaza, and you can almost see tumbleweed rolling around. I have no relationship with the place either, other than turning up every couple of years and cracking some jokes.

So it remains a riddle as to why the gigs always go so beautifully there.

Admittedly, all I remember about my previous visit was a woman shouting, 'My husband wants a penguin!' from the crowd. I think I was talking to her husband at the time; I think he sold mobile phones. I have no idea how we took the leap from that to his crazy-pet dreams. Luckily, the husband was happy to confirm that he had often expressed the desire to own a penguin, and we all agreed that having a tiny maître d' round the house would be a good thing.

This year things began more prosaically:

'I work in business continuity.'

A dull silence from the rest of the crowd. 'Business continuity' sounds like arranging bridging loans for expanding call centres. It isn't, of course. It is, actually, the coolest job in the world. Business continuity is the sector of industry which promises to keep your offices and shops functioning after a flood, a terror attack or a meteor shower. Or anything else that happens in a disaster movie that they could threaten your shareholders with.

It's an industry entirely made up of ex-army guys scaring the hell out of accountants:

'Have you made contingency plans for an assault on your offices by suicide bombers/bears/an army of the undead?' barks a man with a scar.

'Well,' the accountant says, looking nervously round to the other accountants, 'we never thought . . .'

'You never thought! Well think about this!' says the army guy as he slides photographs from war-zones across the table, all blood and guts and machetes sticking out of heads.

'Eeeek!' cry the accountants, and they start writing cheques.

A friend of mine works in PR for a large Oxford Street department store and, when I was enthusing about this very subject once, she revealed that she had been given a pass to the organization's secret bunker. It's good to know that, in the event of a nuclear holocaust, she'll still be around to get the word out about the sales in bedding. Her husband was less thrilled, as the invite didn't extend to him or the kids. That's business continuity!

Business continuity is who you call when your CEO is

kidnapped by militiamen, and they come in and tell you the odds of getting him back.

Of course, business continuity is also people handing out flash-card memory key-chains and telling you to back up your emails. That was what my friend here in Derby did for a living.

We moved on to the teacher:

'What do you teach?'
   'Technology.'
   'Wow, very flash. What's involved in that?'
   'It's plastics, metal and woodwork.'
   'I'm sorry. What was that last one?'
   'Woodwork.'
   'When is the last time anyone made technology out of wood? No, in fact, I'll tell you. It was … Look at this big, free horse! What's that scuffling noise from the middle? Never mind. No one is advanced enough to build a hollow horse …'

The performance analyst for the Nottingham police force was unwilling to explain which of the performing arts the lads were doing well in. We guessed tap, but that jazz and contemporary weren't far behind.

The lorry driver didn't want to be typecast as just another lorry driver:

'I have a weekend job too!'
   'What is it?'
   'I play Robin Hood in the Robin Hood Experience in Nottingham.'

Now, I mentioned the Robin Hood Experience in passing when talking about Nottingham. I alluded to the 1970s animatronics, but may have neglected to mention the very real members of staff wandering around in doublet and sackcloth and administering the safe-play archery range at the end of the tour. If you're accurate, they present you with a certificate! I know this because I have one of those certificates.

As we were having this chat, a thunderbolt suddenly struck me. I looked at the lorry driver, and then down the row, then back at the lorry driver again, and saw a beautiful synchronicity:

'Oh my God, has anyone noticed …? In the front row we have Robin Hood,' I said, and pointing to the performance analyst two seats away from him, 'and the Sheriff of Nottingham at the same gig!'

We got most of the first half out of this.

When I came out for the second half, I decided it was time to change the subject. So I started telling a story. I was only a couple of sentences in when I was interrupted by the policeman raising his hand.

'What's up?'

He pointed to a man sitting directly between him and the lorry driver/Robin Hood; a man I hadn't spoken to at all.

'Ask him his name,' he said, with a grin.

I peered down at this stranger.

'What's your name?'

'You're not going to believe this,' he said. 'It's Matthew Merriman.'

I promise this is true.

York Grand Opera House

1 accountant from Lincoln
1 man who teaches staff at a mobile-phone company
1 man who repairs technology

Nothing that happened the following night could quite compare with that, although the Opera House is a proper, plush Victorian theatre. It sits well in the city.

York is pretty, medieval and strangely obsessed with trains. It has both the National Railway Museum and the Model Railway Museum. I got a whole routine out of the Model Railway Museum many years ago when the man behind the counter refused to let me leave my bag in reception, saying, 'Not with what your boys have been up to.'

I didn't get a routine out of the National Railway Museum, although I did get a free ride on the Yorkshire Wheel, sited at the museum. I felt quite the celeb until I realized, on the slow ascent, that I was the only person on the entire Ferris wheel, because the heavy rain had decimated the view. I think I saw a cathedral at one point.

I was wrong. It was a minster, which is like a cathedral, only more camp. And also more expensive to get into – although you can walk into the ticket-selling area, get to the turnstile and announce, 'I'm just looking, thanks,' as if you're shopping around for a cathedral to visit.

York also has a famous street which is called The Shambles. And they sell a lot of fudge here.

The English obsession with fudge is a puzzle to me. Fudge is fine, don't get me wrong; but so many towns around here seem desperately proud of their local variety. There are the seaside towns, obviously, along with most of Devon and Cornwall. Bath is all about the fudge. And to that august and immortal list of Places That Melt Milk, Sugar and Butter Together (Vanilla/Chocolate optional), we can now add the Viking town of York. You can't get away from fudge here. You'd think the streets were built from it, especially given the subsidence in The Shambles. Come to think of it, Fudge and the Shambles would be a great name for a band.

And, despite all this local pride, all the fudge tastes like, well, fudge. Everywhere it's sold as 'Bla-di-bla's Famous Fudge', and it's not even English, it was invented in Poughkeepsie, New York, in 1886.

York has invented enough confectionery, though. Rowntree and Mackintosh were based here, as was Terry's. York City FC play at KitKat Crescent, and the Yorkie bar was named in the city's honour.

You'd think, with all this, as well as Mars in Slough and Cadbury's in the Midlands, that England would be the biggest sweet-eating country in the world. Certainly, as an Irish child, taking a trip over the Irish sea was like winning Wonka's golden ticket. You had sweets here we never dreamed of. Crazy, unnatural sweets that were being stopped at Irish Customs as an affront to God or something. Mint Aeros and giant, giant bars of Dairy Milk and, strangest of all, Caramac. Washed down with Vimto and Tizer and other foreign drinks, we burped our appreciation of the English love of confectionery. We were wrong, though. The Swiss are the real pigs, getting through more than 22lb of chocolate per person each year. Then come the Austrians, then, feasting on the work of other nations, the Irish. As usual, you only made the quarter-finals. You come in seventh.

Grassington Festival Marquee

1 solicitor
1 park ranger
1 landlord
750 people in a tent

After York, we made a quick stop off at the Grassington Arts Festival, one of the many local arts festivals that dot the English countryside throughout the warmer months. The product of an enthusiastic committee and, usually, one crazy visionary, these festivals aren't built to compete with Glastonbury or Hay but to bring some entertainment to the locals and add some heft to their tourism push. There isn't any particular theme to them other than deciding who they're in the mood to invite, which leads to an informal and eccentric mix.

Grassington is a tiny village in the Yorkshire Dales, described on its own website as 'one of the best loved of the honeypot villages' in the area, the honeypot comparison apparently based on their allure to tourists. Y'know, like the phrase 'like flies to shit!' but more Up! Their festival has been running for almost thirty years now, is spread over more than a fortnight and allows me to claim that I shared a bill with Aled Jones, Barry Cryer and General Sir Mike Jackson. I'm not sure if I shared a dressing room with them, but if I did I'm sure that they were just as impressed as I was by the small tent, next to the marquee, with the gas fire. This was no place to be a prima donna. I hung up my two shirts (fifty-eight shows and counting now) and went to work.

The Dales themselves are famously beautiful, although I have only their reputation to go on, since, the night we were there, the entire area was enclosed in cloud. The Yorkshire Dales might be the world's largest wind-farm and oil refinery for all that I could make out in the drizzle. I spent a large part of the gig pointing in random directions and imagining out loud what hideous industrial eyesore was hidden by the fog. I find that the best way to address people who are deeply proud of their beautiful landscape. 'That's the docklands over to the left. And over there is the smelting plant . . .'

Ironically, since the gig was in a big white tent, the one thing I could see was the audience. In a theatre, the stage lights have to be tweaked and lowered even to let me see the first couple of rows; seeing the entire room, eyeball to eyeball, is like running naked into a school assembly. I spent the first twenty minutes talking to my shoes, rather than face the people.

Luckily, the audience didn't care about either the strange lighting, or the nonstop pitter-patter of rain on the tent roof. They were far more interested in the solicitor whose big court case was getting a dog off the crime of worrying sheep.

The informality of the festival is such that I ended up after the show in a local pub with the festival committee and, coincidentally, the local rugby club. I pressed the committee for gossip, and they revealed to me that one of the other headliners, a famous and famously anodyne television presenter, had arrived in the village with his own security detail to fend off stalkers. 'Look at him and his bodyguard, who does he think he is?' was the general reaction, until just before the show started when one of the festival staff found a mysterious man trying to break in at the fence. 'I'm a close personal friend of —' he insisted, until the police were called.

They did tell me who the celeb was, by the way, although I can't be 100 per cent sure because the rugby team had started making me drink yards of ale. It's a very informal festival is Grassington.

Carlisle Sands Centre

1 manager of a fireworks company
1 air-traffic-controller controller:
  'What do you do? Stop them bumping into each other round the office?'
1 student

Very hung over from drinking those yards of ale. Clouds lifted and I saw the Dales look beautiful at last. We crossed the Pennines, bought a football and kicked it around in the summer sunshine outside the venue until I got dragged in to perform in a room that doubles as a basketball arena.

We learned that, when designing a fireworks show, some of them make you go ooh! And different ones make you go ahh!

Getting demob happy now. Only one to go.

Perth Concert Hall

1 man who runs 2,000 vans for Tesco
1 cancer researcher
1 jewellery designer
1 tool line supervisor

This is the last gig of the UK tour until October. We've reached the end of May, done sixty shows and, to finish, driven to the most northerly point of the entire schlep. The landscape opened out more and more around us after we left Carlisle, until we sit now at the edge of the Highlands. The weather is spectacular, we've arrived too early, we've got time to kill, so me and Damon go for a pint.

In the middle of Perth, there is a row of pubs and restaurants with terraces and outdoor seating, filled with tables. We plonk ourselves down at one, I get some drinks and we settle down to enjoy the last of the afternoon sun.

Then a waiter runs out after me and takes our drinks off the table.

'You can't drink them here,' he says.

'What's the problem?' we protest.

'It's the law. You're not allowed drink on the street. Not without food. You'll have to sit indoors I'm afraid.'

'But we're in your beer garden!'

'No, it's still technically the street.'

'Can we order food then?'

'The kitchen is closed.'

'But why do you have this beer garden?'

'It's the council. You can sit out here, they'll let us have the terrace, but you can't drink, because they don't want any public drinking.'

So we swapped our beers for soft drinks, and sat there at the pub terrace, amidst a row of pub terraces all filled with people who weren't allowed to drink. Every few minutes, new people would arrive, buy drinks and then the waiter would run out, take the drinks off them and explain the bye-laws. And each time, the punters would wriggle for a loophole.

'What if I stood and my wife sat and then we . . .'

And each time, the waiter would patiently shake his head and just go, 'The council . . .'

If Perth Council built a giant Ferris wheel, people would admire it, queue up along the river Tay, and as they approached to board, a council member would cry, 'Halt!'

'What's wrong?' the people would say.

'You can look at it,' the alderman would explain, 'but it's not for travelling on.'

It wasn't the only lost opportunity in Perth that day. Truth be told, I wasn't very good that night. Perth has a gleaming new concert hall, modern and geodesic amidst the smart grey stone from which all Scottish cities are built. Modern halls are a wonder of multifunctionality, but you pine for the intimacy of the Victorians. This is not an insurmountable handicap, though, or a justifiable excuse. That night, I just never got any momentum going. I never owned the room, never felt I really had them. After the show, the festival committee came backstage to say hello, and I mumbled something and desperately hoped that I was just spoiled by the truly great nights in Derby and York, that I was being a neurotic performer and that it was better than I imagined.

I don't think it was, though. And it was a disappointing way
to wrap up.

When we got back to our hotel, we immediately asked for
the bar and hit our second wall of bureaucracy of the day.

'The bar is closed, I'm afraid.'

'Can we not get a drink at all?'

'Of course. You can sit in the bar and the night porter can
serve you minibar drinks.'

And that's what we did: we sat in the bar, staring at two
hundred bottles of top-quality scotch we weren't allowed to
touch, while the Eastern European night staff brought
us miniature bottles of Bell's and single-serving bottles of
wine.

It was time for a break.

The following morning Damon and I parted company for
a few months. It was bitter-sweet, with Damon supplying
most of the bitter, seeing as he was leaving me off at
Edinburgh airport so I could fly home while he then drove
the car all the way back down to London on his own.

'Aren't you going to wish me a happy flight?' I said to him
as we parted.

'Fuck you.'

A couple of weeks later, I tuned into *The F-word*. It was all
as I remembered, apart from the bit where Gordon, in
voiceover, went, 'Hopefully this dish will help Dara eat
more healthily on tour.'

Well, thanks, Gordo, that's all my problems solved. Now
all I have to do is talk Damon into travelling everywhere
six hours early in order to arrive in time for the local market
and making sure we only play theatres that have industrial
kitchens on site.

And chervil? You can't get chervil anywhere, for love nor money. Trust me, I've tried. I've spent the last year trying to find it. Greengrocers. Fancy supermarkets, chervil.com. It simply doesn't exist. I think Ramsay just made it up.

Television, eh? It's all lies, y'know.

Chapter 14:
I Remember That Summer in Dublin

We take a couple of months off the tour here, because people don't really go to comedy shows during the warm summer months. Except in Dublin. What Ireland may lack in the number of theatres, the audiences make up for in enthusiastic attendances. Ireland boasts one of the largest comedy festivals in the world, a DVD chart filled with home-grown acts and, most importantly, night after night of full houses. A good-sized comedy tour in England will maybe do fifty shows. A big Irish act, Tommy Tiernan, say, or Des Bishop, will do that many nights in Dublin alone.

All through the summer, I kept returning to the city, weekend after weekend, to one of the greatest rooms in stand-up, Vicar Street Theatre. It didn't start as a comedy room. It was originally built as a music venue for legendary Irish singer-songwriter Christy Moore, but over time the focus changed as more and more Irish comedy acts began to develop their own enthusiastic following.

If a band gets big, they move to bigger and bigger venues, all the way up to stadia. Comedy loses something the bigger the room gets, so if a comedian gets big he just plays the same rooms more often. Some comics have started to try 'arena' shows, and good luck to them, but it wouldn't work for me. In a giant room, I'd have to lose the very closeness that allows me to keep the show spontaneous. I'd also be trading in a number of nights in the perfectly sized room for one of hassle and compromise in a vast one. I love actually doing my job; I love performing the show. I'm not searching for the most efficient way to deliver these jokes to the greatest number of people as quickly as possible.

So every weekend I head over to Ireland to enjoy myself. And, in the process, see how it all compares to England.

Dublin Vicar Street

1 woman who gave me a belt
1 woman who gave me a camera and told me to take a
   photo of her friends
1 man who gave me a set of lurid protective gloves for
   handling asphalt
1 man who makes artificial limbs
1 woman who gave me some crisps

Well, for a start, it's even more interactive. This might be because the room is much more informal, perhaps because it's a music venue, not a Victorian theatre. The show starts later than normal, there's a proper bar, people sit on stools downstairs with a table covered in drink in front of them. This informality suits me; if I walk onstage lamenting the fact that I came out without a belt, I am immediately supplied with one. A lady's belt, unfortunately, with a diamante edging, but all it had to do was keep my trousers up for a couple of hours, and it did the job fine. When I returned the belt at the end, the nice lady had the decency to accept her own belt back as if it was a lovely souvenir of the night.

Having a photo taken is a more usual souvenir, but it's always better if you can get an unusual angle on it, such as from the stage, in the middle of a show. I took one of this group smiling, and one of them looking bored and miserable while tearing up their tickets in disgust. I know which one ended up on Facebook.

The lurid gloves were from a safety-equipment salesman:

'Do you have any of your stuff on you?' I asked.

'What do you mean, on me?'

'I mean, in the back of the car, in the car park, nearby. If you can find any of your stuff during the interval, I'll do the show wearing whatever you've got and that'll be free publicity for you. Anything. If you have a full-length body suit to protect against radiation sickness, I'll wear it.'

He looked at his wife dubiously, and she shrugged. I let it go.

When I came out for the second half, there was a pair of Day-glo heat-resistant gauntlets on the stage.

You can imagine how long I spent pleading with the artificial limb-maker.

As for the crisps, well, they were Tayto. The minute I got to Ireland, that killer routine was resurrected, put in pride of place, and it worked every time. Fuck you, Damon. Fuck you, Dominic Maxwell of *The Times* of London. And every time it absolutely stormed, I would go, 'Jesus, I wish I could do this in the UK too.' But it just doesn't work outside of Ireland.

One night, there was a girl in who happened to have a packet of Tayto on her, and she weaved her way through the crowd after the routine and presented me with it. I had to do the encore spitting out fragments of crisp.

The crime stories were also a treat.

Dublin Vicar Street

1 estate agent who found squatters in the house he was showing
1 woman who confronted two armed robbers in a shop because they were laughing at her sister
1 man who was attacked by a syringe:
  'I know what you mean. Lab equipment is out of control these days. I was assaulted by a Bunsen burner last week.'
1 woman who caught someone stealing her tomatoes
1 man who heard a 'ruffling' noise while he was in bed one night:
  'Ruffling?'
  'Yes.'
  'Were they in Edwardian dress?'
  'Rustling.'

'Do you own cattle?'
1 police officer
'Cardboard squad cars!' screamed the crowd.

The estate agent lost the sale, unsurprisingly.

The armed robbers got away, but not before the young woman ran after their car, while dressed in her pyjamas, and hung on to the door handle as it drove away.

The tomatoes might seem less important, but the woman was quite upset:

'How did you notice that they were stealing your tomatoes?' I said.
    'The alarm went off.'

This is a woman who takes her vegetables seriously.

I wasn't expecting 'Cardboard squad cars!' either, and had to quiz the crowd. It turned out that the news during the week had been dominated by the story of how the Irish police force had placed dummy police cars by the roadside as a deterrent to speeding. Seen from a distance, they would be indistinguishable from the real thing; only when you had slammed on the brakes and passed them at the legal velocity would it be obvious. Thus, not only were you slowing up your journey, you got to feel like a fool as well.

This tickled me enormously, so I ran around backstage trying to find some cardboard. Vicar Street has an excellent sound and lighting team and, with the technical demands of a comedy show extending only as far as a microphone and some walk-on music, they're left idling all night. To their credit, they took the task off me. When the encore came, I was able to walk back out behind a full-sized cardboard car door, with a window cut out and the word 'Garda' written in massive letters along the side. Then I presented it to the police officer. And he presumably drove away in it, calming traffic all the way home.

These are highlights, of course. The average night in Vicar Street was usually pretty interesting just as a snapshot of how Irish society had changed during the last decade. This was the usual breakdown of the front row:

Dublin Vicar Street

2 mobile-phone salespeople
7 IT professionals
4 financial consultants
13 marketing managers

Ireland hasn't had to recover from the slow deterioration of its manufacturing base: we never had one. We jumped straight from farming to tertiary workers. This means that we don't have England's bizarre false nostalgia for an agricultural past. The way that people idealize country living and agrarianism in the UK; you're worse than the Khmer Rouge sometimes. Irish people know farms. You're either from one, or you had to spend your holidays on one. They aren't just something redbrick and twee that you drive past in the Cotswolds.

Nostalgia doesn't do a great deal of business generally in Ireland, at least not with my generation. Things were just too grim and for too long. I wouldn't be exaggerating things to say that my memories of my teenage years are in black and white. The Celtic Tiger, Ireland's economic boom, was years away, and the general presumption was that you would all end up in London, Boston or Melbourne. Even our school and college holidays were commonly spent abroad: working in hotels in London, building cars in the BMW factory in Munich or working in bars in America. Irish young people were trained to emigrate. I never thought twice about this either. They were brilliant summers. Then I moved to England, where young people have six weeks off school for the summer holidays instead of three months. Six weeks! You'd hardly find a flat for the nineteen of you in that time, let alone make any money.

I remember meeting some friends for lunch in Dublin and, unconsciously, the conversation demonstrated just how natural the idea of emigration is to the Irish.

We were discussing the economic downturn, and one of them casually mentioned to me that the papers in Ireland were recommending Saskatchewan in Canada as a good place to move to. Neither of us saw anything strange in this at all; it took my wife, who's English, to point out how strange it is for a national paper to run recommendations of destinations for the population to emigrate to. You certainly wouldn't open the *Telegraph* and see 'Canada! A great place to visit your grandchildren!'

Of course, we had thought that the Celtic Tiger had brought those days to an end. For ten years, the only people emigrating from Ireland were comedians. The Celtic Tiger has since departed and, at the time of writing, it's way too early to start gauging the effect this bust will have on a country which loved the boom so much.

A friend of mine who works in the nightclub industry had an interesting take on it. Having run venues in both England and Ireland, he says that a recession will always progress more smoothly in England because, while the Irish bemoan and deny the downturn, the English respond, and this is crucial and telling, as if they deserve it. In the same way that the English find success difficult to enjoy, and have a tendency to see the worst in everything, when the bad times come, they're ready for it. They decrease spending, tighten their belts, invoke the Blitz spirit and, eighteen months later, they're out the other end of it. We, on the other hand, are still out each night, cursing the recession and dragging it out at the same time.

It's only a theory but, when I put it to my friends at lunch in Dublin, they said, 'Actually, we've decided to embrace the recession.'

This was a year in. The English had been embracing the recession before it even started.

People sometimes ask me: What is the greatest difference between England and Ireland? England's natural pessimism is a contender, certainly. Another good candidate is that the Irish find each other endlessly fascinating, in a way that the English don't. If I hear another Irish accent abroad, for example, a conversation will inevitably start. We regard our mutual Irishness as sufficient excuse to start talking to each other. I don't think the English do that at all.

The Irish would like to think that they take the laurels for charm; but the English are just much more professional. From grand engineering projects, to the media, to the world's most beloved national sporting league, there's a polish to the work that comes out of England that a smaller country like Ireland can only admire.

There is another fun distinction, though, that I've rarely seen mentioned. Irish people like to think they're feisty and anti-authoritarian; English people like to think of themselves as conservative and respectful of tradition. In reality, though, Irish people are conservative and traditional and English people are riotous and unruly. Compared to the Irish, English people are much more suspicious of their politicians, much more likely to throw out governments they're unhappy with and, crucially, much, much more likely to take to the streets when they're angry.

Let's deal with the legitimate means of political expression first. The two countries run their elections in completely different ways. Ireland's electoral system is called PRSTV. That's proportional representation, single transferable vote. For the English here, and many of the Irish, this might need explaining, but one book may not give me enough space. You pick your first choice, then your second, then your third, and so on down the ballot paper. Then there are quotas and multiple seats and bundles and eliminations and distributions of surpluses, and it all goes on for days. The system delivers a roughly approximate ratio of elected representatives to percentage of national vote.

England operates a first-past-the-post system. Tick one box, pile them all out on to the table and, by 11 p.m. on the same day, the results start to come in. Results have only a vague bearing on national polls, elections reducing down to a number of marginal constituencies and Peter Snow waving a giant computer-generated swing-o-meter around the studio.

The Irish system correctly reflects the wishes of the population. It is conservative and vague and regularly leads to hung parliaments and awkward and unstable governments. Elections are followed by a period of closed-door meetings, while opposing parties see which of their cherished beliefs can be most easily compromised for power. Eventually, a 'rainbow coalition' is announced, as if nature could produce a rainbow with a large block of grey, a tiny streak of green and a couple of independent colours bought off with planning permission for a new local hospital. The most telling post-election quote in Ireland is: 'The Irish people have spoken; now we have to work out what they said.'

The English system is fickle, violent and punitive. Every decade or so, it amplifies a few percentage points of swing into the appearance of a once-in-a-generation political revolution. New governments are swept into power on an apparent wave of public acclaim, and whole new eras are declared. English elections are a moody teenage girl, throwing herself on her bed and screaming, 'I hate him!'

Here's another example of how the English, contrary to appearances, are excitingly anti-establishment. There is a notion of us Irish being big fighters. We've had some top boxers certainly; our native sports are certainly 'robust', but when it comes to taking on the ruling powers, well, we don't even come close to the English. For all the talk about England being a nation built on fair play, tolerance and obeying the rules, you love a bit of a scrap. Particularly in the name of political change.

At the Hay Literary Festival in 2006, Andrew Marr, discussing his television series *The History of Modern Britain*, said that every single episode could have featured footage of a policeman, on horseback, wading into a rioting crowd. Not the same policeman, of course, and hopefully not the same horse, but the point was clear. The English love a good riot. And despite outraged newspaper columnists trying to pretend that violence in England was invented by happy-slapping teenagers, there's been rioting in England for centuries, and it was usually about money.

Take the Peasants' Revolt in 1381, for example. It erupted in Brentwood in Essex, due to anger about a poll tax and conditions for agricultural workers. The peasantry marched on London and killed a number of King Richard II's administration, including the Archbishop of Canterbury. The king originally agreed to meet most of the rebels' demands but, when Wat Tyler arrived for negotiations, he was stabbed in the throat by the Lord Mayor of London.

It is difficult to imagine how mind-blowing that chain of events would be if it read: 'G8 protestors attacked Buckingham Palace, killing the Archbishop of Canterbury, Rowan Williams. The attacks were only repelled when the leader of the protests was stabbed in the throat by the Mayor of London, Boris Johnson ... who then held a press conference, where he made it sound like a charming mistake.'

Rioting as a response to loss of livelihood is a common occurrence throughout English history. Let's fast-track to 1811, when the textile workers of Nottingham decided they'd had enough of industrial development and destroyed the offending machinery and mills. The revolt spread to Lancashire and Yorkshire in 1812. The social historian Eric Hobsbawm has pointed out that, at one point in the Luddite disturbances, there were more troops defending machines in England than there were fighting Napoleon in Spain.

In 1830, there were the Swing Riots, in which agricultural labourers in Kent rose up and wrecked the threshing machines that were putting them out of work. There were 'The Days of May' in 1832, when rioting swept across the country in support of the Great Reform Act.

In August 1919, about a thousand police officers in Liverpool, Birkenhead and Bootle went on strike for improved pay and conditions. The strikers marched on the police stations manned by their non-striking colleagues and, while the two opposing groups faced off, the city descended into widespread looting and street violence. After several days of chaos, the army, some tanks and – my favourite detail – three warships restored order. When you start wheeling out the warships to deal with failed contract nego- tiation, well, that's when you've got to have a long look at your Human Resources department. Interestingly, General Macready – the then Commissioner of the Metropolitan Police – suggested this particular strike was probably caused by 'the presence of many Irishmen in the force, a class of men who are always apt to be carried away by any wave of enthusiasm'.

This is a little harsh, given, by contrast, the absence of rioting in Ireland. We don't have a history *without* violence, of course, but much of it was directed into uprising against the English themselves and, since our own civil war at the start of the 1920s, the taste for that kind of public violence seems to have disappeared. There has hardly been a riot worth talking about. For all our reputation, the Irish are the conservative ones, with hardly a paving stone torn up in anger. That hasn't been the case in England in the last ninety years.

The 1984–5 miners' strike, for example, was famously violent. At the 'Battle of Orgreave' in June 1984, around five thousand police in full riot gear and with large numbers of police horses fought a pitched battle with an even larger number of striking miners, with hundreds of injuries sus- tained on both sides. More than eleven thousand arrests were made during the period of the strike.

As well as industrial disputes, there have been racial ones too.

In August 1958, the Notting Hill Race Riots erupted when young white men began victimizing Caribbean immigrants in the Notting Hill area. The violence started when a group of youths attacked a white woman who was part of a mixed-race couple, but quickly degenerated into more serious mob violence with hundreds of young men – many dressed in distinctive teddy-boy clothes – attacking houses and shops they believed to be owned by immigrants. There had been an even bigger race riot in Nottingham a few days earlier, with more than a thousand rioters on the streets.

Then there are the riots that seem to have taken place for no good reason at all. In May 1964, rival groups of mods and rockers met at the popular seaside towns of Bournemouth, Brighton and Margate to beat the lard out of each other. In Brighton that Whit weekend, about a thousand youths fought each other on the prom and beach. It probably says a lot about the English attitude to this kind of thing that, when the fighting started up for a second day, thousands of spectators jockeyed for a good viewing position on Brighton's Marine Parade and Aquarium Sun Terrace.

So yes, the English are willing to take to the streets – as they also did for the Sacheverell riots, the Bristol Bridge riots, the Scuttlers, the Tonypandy riot, the Brixton, Toxteth and Broadwater Farm riots, the Wapping print strike, the Bradford Race riots, the Poll Tax riot, the G20 riots and so on.

And we haven't even mentioned football yet.

Dublin Vicar Street

1 journalist from the *Irish Sun*
1 electrician
1 man who makes 'mezzanine' floors
1 accountant

Nothing special about that line-up. I only mention it because it was the day of the All-Ireland Hurling Final, which I attended and enjoyed, and I had to do the show despite being sun-kissed and slightly woozy from drinking. It was never going to be the best show I've ever done. I can recall a moment midway through the second half where I felt as though what little energy I had would have been far better spent in a pub somewhere, continuing a debate about whether the Kilkenny team we had just watched win a three in a row were the best in history. I shook it off.

Sport and comedy shows tend not to mix very well. I was onstage in Vicar Street the night of the Liverpool *v.* Milan Champions League final in 2005. Me and the stage crew were watching it backstage and, when the show started at eight thirty, I made an announcement from the stage that Milan were already 3–0 up. There was a palpable wave of relief from the crowd that all they'd missed was a one-sided walkover. But when I came out for the second half and announced Liverpool's historic comeback and that we were in the last few minutes of extra time and heading to penalties, the mood changed sharply.

Every man in the room stared bitterly at me. 'I have missed a classic,' they were all thinking, 'for this.' Now, that is a tough crowd to impress.

Even though I am very happily settled in England, the one time that I sorely miss Ireland is on the day of the All-Ireland Hurling Final. This year, I was lucky enough to have a show in Dublin that day, and blagged a ticket for the match in the afternoon.

There is a mysterious art to obtaining a seat at the All-Ireland final. There is no booth, or box office, or phone line that sells All-Ireland final tickets. I think the GAA, which organizes the sport, just releases all 82,000 into the wild as a yearly test of cunning and contacts. This means that the supporters are mixed and mingled and multi-generational in a manner that would be unthinkable for the equivalent fixture in the Premier League. And, despite the passion of the supporters, and even with drink taken, there is no history of crowd violence at GAA matches. The fact that there are as many pensioners and kids attending as there are young men does tend to take the ire out of the occasion, for a start. It's difficult to 'kick off' if you've got your Uncle Seamus and Aunty Nora on one side of you and a group of eleven-year-olds on the other. Even if they are all screaming blue murder at the ref.

As I regularly attend football matches in England, it might be worth pointing out a couple of the differences between the two national sports which could explain this unique atmosphere, both impassioned and benign.

The Irish national games are amateur, the players represent their counties of birth and are followed fervently by their townspeople, neighbours and families. The sacrifices required to represent your people like this shouldn't be underestimated. The absence of violence in the stands is in stark contrast with the blood and thunder on the pitch. Hurling is a heroic and dangerous game. In contrast to soccer, few concessions are made to injuries of the players. In the likely event of a player getting injured (there's a lot of wood flying around here), they lie on the field while the game continues and they recover; or they are brought off the field as a 'blood' substitute, patched up and sent back out. There is no 'simulation', as it is euphemistically called in soccer; there isn't any advantage to rolling around the turf pretending to be injured. If you're genuinely hurt, get off the field and let somebody take your place.

And, for a stadium filled with noise, there is another alien detail to soccer fans. (It's not just America that calls it soccer, by the way: saying 'football' in Ireland usually refers to Gaelic football, hurling's sister sport. It's worth noting that 'Association Football' has had worse names in Ireland. The Christian Brothers who ran my school used to call it '*Peil an Banríon*', the Queen's football, or, even more damning, '*Peil Luther*', Martin Luther's football. There was no doubt but that you were going to hell for playing it.) There is no chanting or organized singing at GAA matches; there is none of the to-and-fro wit of England's vibrant terrace culture. This is mainly because of the difference in scoring systems. Soccer can be a thrilling sport but also dull and uneventful a lot of the time. It's not surprising that, for long periods of a match, the crowd has to make its own entertainment. Hurling will usually feature about twenty to thirty scores in a match, and there is no such thing as 'possession hurling'. Action is occurring almost constantly, so the predominant crowd noise is a screaming din, peaking as the ball heads goalwards.

The only soccer-style song I can recall at a hurling match is a tribute to Offaly's Dooley brothers Billy, Johnny and Joe, who were the backbone of the country's All-Ireland winning forward line in the nineties. It is sung to the tune of 'That's Amore'.

> When the ball's in the sky,
> In Croke Park in July,
> That's Joe Dooley.

> When the ball's in the net,
> And Kilkenny are beat [*pronounced 'bet'*],
> Johnny Dooley.

And so on. Rather than being sung during the match, though, this is more often heard hours later in a pub, along-side the retinue of county songs which exist independently of sport: 'The Rose of Tralee', 'Molly Malone', 'The Fields of Athenry' – every county has a song. Ireland's thirty-two counties have a very sharply defined identity, far more than the counties of England. Possibly due to more than a century of organized sporting competition along county lines, there is a real sense of identity to Cork, or Dublin, or Kerry, or Galway. There are ancient bragging rights at stake in these matches; fresh chapters in the endless tussle for superiority.

Other than at the extremes from London (Yorkshire and Lancashire, Devon and Cornwall), English counties have little enough distinct identity. Wiltshire, Hertfordshire and Rutland anyone? It's Dara's First Law of Identity again. If they've competed in sports, they'll have some strong sense of who they are.

Irish counties compete for perceived personality traits as clearly defined as those we ascribe to our neighbouring nations. There's the spendthrift county, the backward county, the imperious county. The famous Irish actor and comic Niall Toíbín used to do a routine in which he would perform all thirty-two different county accents.

It's this sense of place that underpins the Irish sporting experience. Unlike the superbrands of the Premier League, Irish county teams haven't detached themselves from their communities. You get your county by birth, and you're stuck with it. There's no reason to get violent; it's not like it's going to change things. It's part of who you are. 'Sure what do you know,' someone will say, 'you're only a Kerryman.' Or a Corkman. Or a Dub.

Why do I mention all this?

Well, if Monty Python had set *Life of Brian* in Dublin and written a routine called 'What have the English ever done for us?', they would have a short enough list. Tithing, famine, poverty and immigration. It's not even as if the roads are that great. Or the trains.

But, if you really had to make a list – were forced to – at the head of it would be the counties.

That's the punchline to this eulogy for the Irish county. It was a gift from the English. Henry II, to be precise, so you could argue that it's a gift from the Normans, but who are we kidding? You came over eight hundred years ago, set about organizing the place and divided it up. From 1192 on, there followed four hundred years of map-drawing; piece by piece, the thirty-two counties took form, all the way up to the creation of the final county, Wicklow, in 1607. (That's the county I'm from, by the way.)

England devised the counties and then, in our style, we made them our own. We filled them with histories, song and stories and spurious personality distinction. We took the smallest of local differences and, in the manner of a country whose roots lie in hundreds of local kingdoms, we made myth and legend of them. The amplification of such local rivalries and identities may seem a bit ridiculous if you look at it rationally. I mean, are the people of Leitrim that different from the people of Mayo, or Roscommon, or Longford? Of course not. But try telling them that. And when you meet an Irish émigré, see how quickly they tell you what county they're from.

The Irish poet Patrick Kavanagh wrote about this Irish tendency to craft epics from local stories:

> Homer's ghost came whispering to my mind.
> He said: I made the Iliad from such
> A local row. Gods make their own importance.

That reverence for the local may be the greatest difference between our two countries, and its roots go all the way back to how the English carved up the country. There's an irony there, somewhere.

Then again, what do I know? I'm only a Wicklow man.

Chapter 15:
Sullen Teenagers and Samurai Swords

The English tour resumed in October with a collection of bonus dates and, to mark the approach of winter, we hit the beach resorts. In a bizarre confluence of shows which Damon christened our 'Everyday is Like Sunday' tour, we played one faded seaside town after the other. I grew up in a faded seaside town, a town called Bray in Co. Wicklow and, while there may be many of you who would envy me the easy access to a set of dodgems and a chance to walk along the prom now and again, being a shy teenager was dull enough without having to spend it in a museum exhibit marked 'Decline'.

My home town was built for daytrippers from Dublin, though, and settled into its retirement as a suburb quite easily. It didn't have the infrastructural investment in summer fun that places like Skegness and Rhyl still have on show; these places look like industry towns pining for raw materials long after the raw materials decided to go to Spain on package holidays instead.

The proms are still twinkling away, though. British holiday resorts are unflagging in their devotion to using massed light bulbs as a lure. Even in October, on a cold night on an unfashionable coast, the light bulbs are on, the machines are beeping and flashing and the tuppence pieces are all teetering on the edge waiting for that one addition that sends them hurtling.

There is an aching poetry to an old seaside town. The pleasures on offer may seem simple and unsophisticated, but it's too easy to look at a shopworn promenade and only see decay. There's a far more poignant question asked by the bright lights still shining. There's a confused lament to the holidaymakers who've abandoned these towns for faraway shores, that it shouldn't just be nostalgia that keeps these places going.

If all this was fun once, how can it not be fun any more?

Skegness is a small town, probably Viking originally (hence the beautiful name), based around a small harbour, and it remained a small fishing village, until the railway arrived in 1875. In that revolution for leisure-time England, Skegness suddenly became a popular tourist destination for workers from the Midlands.

Skegness achieved legendary status as home to the first Butlins holiday camp, opened by impresario Billy Butlin just north of the town in 1936. The idea was to provide cheap holidays for families, with no-frills chalets, three meals a day, and activities and entertainments included in the price. There was an emphasis on fun activities (knobbly-knee contests, egg and spoon races) and group participation. Overseen by the camp's famous redcoats, this was the kind of organized, regimented fun that seems very typically English to Irish eyes. We like a bit of fun, don't get me wrong, but if that man comes to us with the megaphone one more time, they'll have to remove it from his arse if they want to use it again. It's like the way that English pubs are burdened with purpose, like quizzes or open-mic nights, or – heaven forbid – food. What's with all this multitasking? Irish pubs just serve drink and people sit around and talk.

Are knobbly knees a good thing? Or a bad thing? How did you win that contest exactly? Watching *Hi-de-Hi*, I could never work that out. The 'bonny baby' was a rationing thing, wasn't it? If you had a fat baby in Britain in the late forties, you were to be applauded. Present the same fat baby now, of course, and they'd put you on *The Jeremy Kyle Show*.

Not that we didn't have a Butlins in Ireland. There was a holiday camp in Mosney, north of Dublin. Currently, it's a refugee camp for asylum seekers. Organized fun just isn't our thing.

At one point, Butlins Skegness housed ten thousand campers and was one of nine Butlins camps across the UK. Now they're down to three, and that there are even three left would come as a surprise to many. The remaining camps – Skegness, Bognor and Minehead – have been upgraded, probably to the point of being unrecognizable. Skegness now has a spa with hydrotherapy and beauty treatments, but it also has weekends focusing on the young, drunk, can't-afford-Ibiza market. And if you're wondering what could be more fun than going to Butlins, how about going to Butlins with thousands of evangelical Christians? Butlins Skegness and Butlins Minehead co-host the Spring Harvest Christian festival over Easter, with fifty thousand in attendance.

You could also go to the extremely popular eighties retro weekends, featuring artistes such as Bad Manners, Doctor and the Medics and Sonia. Are we surprised that that one is so popular? It's like a nostalgia overdose. In one weekend, you can re-live both the eighties and the fifties.

Before the show, the lights won me over. I wandered into one of Skeggy's amusement arcades and was amazed to find signs up advertising a sale on video games. 'Three games for 50p' is an impressive return against inflation, even for an industry rendered obsolete by home consoles. I eagerly dropped my 50p into a Star Wars machine so that I could blow up the Death Star once more, for old times' sake. Sadly for the Rebel Alliance, there was no *ping* from the machine and no credits appeared on the screen. And, to add insult to injury, no 50p came rolling out of the slot. I banged the machine a couple of times in an increasingly vigorous way, until people began to notice. I hadn't caused a scene or anything, but suddenly realized that I probably looked a little intense.

I find that, in those circumstances, it can be very difficult to explain that it's the game you want, not the 50p. I stepped away from the machine and scurried back to the theatre.

Skegness Embassy Theatre

1 warehouseman who transports steel in Sheffield
1 semi-retired plasterboard worker
1 police officer
1 Scouser who came to Skegness to run a guesthouse

The Embassy Theatre sits on the prom, next to a darkened funfair, and across from a run of shimmering arcades. The crowd was filled with people with solid jobs involving plaster and steel and scrambled eggs.

We disqualified the police officer from the crime-stories section. Somebody at the back was telling us about a burglary, which I was energetically re-creating onstage when a man in the front row shouted, 'Your pants have split!' A quick rummage confirmed this and, while most of the room were laughing, the front rows had a different expression. It wasn't an eruption of joy at this unplanned moment; it was the relieved look of a siege being lifted.

'They've been split for a while, haven't they?' I said.

Lots of nods in the front seats.

'Sorry about that.'

'Actually,' ventured a polite man, right in the middle, 'it was particularly bad when you mimed going to the toilet.'

And this wasn't any old mime of going to the toilet. For reasons far too complex to explain here, it was actually the mime of an adult crouching down to use the toilet of a pre-school child. It was a long, long descent; and then I held the position to – unfortunate phrase – milk the laugh. And I had thought that it went particularly well that night.

I left Skegness with neither my dignity, nor my 50p.

Rhyl Pavilion Theatre

1 retired police officer
1 lorry driver
1 man fired from a courier company for opening the
  parcels:
  'It was Christmas Day every day for you, wasn't it?'

Carol Vorderman grew up in Rhyl.

This wasn't important to my gig there, or indeed to the
lives of the people of Rhyl, but I thought that telling you that
little fact might save me having to describe the town. I didn't
see the town. It was already dark, windy and rainy when
we arrived on our now quite wintry tour, and any of the
whimsical poignancy and optimism of the other deserted
seaside resorts wasn't much in evidence here. Even the Sun
Centre, in the same complex as the Pavilion Theatre, was
closed, which I was particularly unhappy about.

In an attempt to overcome the basic problem all seaside
towns have in the UK, Rhyl has built an indoor alternative.
The Sun Centre has a monorail, a beach and a surfing
pool, all in a controlled environment under a massive roof.
It's been around for a while now, long enough, in fact, that
I threw up there as a twelve-year-old. I was returning to
Dublin from a trip to Old Trafford with my under-twelve
football team (a dull nil–nil against West Ham, if you must
know) and, to kill time before the 3 a.m. ferry from Holy-
head, they took us to the Sun Centre. The exact order of
events was: run, scream, splash; slide, scream, splash; chips,
gobble, gobble; run, scream, splash; feel queasy, puke,
pause; run, scream, splash.

Having thrown up on Rhyl once already, I'm going to avoid the temptation to do it again. It deserves better than that. Despite the Sun Centre, Rhyl has been hit worse than the other towns here by the change in leisure habits.

The pier and the original five-domed Pavilion Theatre were demolished in the seventies. Ocean Beach funfair closed in 2007. There was a failed campaign to save the rollercoaster and flume ride from the original funfair to send them to Margate, which is similarly trying to regenerate itself to former glories, but the funding fell through.

Still, Rhyl has got a fighting spirit. It's the place where John Prescott punched a protestor, Craig Evans, who threw an egg at him. In many countries, this would probably be a very shocking event, so it says a lot about this country that the lack of any real clamour for resignations amidst the usual point scoring shows that it was broadly regarded as a fair exchange. Evans chose the terms of engagement; Prescott responded in kind, and the precedent was set. Your political life is prone to occasional outbursts of violence, as I've mentioned before, but we learned that, here, politicians will punch back.

It wouldn't be Rhyl's first fight against invaders.

The town sits at the northern end of Offa's Dyke, the massive eighth-century earthwork roughly following the line of the current Wales–England border. It was believed to have been constructed by Offa, the head of the Anglian kingdom of Mercia, to protect against invasion from the Welsh kingdom of Powys. This was back in the day, when an eight-foot ditch was enough to confound invaders. Interestingly, the Anglo-Saxons probably should have been watching their backs rather than digging ditches, and ended up being overrun by Vikings and Normans instead. In fact, the dyke may have had the opposite effect to the one intended. Genetic research published by UCL in 2002 indicates that the Welsh gene pool is quite distinct from the English, and possibly a closer match to the original Britons; the English are closer to the Dutch region of Friesland.

Even the week I was there, Rhyl had reason to be wary of visitors from across the border. The front-page story in the *Denbighshire Visitor* (an insecure name for a local paper if ever I heard one: move into the area and commit, for Christ's sake) the day I was there was 'Outrage over TV Ghost Show at Hospital'. The local town of Denbigh was the site of a former mental-health hospital which was being visited by *Most Haunted Live*, Living TV's ludicrous fake paranormal investigation show. If you haven't had the pleasure, it's all night-vision cameras and presenters looking scared and noticing how cold it seems to have suddenly become. It's a ridiculous piece of tosh, of course, but it brought the world Derek Acorah and fuelled the boom in stage psychics clogging up theatres all over the country, feeding off the bereaved with made-up messages from their dead, as I've bemoaned earlier. Living TV's crime in this instance was to call the series 'Village of the Damned', which was news to the people of Denbigh, who had been going about their business all this time, unaware of being damned. It was particularly galling to the local councillors, who had planned to convert the building into apartments.

'Who's going to live here after this?' asked Cllr Graham Maudsley.

It might be time to start digging that ditch again.

I kept my demands to a minimum when I got to Rhyl. I kept dropping hints about opening up the Sun Centre just for me, but nobody was biting so I let it go. It might have been a bit tragic, just me in a waterpark, all on my own. But for old times' sake: run, scream, splash; slide, scream, get stuck; stay stuck, start to worry; shout 'Hello?', 'Anyone there?', 'Hello?' . . .

Bridlington Spa Centre

1 dentist
1 fork-lift-truck driver
1 student of musical technology
1 trainee teacher
Mike the design engineer

Further up the coast, then, to Bridlington. Charlotte Brontë had her first view of the sea here and burst into tears at the sight. I wasn't quite as emotional, but it is a beautiful bit of coast, and there is little doubting the power of the ocean here, since this area has the highest erosion rates in Europe.

It was a tiny town before the discovery of a mineral spa source prompted the building of a first hotel in 1805, and the town expanded as part of the leisure boom of Victorian Britain. The Spa Centre, opened in 1896, was a little bit of everything. For sixpence, visitors could stay all day, walk in the gardens, bathe in the mineral baths, have a meal, listen to the band at the bandstand, attend a music-hall concert, the theatre, or go dancing.

As the industrial north declined, and cheap package holidays became available to destinations with beaches that didn't front the North Sea, Bridlington's holiday boom started to decline, but Bridlington has really tried to modernize.

They had a Bridlington Eye here, yet another of these Ferris wheels that keep appearing all over the country. It may just be the same Ferris wheel, of course, but I've seen it at least nine times now. A Ferris wheel in Bridlington might have been a bitter-sweet experience, of course, given the amount of erosion. People probably took one aerial look at the coastline and then ran home to fill sandbags.

The Spa Centre was gleaming after a multi-million-pound restoration, and attracting all the big acts.

'I see you've had Ken Dodd here, then,' I said to one of the ushers when Damon and I arrived.

'Oh yes. Ken's an old favourite here.'

'How long was he onstage then?'

'Well, we did have one complaint from a customer who said that the new seats were going to give her deep vein thrombosis. I said, it's not the seats that are giving you DVT, it's Ken.'

A quick wander round the town gave me the measure of the place. This being months out of season, most of the seaside shops were closed, denying me the chance to try Bridlington Fudge, which I'm sure was also the best in the country.

In a glorious manifestation of retail optimism, however, the ice-cream parlour was open. There were tubs and tubs of gelato, overseen by the world's narkiest-looking sixteen-year-old girl, sullenly posted at the deepest part of the counter, an ice-cream scoop in her hand and her face in a grim rictus that said, 'If you walk in here and make me work, I will scoop out your fucking eyeball.'

Sixteen is a terrible age to be living in a deserted seaside town. It's the claustrophobia that gets you. All through my teenage years, I couldn't escape the feeling that life was happening just over the horizon, somewhere else. The whole place just screams, 'Leave. Leave. This place is old and dead and you are new and alive. Leave!' I brought this up during the show, of course:

'Any teenagers in?'

Big cheer.

'Bet you can't wait to leave.'

Bigger cheer.

This says a lot more about teenagers than it does about Bridlington. It's a bright and cheery town with a gorgeous harbour and top-notch fish and chips, and one of the finest audiences I met all year. There wasn't a single person I spoke to who didn't add something to the collective store of knowledge.

From the dentist, we learned that the pink liquid you spit out after a procedure doesn't start out pink.

'It goes in blue,' he explained. 'It comes out pink.'

Do you want to know how high a fork-lift can lift? Fourteen foot:

'Have you ever taken it to fourteen feet?'

'No.'

'You've got to push that envelope, man.'

'"I'm taking it to fourteen feet."

'"Don't be a fool, John, you'll tear us apart."

'"I don't care! I've got to see fourteen feet. It's thirteen and a half now. We're nearly there!"

'"For pity's sake, John, you're going to get us all killed!"

'"Almost there ... almost there ... My God ... It's full of stars."'

No, we'll never know what happens beyond the fourteen-foot event horizon, because our fork-lift-truck driver in Bridlington hadn't got near it:

'How high have you gone?'
  'Twelve foot.'
  'Why did you stop there?'
  'That's how high the shelves are.'

Fair point.

The jewel in all this nonsense was, surprisingly, Mike the design engineer. It was surprising, because he held out for six or seven questions, in which we learned that he worked in aeronautics for Rolls-Royce in Derby, to a fair level of indifference from the crowd. Then I remember the one strange fact I had heard about Rolls-Royce in Derby, a fact I learned on an episode of *QI*. And since it's safe to presume that Stephen Fry could say anything on that show and we'd just accept it as gospel, here was a chance to test his integrity:

'Do you have a cannon that fires chickens into an aircraft engine to simulate birdstrike?'
'Yes. Yes we do.'

Stephen Fry speaks the truth.

It's not difficult to get an audience's attention with news like this. Or my attention. Suddenly all the questions in the world are jumping up and down in my head and my brain is trying to get them to form an orderly queue:

'Where do you get the chickens?'
'Sainsbury's.'

Supplementary question! 'Why Sainsbury's? Why not

Morrisons, or Lidl, or Iceland? Who needs free-range at a time like this?'

'This is Rolls-Royce, y'know . . .'

'Do you take the elastic off their legs? You know, to give them a chance? No, wait, answer this one. If a chicken makes it through, does it gain its freedom?'

'No chickens make it through.'

'What's behind the engine?'

'A housing estate.'

'What's the machine called, that fires chickens into an engine?'

'I don't think it has a name . . .'

'It must have a name! What's written on the sign on the door?'

'Keep out.'

Mike was a joy. He even told me the greatest story of industrial espionage. A competitor to Rolls-Royce in the jet-engine trade heard about their technique of testing bird-strike and decided to buy their own cannon. Loading it with chickens, they started the engine up and, when it had reached full speed, blasted the birds through it. There was an almighty explosion as the humble birds tore through the engine, rendering the plane as flightless as they were.

The boffins went back to their calculations, checked their notes and scratched their heads as to why the chickens had done so much damage. They assessed windspeed, turbulence, ballistics and tensile strength, and there was no answer; until the man operating the cannon suggested, 'Next time, should I defrost the chickens?'

Thanks to Mike the chicken man, the first half of my show ran fifteen minutes over, and that was with me dropping huge chunks, even as I was talking to him. When I came out for the second half I said, 'Enough with the chickens, I have a show to do!' and determined to get it back on track. Then we hit the crime stories:

'Has anyone here ever interrupted a crime?'

First up, the story of an eight-year-old throwing bottles at the school. He was asked to stop, didn't, so the police were called:

'That sounds like a merry piece of high jinks! What happened then?'

'They took him away and placed him in a secure containment unit.'

'Oh.'

'It's actually a very sad story.'

'Well, thanks for bringing it up at a comedy show then. Let's move on. Anyone else?'

Next up: 'My mate went mad with a samurai sword.'

There were audible murmurs of discontent through the crowd. My antennae were working overtime. This might also be a bad story:

'Did anyone get hurt?'

'Yes.'

Let's move on. Please God, let the next one be silly:

'My wife was held hostage in a limo for four hours.'

Bingo:

'Where did this happen?'

'In Flamborough.'

(Flamborough: small town along the coast, known for its lighthouse. Not previously noted for limo violence.)

'If you don't mind me asking, why was she held hostage?'

'I don't know.'

'What?'

'I never found out.'

We were discussing how one could possibly forget this one detail, and whether the limo driver's motives were political and whether you can escape through the sun-roof of a limo; all of this, when a deeper voice calls out, 'I'm his brother-in-law and this is the first I've heard of any of this.'

And yes, maybe this man was lying to me and maybe he was making the story up as he went along and maybe I shouldn't have taken him at face value, but here's my argument for it being true. If you, on the spot, off the cuff, had to come up with the first line of a crime story, would it be anything as brilliant as 'My wife was held hostage by a limousine driver'?

And who doesn't like the idea of a woman coming home four hours late to her husband and him asking why, and her going, 'Well, you're not going to believe this but I was held hostage by a limo driver,' and when he asks why she just looks at him and says, 'Darling, we'll never know ... Is that the time? Yaawwwnnn. Goodnight.' And he just shakes his head, mutters, 'My wife, eh?' and kisses her goodnight.

After the gig, I Googled 'Bridlington' and 'Samurai swords' and two stories came up, some months apart, involving the brandishing of Samurai swords, one in a drunken fight, the other in an armed raid on a dairy – neither of which would have contributed to the gaiety of the evening.

Bridlington was a joy to visit and, frankly, once they sort out the erosion and all those ninjas, I think they're going to be fine.

Chapter 16:
We Come in Peace

Bradford St George's Hall

1 lawyer from Grassington come to see the show again
1 café owner from Cork
1 steelworker
2 lady teachers
1 doctor:
 'What kind?'
 'A surgeon.'

'*What kind?*'
'*Bottoms.*'

Bradford had a bizarre smell when we arrived, just the faint hint of burned coffee grounds in the air. We later found out that this was due to a local mill burning down in a spectacular fashion. It wasn't the only business being mourned in the town. Only a week earlier, the Bradford & Bingley Building Society had been nationalized and its retail division sold off to Spanish bank Santander. It's easy to forget from the arid discussion they receive in the financial pages, but British building societies have their basis firmly in the communities from which they take their name; at one stage in the 1800s, almost every town in the country had a building society named after it. For them to have risen to the status of international banking institutions doesn't make them less of a local concern. When I perform in Halifax, the audience will always include a large number of HBOS employees; similarly the De Montford Hall in Leicester will always have a gang from Alliance & Leicester in. These institutions have a real standing in the heart of their communities.

So, emotions were a little raw in Bradford about the fate of their bank. Luckily, I was able to give these good people some of their pride back. I blamed the people of Bingley. The headquarters are there, it's probably their fault. After all, Bingley has little else to be shouting about; it is described, controversially, on its website as 'the Throstle's nest of Old England'. (Oh really, Bingley? Are you sure no Throstles nested anywhere else? Can you back that up?) It does have the Five Rise Lock, of course, an engineering marvel of the 1770s which, when it opened, was greeted in the *Leeds Intelligencer* with the report:

This joyful and much wished for event was welcomed with the ringing of Bingley bells, a band of music, the firing of guns by the neighbouring Militia, the shouts of spectators, and all the marks of satisfaction that so important an acquisition merits.

People that excited by a canal gate shouldn't be left in charge of a massive international financial institution. I'm sorry, Bingley, sometimes live comedy is a numbers game and I had to ditch you for the good of the gig.

Not that the gig was in any danger. This is Yorkshire, after all, where audiences love to talk (except, of course, in Sheffield – Oh Sheffield, why hast thou forsaken me?). The first crime story, for example:

'My neighbour was being burgled, but when we went to investigate, the burglar had left his keys in his car, so we stole them.'

'Nice move. What happened when the burglar came out?'

'He took umbrage.'

'So what happened?'

'We wrestled.'

[Brief sidebar question] 'When the burglar walked out, what had he in his arms? What had he stolen?'

'A Dyson vacuum cleaner.'

[Back to the action] 'So what happened when you wrestled?'

'He ran off.' [Big audience cheer.] 'And then came back with a knife.' [Audience cheer disappears, replaced by loud murmur.] 'So we threw the keys at him and he got away.'

Dyson do a great vacuum cleaner but I wouldn't take a knife for one, not least my neighbour's.

Another person raised their hand:

'Madam, do you have a story you'd like to tell?'

'Yes! We heard a car thief stealing our car so my husband ran out to stop him.'

'What time of the day was this?'

'Midnight.'

'So what was he wearing?'

'Well, emmm, let's just say he grabbed whatever he could on the way out. He ended up in a waxed jacket, underpants and hobnail boots.'

'So he looked like an industrial flasher. A flasher who pays attention to safety in the work place . . . Our car is being stolen! Quick! To the dressing-up box! You're allowed four items! A Stetson, a posing pouch, one stiletto and a four-foot-long clown's shoe. Perfect! That's funny.'

The woman interrupted me:

'That's not the end of the story!'

By this time I had noticed her husband, who was beginning to squirm in the chair beside her. In the way one would when one's tale of heroism was about to turn:

'So, what's the end of the story?'

'He chased the two thieves out of our cul-de-sac, and on to the main road and . . .' She started giggling. 'He got arrested for indecent exposure.'

She just about got that out before bursting into laughter. As the audience joined her, she turned to her partner and managed to mouth, 'Sorry.'

Credit where it's due, he stood up when asked and took the applause. He may be on a register, but he's got a sense of humour about it.

Bradford gets enough grief. It was once famous as the 'wool capital of the world' and, in the nineteenth century, when wool was a high-tech industry, this was like calling it Silicon Valley. Since then, it has suffered the typical problems of post-industrial Britain. Most of the old wool-trade buildings were knocked down in the fifties and sixties and replaced with office buildings and pedestrian subways.

Bradford still has plenty of open spaces and old buildings made of beautiful stone. It has the nicest Waterstones in the country, in a converted church, filled with air and light. (I didn't check, but I am really hoping that the science section is right where the altar used to be.) The theatre I was in for tonight's gig, St George's Hall, is also one of the more interesting buildings in the town. It was opened by Queen Victoria in 1853. In 1854, Charles Dickens gave a debut reading for *Bleak House* to 3,700 people here. He described it as 'a tolerably easy place – except that the width of the platform is so very great to the eye at first'. Dickens never played the Hammersmith Apollo. That would have wrecked his head completely.

Speaking of having your head wrecked, in 1910, a political speech by Winston Churchill from the stage here was interrupted by suffragettes who had hidden under the stage the previous evening and burst up through the trap door. There is no record of whether they went 'Ta-daa!' when they appeared. But then it's unlikely they were dressed like magician's assistants at the time. Great girls, the suffragettes, but you could never get them to gussy up.

The afternoon of the show, Damon and I had been to the National Media Museum (the most visited museum in the country outside of London; and where the woman who sold us the tickets recommended the telly exhibition 'because you can try reading an autocue'). Then, in the evening, we had a slap-up Indian meal, and watched two girls having a sort of fight while some lads cheered them on. The next day we went to see some Hockney paintings. It was like being on a mini-break. While we were there, the city was lit up for Diwali, the Hindi festival of light, and it was all a delight.

Of course, in 2001, Bradford had the worst race riots in the UK in twenty years. Up to a thousand youths took to the streets over a three-day period. The uprisings were triggered by riots earlier that summer in Oldham and Burnley, and specifically by clashes between the Anti-Nazi league and the National Front. Two hundred and ninety-seven arrests were made and two hundred sentences handed out.

Bradford has one of the highest levels of Muslim inhabitants, particularly Pakistanis, in the UK. It also has high levels of Hindus, Sikhs and non-conformist Christian groups, and it has the Bradford Mela – a celebration of Asian culture, the largest such festival outside Asia. Then again, in 1989, *The Satanic Verses* was publicly burned here.

So, it might seem natural to raise at this point England's attitude towards race and integration. Let me describe one more stop on the tour first, though – somewhere that might put that discussion into a different context.

Wolverhampton Civic Hall

1 fireman
1 journalist
1 Honda salesman
1 man who sells computer qualifications
1 man who markets hospices and baths, although not at
   the same time

I reached the Civic Hall after two nights of violence and bloodshed. Two days before I arrived, the venue had hosted an event listed as 'The Unmasking of Kendo Nagasaki – Live Wrestling!', which, according to the website, 'features the unmasking of Kendo Nagasaki', so, frankly, if Kendo Nagasaki didn't get that mask off, you could probably ask for your money back.

The Civic Hall has been in the grappling business all the way back to when it was the main venue for the legendary live television broadcasts of the seventies. The era of Big Daddy, Giant Haystacks and a front row of bloodthirsty grannies baying; it was among the most bewildering things to watch from Ireland. Did you all believe it? You certainly elevated the participants to the status of proper sportsmen. The Queen and Margaret Thatcher were rumoured to be Big Daddy fans. At one stage he was even offered his own kids TV show.

Daddy's Union Jack hat and trunks probably limited his support in Ireland, and the one we could get behind, Mick McManus (real name Michael Matthews, from London), was one of the bad guys, famed for his black trunks and his catchphrase, 'Not the ears, not the ears.' Irish playgrounds were not filled with kids screaming, 'Not the ears, not the ears.' But McManus let the side down by twice being beaten by another wrestler who tickled him to submission while he had him pinned.

Kendo has endured longer than all of them, and this is despite a series of unmaskings. In 1975, Big Daddy exposed him in a televised bout and, on 20 December 1977, Kendo held a 'ceremonial unmasking' for ITV in the Wolver-hampton Civic Hall. His most embarrassing unveiling was much more mundane. A plumber working at his house recognized his manager and put two and two together; and taking Kendo's real name off the invoice, he started to hand out leaflets outside bouts that said 'Kendo Nagasaki's real name is Peter Thornley, and he lives at this address . . .'

Peter Thornley continued to fight, though, later becom-ing a close friend of the artist Sir Peter Blake, who painted him for a BBC series called *Masters of the Canvas*, which must have been invented in a panicked moment during the meeting:

'I don't like any of your ideas. What else have you got?'

'Well, artists use canvas . . . And you know who else uses canvas?'

'Wrestlers! Of course, that's brilliant. Give me six one-hour documentaries right away!'

'Great! I was going to say tent-makers, but your idea is much better . . .'

So, the same week I was on, Kendo hit the floor one last time at an event where, this being wrestling, no real injuries occurred. The following night was less successful, however. Michael McIntyre was enjoying his encore after a successful show when gravity struck during a routine about skipping and he was left crumpled on the stage.

This initially got a big laugh, until it became obvious that Michael wasn't getting up, having dislocated his shoulder. The theatre manager had to finish off the show, thank Michael and tell the audience to leave. However, the Civic Hall isn't one of those theatres with a proscenium arch at the front, nor with a big red curtain that can fall to cover the stage. The crowd left with Michael in full view and a gathering of staff in attendance. Needless to say, comedians are a tiny and gossipy community, so I made sure to interview everyone who had been in the audience that night, located the exact spot onstage where he had lain and had to be restrained from drawing a chalk outline around the body. I did re-create the ending of the show for my crowd and generally got a good couple of minutes' laughs out of the whole event.

Later that month, I met Michael on the set of *Live at the Apollo*, and felt I should come clean.

'I was on in Wolverhampton the night after your accident. I did a couple of jokes about you, I just thought you should know.'

'I already know. In fact, five different people have told me.'

Great crowd in Wolverhampton, but can't keep a secret to save their lives.

Not a very forgiving town either. We dug out a copy of the local paper, the *Express and Star*, and found, thrillingly, an editorial calling for witches not to be pardoned. This is particularly ironic in a town whose coal and iron industries caused so much local pollution that it is generally thought that J. R. R. Tolkien used it as the model for Mordor in the *Lord of the Rings* trilogy. Orcs, yes; witches no, in the Black Country.

Rock stars get a thumbs-up here too, locals including Robert Plant, Slade, Goldie and Edward Elgar. In fact, the Civic Hall had the most 'rock and roll' dressing room of the tour, with a built-in sauna. I have no need for a sauna before or after a gig, particularly if I think that it's still moist from the sweat of Michael McIntyre. Or Kendo Nagasaki. Or Edward Elgar.

I could just wait a couple of weeks and share the sauna with bloody Ken Dodd, posters for whose upcoming show greet me on the way into the theatre. At this stage, I'm almost too scared to ask the stage hands about him, for fear of being treated to even more awestruck reminiscences of nine-hour-long shows. It's beginning to eat away at my confidence this, knowing that, as I perform the longest and most comprehensive tour of my life, a man in his eighties is matching me stride for stride.

So, we have some Saturday-afternoon wrestling, the Doddster in a Union Jack coat and Edward Elgar. Wolverhampton is shaping up to be the most English town in history. And why did I hold off discussing multiculturalism in Bradford until I told you about my time in Wolverhampton? Enoch Powell, of course.

In 1968, Powell was the Conservative MP for Wolverhampton South-west when he made his famous 'Rivers of Blood' speech detailing the dangers of mass non-white immigration into the UK. Polarizing public opinion at the time and finishing off his cabinet career, it was a performance filled with apocalyptic language:

'We are watching a nation busily engaged in heaping up its own funeral pyre.'

As an immigrant myself, this kind of rhetoric always excites me enormously. To have been even a small part in this foreign tide, well, it's always nice to belong, isn't it?

The fact is that the United Kingdom is still over-whelmingly white, with 54.2 million white people in the total population of 58.8 million in the last census in 2001. Asians make up easily the largest ethnic sub-group in the United Kingdom, but in 2001 only about one in every twenty-five people was Asian. Even more surprisingly, in 2001, only about one in fifty British people was black – just 1.1 million people. That number was split pretty evenly between Black African people and Black Caribbean people. Including people of mixed black/white origins and increased immigra-tion from African countries since 2001, the number is now probably close to 1.8 million, but that is still only one in every thirty-three people in the UK. There are a quarter of a million Chinese people and a quarter of a million people from other ethnic groups, and that's it.

This does make the United Kingdom the most multi-cultural of the major European states but, at most, about one in ten British people today are non-white, compared to about half of all Brazilians, one in four Americans, one in six Canadians and one in eight Dutch people. None of those countries has reported rivers turning red.

As for the oft-repeated assertion that 'the island is full', well, in my mind the evidence is mixed. Population density is fairly high in the UK, at 246 people per square kilometre and, although that's lower than Holland, Belgium and Japan, it's true that there is more room to breathe in France, Germany, Spain and just about everywhere else all the way down to the US (31 people per square kilometre) and to Australia, where isolation reaches heartbreaking levels, with

2.84 people per square kilometre (not much more than 1 per cent of the population density here).

Here's my non-scientific, anecdotal counter-argument.

I once blagged a lift on a helicopter from Manchester to London with Barry Humphries. The presence of Dame Edna isn't vital to the story, but I still thought you'd like to know. Anyway, this is England as seen from the window of a Sikorsky: Manchester – outskirts of Manchester – fields – fields – village – fields – motorway – fields – something that looked like Alton Towers – fields – the odd small town – yet more fields – outskirts of London – London.

This island is a long way from full.

Back to Enoch. He also said:

'As I look ahead, I am filled with foreboding. Like the Roman, I seem to see "the River Tiber foaming with much blood".'

An easy explanation for the rivers running red is that it's probably blood from all those swans the immigrants keep eating.

This story is a perennial favourite among certain sections of the press. It plays on the English love of animals, fear of foreigners, and the fact that all the swans in Britain are, for no well-explained reason, owned by the Queen. Somebody should explain this to the immigrants. Don't touch the swans; but the Canada Geese are fair game – unless the Mounties spot you.

Of course, there are no witnesses to this widescale swan-feasting. There is no footage, or proof. But, apparently, there are campsites surrounded by 'thousands of feathers' (the *Sun*, April 2008) and carcasses.

The average Mute Swan weighs between 20 and 30lb

(unplucked). Even allowing for the weight of its legendarily powerful neck (although I get confused: can a swan break your arm with its neck, or break your neck with its beak?), that's twice the size of the average family turkey. Now try cooking your giant super-turkey on a campsite:

'I have brought home swan!' the cartoon Eastern European immigrant tells his wife.

'But Wladyslaw! We have only one-ring fire. You are bad husband. Next time, steal pigeon.'

> *'The sense of being a persecuted minority which is growing among ordinary English people in the areas of the country which are affected is something that those without direct experience can hardly imagine.'*

In the coverage of the 2001 census, much was made of the fact that there are now areas in the UK, mainly in London, that have majority non-white populations. It's also been suggested that, in Leicester and Birmingham, white people will be in a minority within a couple of years. The 'are we celebrating this or are we worrying about it?' way in which these stories are reported in the media illustrates a real ambiguity about multiculturalism in the UK today. The continued immigration since the 2001 census, allied with the increased suspicion of many ethnic groups since the attacks of September 11 and 7/7, have created an unpleasant note of xenophobia.

This is of some concern, because, apart from some obvious exceptions, there is still a real sense that the English have done a better job of getting past the race issue than many other countries. If you asked British people to say the first thing that came into their heads about Lenny Henry,

Naseem Hamed and Naomi Campbell, I think you'd get more people who said 'Comedian', 'Boxer' and 'Super-model' – or, possibly, 'Black Country', 'Sheffield' and 'Tetchy' – than said 'Black', 'Arab' and 'Black', or even 'Black comedian', 'Arab boxer' and 'Black supermodel'. I'm not sure you'd get the same if you said Chris Rock, Bernard Hopkins and Tyra Banks to a group of Americans. Americans are simply more aware of race.

Jeremy Paxman, in his book *The English*, makes the good point that British regional accents have probably helped integration. It's very hard to listen to a Scouser or Geordie of any race and not simply think of them as a Scouser or Geordie.

Bringing it back to Wolverhampton, thousands of Sikhs came here after the Second World War, and the Sikh population is now about twenty thousand strong (this is roughly one in every twelve Wulfrunians). In 1965, Wolverhampton had the first major row about the wearing of turbans by Sikhs at work, which ended with Sikhs at the bus company being allowed to wear them in 1967. By now, though, this massive Sikh population speak like the rest of the Yam Yams, in a dialect that even Brummies don't always understand, a dialect that has many throwbacks to Middle English. And if that scholastic fact doesn't convince you, they also all sound like Noddy Holder. And who's afraid of Noddy Holder?

Maybe it's a very English characteristic to focus on the fact that there may be some people out there who have racist views instead of noting with pride that there are tens of millions who don't. Similarly, the British National Party won just 0.7 per cent of the national vote in the 2005

Westminster election and got a hundred local councillors of various kinds elected in the 2008 local elections, but this was still only 1 per cent of the total available. The cheering thing is that, instead of dismissing this as inconsequential, the English agonize over what these minor peaks in support for the BNP mean for the future of their country.

Even the BNP's winning of seats in the European parliament has to be taken with a pinch of salt. Ireland is quite pro-Europe, and quite moved by the European election. By contrast, the English couldn't care less. What was the turn-out? About 33 per cent? It was an election that only the extremists voted in and, hey presto!, some extremists got elected.

The truth is that, after the initial shock and scare of each new wave of arrivals, England has generally moved on. The *Windrush* panic has given way to a general acceptance of Black Caribbean culture. The Eastern European or asylum-seeker panics will go the same way. If the English have demonstrated one thing in their history, it's an ability to steal the best bits from each newly arrived culture. Balti, anyone?

The fact is, multiculturalism is a lark if you engage with it. In the last year, I have attended an Indian child's first birthday (along with three hundred friends and family, and a day-long binge of food and music) and a Jewish bat mitzvah (slap-up meal, loads of dancing and funny, funny speeches). The last 'English' children's party I went to, by contrast, consisted of a lot of middle-class parents making nervous small talk while their toddlers stared blankly at each other.

I've done living in a monoculture. It's a lot less fun and it warps your head. Take it from me, there's something wrong when you regard Protestants as being a bit 'exotic'.

'We must be mad, literally mad, as a nation.'

Norman Tebbit once said that the real test of whether integration was working was the 'cricket test', i.e. whether immigrants cheered for England when they played the old homeland – India, Pakistan, or the West Indies – in cricket. The fact is, most immigrants very quickly come to see Britain as their homeland. In the 2001 census, the vast majority of people in almost all ethnic groups described their national identity as being British. This included almost nine in ten people from a Mixed or Black Caribbean group, around eight out of ten from the Pakistani, Bangladeshi, or Other Black groups, and three-quarters of the Indian group. Just as you would expect in a successfully integrated society, second-generation immigrants were particularly likely to describe their national identity as British.

Interestingly, members of ethnic minorities were much more likely to describe themselves as British rather than English, Welsh or Scottish. This must surely be the perfect result for the isolationist Little Englanders. Immigrants with a loyalty to the island, but who aren't interested in diluting the golf club. No need to change those lists of membership requirements, then.

Predictably enough, the group with the lowest rate of describing their national identity as being British were the Irish, at just 13 per cent.

The Irish have, you see, found a way of failing the cricket test twice – not only neglecting to support England when she plays Ireland, but also cheering against England when she plays anyone else. Indeed, it is a notable day for any Irishman living over here when he realizes that cheering against England at all possible opportunities is probably a bit childish and unfair on his many English friends and family. So he cheers inwardly instead.

In the 2001 census, there were almost 691,000 Irish people in Great Britain in 2001, accounting for 1 per cent of the total population. In terms of ethnic groups, only the Indians and Pakistanis were larger. We look like you, we speak the language and we're everywhere. We're on your trains and in your offices. We're marrying your sons and daughters and raising your children. Look around you. There might be one of us right here, sitting in the room with you. Fear us, Britain. Fear us!

Enoch Powell certainly did, spending the latter years of his political career as an Ulster Unionist MEP.

He died in 1998. Sadly, he never got to see how modern Britain looked when, as he put it himself, 'the black man had the whip hand over the white man'. Of course he didn't; none of us have. But he wasn't forgotten. In a BBC poll in 2002 he was voted fifty-fifth on the list of 100 Greatest Britons. He was one place ahead of Cliff Richard.

Chapter 17:
We're Only Here for the Piers

Brighton Dome

1 computer programmer for *Second Life*
1 travel technology helpdesk supervisor
1 man who worked with 'banking needs'
1 teaching assistant and her husband who was ...
1 double-bass player

If ever there was a place with an identity crisis it's Brighton. On the one hand, it's artistic, bohemian and gay, with boutique hotels and lanes filled with antique shops and a thriving music scene; on the other hand, it's England's coolest commuter town. Only an hour away from the capital, vast chunks of the population trek northwards every day in a migration begrudged by the locals, who stay put and complain about the rise in house prices. Unfairly, probably, since the only way Brighton can afford its extravagant lifestyle (there are a LOT of antique shops) is from having people make cash in London, Monday to Friday, and then spend it on the south coast at the weekend.

It's like some dysfunctional family unit: the hard-working elder brother keeps the money coming in, while the flighty younger sibling dresses extravagantly, runs an indie label and dances all weekend. One is kept solvent; the other basks in the reflected cool.

You know that feeling you get during a beautiful tropical holiday when you turn to your partner and say, 'This is incredible, darling, why can't we stay here all our lives?' and he/she says, 'Don't be ridiculous, what would we do?', and the dream crumbles. Well, that's what Brighton is like for Londoners. An hour before leaving the chintzy pub on the Sunday afternoon of your weekend away, one of you will turn to the other and go, 'We could live here, y'know,' and your partner goes, 'You're right! All we need do is outbid some local fisherman for a cottage in Hove, and you can spend fourteen hours a week in trains!' 'It's a crazy dream but it might just work!'

Brighton *is* cool, though, and did well on the all-important 'how good is your fudge?' index. It is also the best surviving of the great British seaside resorts; as it should be, since it is probably the oldest.

People began to stay there to take the fashionable

seawater treatment in the eighteenth century. It was a particular favourite of the future George IV when he was Prince Regent, and his patronage made the small town popular with the elite, which is ironic, because he originally liked the privacy of Brighton for his various affairs with young ladies of the court. He built the Brighton Pavilion, one of the most exuberantly bizarre buildings in the country, and his patronage played a large role in making the seaside a fashionable destination for the English. Then, as ever, it was the railways which opened this elite resort up, with the first daytrippers arriving in 1841, despite objections from horrified local shopkeepers, who campaigned the rail companies to raise their fares and price the ordinary Londoners out. So, nothing much has changed in 170 years then.

Brighton is also a great place to enjoy one of the most singularly English pleasures: a walk along the pier.

Nowhere else in the world has quite embraced this piece of nineteenth-century whimsy. Walk out over the waters! Feel the small thrill of being on dry land and yet! And Yet! Sort of . . . not! You can see the waters churn through the gaps in the boards! A watery grave could be only moments away! In the meantime, have some candyfloss and watch some mainstream comedians.

Like the skyscrapers of the nineteenth century into the skies, around the country the piers extended further and further into the ocean, in some King Canute-style effort to extend man's dominion, and then sell fish and chips there. At one stage, there were over a hundred piers in England and Wales; that figure has dwindled to less than fifty now, with fire, and safety concerns, leading to more and more being closed.

Typically of Brighton, though, even when it comes to

piers, they get to have it both ways. On one end of the beach, enjoy the melancholic decline of the ruined West Pier, closed in 1975 and subject to a couple of arson attacks since then, sitting on the water, a majestic ruin. Or, if you'd all like to turn your head to the left, all gaudy lights and compact funfairs, Brighton Pier (formerly the Palace Pier), finished in 1901, one of the last and longest of the Victorian entertainment piers, and intended as the zenith of the entertainment pier industry.

It still does a roaring trade today, and I am a fan, having been drenched on the log flume and petrified on the tiny rollercoaster and then demanding that the entire filming of *Three Men in Another Boat* be delayed until we played the Dolphin Derby game one more time. Which I won, and then we could move on.

All of which makes Brighton a lot of fun to visit. However, you can have too much fun. My gig there, as part of the excellent annual comedy festival, after starting well, descended into madness in the second half. I threw out one of my usual questions: 'What do you NOT want to have happened in your home, before you moved in?'

At first the standard answers were coming back. Murder, first, as always, then Brothel, Crack Den, Fire and Flood. All the usual horsemen of a domestic apocalypse. Then the answers started to accelerate, as the crowd began to embrace its role in this moment of interactivity. I hardly had time to distinguish between Death and the Deaf (never underestimate the pleasure in deliberately mishearing an answer) before one man roared 'Students!' at the top of his voice. Brighton has a large student population, of whom he seemed to be one, as they all cheered round him at the reflected glory of having wedged themselves into the show.

I hardly had time to turn and address this answer before somebody on the other side of the room started shouting, 'Asbestos', which seemed a far more interesting thing to talk about than 'Students'. The floodgates were beginning to open now, and I got the distinct feeling that some of the crowd were so caught up in the thrill of naming things that my part in the conversation, where I turn their answers into something funny, was being happily ignored.

They were just thrilled to get an acknowledgement. They shout, 'Students', I say, 'Students', they cheer. Was there a point to this? Of course not. This is the drunk logic: 'I made the man say "Students!" That was me! I was part of the show!'

This is a risk you'll always run opening things up to the floor, especially as the night gets later and drink begins to take hold. I did a late show at the Kilkenny Cat Laughs Festival a couple of years ago, and by the time I got onstage it was long past midnight and the crowd were getting pretty jolly. It was only a twenty-minute set and, up until the last five minutes, things were going well. Then I decided to finish on that national-characteristics game I mentioned at the start of the book, which as well as making a terribly clever point about how we bracket the people of the world with ludicrous thumbnails of a personality, usually allows me to speak about how the people of Kyrgyzstan are all controlling and ticklish, and the Togolese are ravenous and judgemental, depending on the crowd's suggestions.

Any subtle commentaries got flushed away pretty fast in Kilkenny that night. When I threw to the floor, 'Name a far-away country,' every wag in the room started bellowing Irish counties.

'Cork!'

'Ha ha, yes, very funny, but no, I need a country from very far away.'

'Monaghan!'

'Leitrim!'

'No, no,' I tried again. 'A country, from far away, that we don't know much about . . .'

'Cork!'

'Wicklow!'

'Cork!'

'No wait . . .' I said, and realized that I was beginning to sound more and more like a supply teacher, or that sober guy at the party who's trying to get everyone to play Twister according to the rules. 'A country . . .'

'Cavan!'

'Galway!'

'Wicklow!'

'Wicklow!'

Me being from Wicklow made shouting it out incredibly funny to one lad in row three. Unfortunately, we were getting to the point that even the punters who weren't shouting out 'Donegal!' had forgotten what the point of the routine was, and it was long past the point where I could save the show.

'Waterford!'

'Okay, let's just knock this on the head, shall we?'

'Wicklow!'

The really sad thing is that there are probably four hundred people from that gig out there who think my closing routine involves enticing the crowd to shout place names at louder and louder volumes until I eventually slink off. To this day, they must wonder how I've made a career of it.

Meanwhile, back in Brighton, I've been given an escape route. Somebody has shouted 'the Irish' as the one thing they don't want to have happened in their home. I ride the white horse of mock indignation to safety.

Getting the show back on the rails is surely only a respite, though. In my head, a voice is going, 'You got away with that one, but you've got to ask them for crime stories in a minute. The ending of this show is fucked.'

And lo, it came to pass:

'Anyone here interrupt a crime?'

'I was in a shop when people came in to rob it.'

'Wow. What you do?' I said, hopefully, expecting the usual story of derring-do.

'I hid my bag behind a fridge and waited until it was all over.'

'So, in no real sense did you actually interrupt a crime, did you?'

'Nope. But I got my bag back.'

'Inspirational. Anyone else?'

'I was smoking a spliff.'

'And who interrupted you?'

'I did.'

'What?'

'Well, I hadn't finished it and needed to go, so I just stopped it halfway.'

'No, that's not . . . no, y'see . . . Anyone else?'

'An old woman was being robbed and I shouted, "I'm coming!"'

'This is more like it! And what happened?'

'I walked her home, and she gave me . . .'

And he paused just a tiny bit too long, allowing someone to shout, 'Gonorrhea!' at the top of their voice. And the place erupted.

By this stage they were making their own fun.

Bournemouth Pavilion Theatre

1 IT trainee
1 designer:
> *'Designer of what?'*
> *'Helicopter . . . bits.'*
1 newsagent
1 councillor:
> *Entire audience: Boo.*
> *The councillor: No, not that kind of councillor. I'm a counsellor.*

For all the underlying tension between the locals and the London blow-ins, Brighton is a happy place. Next up, though, is the happiest place of all, at least according to a major survey in 2007. Four out of five people in Bournemouth (81 per cent) said they were happy with their lives, nudging them ahead of such top five joy-centres as Llandudno, Plymouth, Tunbridge Wells and Derby. Walsall was the least happy town in the survey. Of course, surveys are normally bunk, based purely on the deeply unscientific method of asking people in a shopping precinct their opinion; but the interesting thing about both these pieces of research was how much play they got in the media, with local people queuing up to explain why Bournemouth was so great or what was wrong with Walsall – evidence that the English believe that some places really are happier than others.

Bournemouth does make a good case, though. For a relatively young town (it was founded in 1810), it has a ludicrously rich literary pedigree. *Tess of the D'Urbervilles* is set here. Robert Louis Stevenson wrote *Dr Jekyll and Mr Hyde* and *Kidnapped* while living here. Henry James was a frequent visitor at Stevenson's house, and his short story 'The Middle Years' is set in Bournemouth. Oscar Wilde and Paul Verlaine both taught at schools in Bournemouth, Verlaine coming here in 1876 after his release from prison for shooting the poet Arthur Rimbaud in the wrist (which is probably a poorly chosen place to shoot your gay lover). Oscar Wilde was a regular visitor, and Bournemouth was one of the many places he 'Bunburied' to, in order to conduct his second life away from his wife. ('Bunburying' is the process, described by Wilde in *The Importance of being Earnest*, of inventing an imaginary, illness-prone friend who you can use as an excuse whenever you want to go off and party at short notice. These days, you'd have to give them their own Facebook page.)

And for a town once described as 'God's waiting room', due to the number of retirees living here, it's also quite the place to party. This may be due to the number of surfers in the area. Bournemouth has developed an unexpected reputation among this community, and is reciprocating, building an artificial surfing reef down the beach in Boscombe in order to crank up the waves and thus lure more of the boarders in. This is probably a smart move. As youth subcultures go, surfers are pretty mellow and benign. They talk a lot of quasi-spiritual nonsense, and I'd sooner eat my leg than join in but, like climbers, or divers, say, they're quite self-reliant and don't tend to smash places up. You don't hear many headlines about 'Surfer Rampage Destroys

Town'. We were there on a mild winter's day, and there were a half-dozen surfers in the water, sitting astride boards, bobbing along and looking extremely relaxed. As well they might, given that there wasn't a fart of a wave to be seen. You could have skimmed stones to France that afternoon, but still the surfers bobbed and still they waited, and even I, watching them from the pier above, began to feel more relaxed.

This mellow vibe must be contagious. In 2008, Bournemouth was the safest major urban area in England and Wales, with the lowest levels of serious crime; this might be why it's a relatively safe, welcoming place to go out, as well.

I was gigging in Bournemouth a couple of tours ago and, staying over for the night, was driven out of the hotel by boredom and sought company in the bars along the main drag. Luckily I fell in with a group of twenty-year-old lads and their pretty lady friend. I was curious about life on the coast, and they were asking about comedy, and so we chatted away quite happily, until one of them turned to the girl.

'Oh, tell him what happened last night . . .'

'What happened last night?' I said.

'Well, I was with this guy,' she started, with a fresh-faced candour, and it was clear that they all knew 'this guy'. I was trying to divine what 'with' meant, of course.

'We were asleep, and something woke me, and I turned around and he was awake and I realized . . .'

And all the lads were waiting for the punchline . . .

'He had tossed himself off, all over my back!'

And they all laughed and turned to me, and I laughed, and they were looking at me for a response and I could not think of a single thing to say. There are very few times in a pub conversation that I can't hold my own. You tell me a story and, if the mood is on me, I'll be able to start with, 'That's funny, because that reminds me of the time ...'

This was not one of those times. I couldn't think of a single ejaculate-based story that I wanted to tell this twenty-year-old girl. Or at least not one that wouldn't suddenly make us all feel really creepy.

In the end I just turned into Alan Partridge:

'Tcch ... Men, eh? With their jizz ... ummm. Drinks, anyone?'

So has Bournemouth found the key to happiness? A few high-culture mentions and a well-waxed board? Happiness is a thorny problem, particularly in these parts. The media would have you believe that England is permanently in a state of discontent. Your fundamental unhappiness is sold to you here as a given and has been for generations. George Cheyne, the English doctor and writer, who was also one of the foremost proponents of taking the waters at Bath, suggested that the English were a people prone to unhappiness. In his influential book of 1733, *The English Malady*, the malady in question was that of melancholy and nervous unhappiness. Cheyne's contention was that this melancholy was a condition of the English way of life. This seems to have been a generally accepted view among Europeans – in Cheyne's explanation, the title for the book came from 'all our neighbours on the continent, by whom nervous distempers, spleen, vapours, and lowness of spirits are in derision called the English Malady, and I wish there were not so good grounds for this reflection'.

Nowadays, however, you can't walk down the street without someone asking you how happy you are on a scale of one to ten, which means that we know a lot more about English happiness than we used to.

Surprisingly, the first thing that really stands out in all the research on happiness is that the English are, in their own estimation, a surprisingly happy bunch of people. Survey after survey suggests that roughly nine out of ten people here are happy. A Gallup poll was conducted in 2006, for example, in which 56 per cent of the population were 'fairly happy' and 36 per cent were 'very happy'.

Another thing we now know is how well the UK compares to its continental neighbours. True to form, the United Kingdom finds it very hard to win these things, but it's certainly not bottom of the pile. In a major survey of Europeans conducted in 2007 by the European Foundation for the Improvement of Living and Working Conditions, the United Kingdom came joint ninth (with Belgium) in terms of happiness, and tenth in terms of life satisfaction. Overall, Britons rated themselves at 7.8 out of 10 on the happiness scale, only half a point behind the happiest nations, Finland and Denmark, who each scored 8.3. The Irish were happier, too, along with Sweden, Norway and the Netherlands, but the United Kingdom was well above the least happy nation (Bulgaria on 5.8) and also above the average for both the twenty-seven countries surveyed and the fifteen older members of the EU.

(As a sidebar, it's worth noting that the Scandinavians are nowhere near the most suicidal people in the world. That hoary old chestnut can be laid to rest. I'd have kept that point for a book called *Tickling the Swedes*, but by the look of these figures, they don't need any more cheering up.)

Similarly, in the first major attempt to rank all the nations of the world by happiness in 2006, the United Kingdom came forty-first.

So there seems to be something of a contradiction between the historical and media view that the English are desperately prone to unhappiness, and the evidence that they themselves say that they're happy. In other words, if I ask you anonymously in a poll, you're happy, but if I'm hosting a late-night radio phone-in show, you can really get your teeth into how miserable you are.

One possible way to reconcile this is the theory about happiness in England put forward by American journalist Eric Weiner in his book *The Geography of Bliss*. Weiner's contention, after a year-long, worldwide research trip, was that the English people are only happy when they're unhappy. Weiner suggested that the British are a grumpy people but '... most Brits, I suspect, derive a perverse pleasure from their grumpiness ... happiness is a transatlantic import. And by transatlantic, they mean American. And by American, they mean silly, infantile drivel ... for the English, life is not about happiness but getting by.'

And this I can agree with. In England, and indeed in Ireland, that happy-clappy, up-with-people! insincere smiley horseshit the Americans train their service industry and politicians to talk in, well, that just feels creepy; for example, when you really think about it, I mean, just mull the words over and over in your head, doesn't 'the pursuit of happiness' sound like the weirdest thing to put in a constitution? No, that stuff doesn't really wash here. And it has saved us from the ludicrous delusion that 'happiness' is a state of joy, and that we deserve that. We don't, and the chemistry of our brains can't possibly supply it. There's only so much serotonin to go around. The healthiest definition I have heard about happiness was attributed to Alain de Botton, who simply said, 'Happiness is no pain.' If you can achieve a life without pain, well done. We have that concept in Ireland. You've probably heard an Irish person use the word 'grand', as in 'How are things?' 'Grand.' This means, 'Fine, perfectly fine. Nothing special, let's not go on about it, but fine.'

If an Irishman is selling you his car and describes its condition as 'grand', then run a fucking mile. But if he's on his deathbed and that's how he describes his life, well, good for him.

In the meantime, of course, there's nothing to top a good moan, and this brings us neatly back to the English and, specifically, to Bertrand Russell, who said, 'Men who are unhappy, like men who sleep badly, are always proud of the fact.'

So, possibly, nine out of ten English people are happy because they aren't. And the other 10 per cent? Well, when they find out that they aren't really happy, they'll be thrilled.

Swansea Grand Theatre

1 unemployed IT worker
1 bicycle repairman for Toys 'R' Us
1 barrister
1 man who works at the land-registry office, with his
    mate, who moonlights as . . .
1 bouncer at Lavalounge

Just a quick endnote on happiness from one of the final towns on the tour, and one reached on a freezing mid-November day, the coldest day on the tour since we set off the previous March.

Swansea is the second largest city in Wales, originally thought to have been founded by the Viking king Sven Forkbeard, the King of Denmark and father of King Canute. By the nineteenth century, it was a major centre for coal and copper smelting, so much so that it became known as 'Copperopolis'. There was mass immigration from Ireland after the Great Famine and, by all accounts, the city was an appalling place to live during the nineteenth century. There was no sewerage system at all until 1857, so they had to endure several cholera outbreaks, and Swansea also has the dubious distinction of hosting the UK's only outbreak of yellow fever (in 1865).

Despite industrialization, the medieval centre of the town was preserved into the modern era. However, in February 1941, three consecutive days of raids by the Luftwaffe completely levelled it, and large areas of the rest of the city centre. 'Our Swansea is dead,' wrote Dylan Thomas, who also described the city as an 'ugly, lovely town'.

Thomas is one of their famous sons, although in lists of the most famous former resident he is often beaten by 'Swansea Jack', a flat-haired retriever who saved twenty-seven people from drowning in the Swansea docks between 1930 and 1937. He received a silver cup from the Lord Mayor of London for his heroics and, in 1937, was named 'Bravest Dog of the Year' by the *London Star*. There is a large monument to him on the promenade in Swansea. Catherine Zeta Jones sometimes comes first too. Although she has yet to earn a statue.

Swansea also came close to the bottom of that 2006 poll to find the happiest place in Britain.

Like all the destinations in this book, I can only speak for
that snapshot I see when I pass through the towns. I make
no claims for authority, other than to say, I was here for one
evening and this is how it was. As you'll have noticed, I
often see towns when they are shut, or deserted, or during
the winter months, when they are in darkness and unrecognizable. A lot of the time, it's just not worth wandering
out of the theatre, because it'll just be another cold and
deserted identikit British highstreet. But occasionally, just
occasionally . . .

When we arrived in Swansea, the streets were thronged
and families were out and lights were gleaming in the trees. I
scampered away from the theatre and found myself in the
middle of the annual Christmas parade, which was weaving
its way slowly through the city centre. I'm not sure if every
mid-sized city in Britain has a Christmas parade; I suspect
not. I would also be shocked if it was greeted with anything
like the numbers and the glee I saw that night in Swansea.
The crowds were five deep on either side, stamping their
feet for warmth, and hoicking their kids up on their
shoulders to get a better view of the passing armies of elves
and drummers and waving Santa Clauses.

Giddily, I joined the crowd in catching the tail of the
parade and then circling through backstreets to get down to
the front again, to hear the arrival of the drummers I had
already seen. People were wearing glowsticks on their heads
and all the trees had just been lit up, and even I, in the town
for only a few minutes now, could see the transformation.
It was joyous, and infectious, and I rang home from the
parade just to share it, and also to say that it was almost
Christmas and this tour was almost over and that I would be
home soon.

Like I said, I can't claim any authority. But I was only in Swansea for one night and the place looked deliriously happy. So let's give them that one.

Chapter 18:
A Classic Act in a Classic Venue

Leeds

Before the end, though, a pilgrimage.

One of the minor disadvantages of gaining any success as a live comic is that the move to theatres takes you away from the rest of the community of comics with whom you used to spend your working nights sharing the bill. This means less drunken fun. It also means fewer chances to see other comics perform.

Although it may seem a little perverse to take a night off and spend it at someone else's comedy show, it's the only way to catch up with the work of your peers. As this year of my tour progressed, I had made trips to see Bill Bailey, Ed Byrne, Omid Djalili and others. Before I finished on the road, though, there was one show left to see.

This would be no peer of mine, however. I wouldn't have the cheek to place myself in this company, at least not until I have shown that I could keep doing this for at least another forty years. And, equally, spend at least a couple more hours onstage each night.

It was time to catch the Ken Dodd show.

The question was, where best to catch it? Ken's website was a long list of dates, passing through as many towns as I've been writing about in this book. One stood out, though. I've mentioned a few times about Yorkshire being the easiest place to find a chatty crowd (that night in Sheffield excepted – Oh Sheffield, what must I do to draw you out?). In Leeds, you get all that natural charm, and also one of the most legendary rooms in showbusiness. It's one of the oldest theatres in the country, a proper Victorian music hall dating back to 1865 (its original name was 'Thornton's New Music Hall and Fashionable Lounge') and still regarded as the best venue for stand-up in the nation. Steeped in history, it is popularly known as the filming location of the variety spectacular *The Good Old Days*, and there are pictures on the walls of the times Charlie Chaplin and Houdini performed there. With the crowd tight around you, it's a room built for the spoken word, both from the comic to the crowd and, to an astonishing level, from the audience back to the comedian. Offered as evidence, this is from the first of two shows I did here in 2006:

Leeds City Varieties

1 man who sells alarms to pensioners:

'Wouldn't it be more accurate to say that you sell "alarm" to pensioners?'

1 pension actuary:

'You two should join forces. You petrify them with the crime stats and, five minutes later, he arrives to sell them a burglar alarm.'

1 market researcher

(Midway through the show his phone rang; it was news about detergents.)

1 man from the trade association for road hauliers

(His wife would sleep with the Milky Bar kid, given the chance.)

1 teacher:

'What do you teach?'

'I teach business to stupid nineteen-year-olds.'

1 nurse called Andy

I asked Andy what the greatest thing was that had ever happened to him:

'Somebody once handed me an amputated leg,' he said.

'Well, you'd obviously dropped enough hints. Was it your birthday and Christmas presents all at once? Did they wrap it well?' (At this stage I'm standing shaking an amputated and gift-wrapped leg and going, 'What is it? Is it a leg? Oh please, let it be a leg! That would be the best Christmas ever!')

The great thing about Leeds City Varieties is that this was the quiet night.

Leeds City Varieties (the following night)

1 piemaker (who gave me an éclair to shut me up)
1 offshore engineer
1 nurse (who arrived late from an emergency):
> *'Did you tell them you had tickets for a show?'*
> *'Yes.'*
1 Liverpool man who works in job ads
1 financial adviser
1 plasterer

This doesn't look as good, but I'm cutting to the chase. I met the plasterer midway through the show. His name was Keith, and he worked for a company called M&K Ornate Plastering:

'Why is it called M&K? Why isn't it called K&M?'

'M is the one with the van.'

As if this wasn't great enough, he then approaches me onstage, mid-show, with a business card, if I ever move to Leeds and suddenly inherit a lot of ornate plastering in disrepair.

I explained that I wasn't really in the market, but what the hell, we had five hundred people in, did anyone want the number?

'Yes!' shouted a woman from the left balcony.

So I read out the number.

'0778 123 ...'

And I moved to continue the show.

'Did we all get that? Great! So anyway, I was talking about . . .'

'Wait!' shouted a woman from the opposite balcony. 'I didn't have a pen. Read it out again!'

So I read out the number a second time: '0778 123 . . .'

I tried to resume the show again.

'Where were we? Ah yes, I was just about to tell you about the time when I . . .'

'So,' shouts a woman from the back of the room, 'it's oh-seven-seven-eight . . .?'

And I collapsed on the stage in a fit of the giggles.

I rarely corpse onstage. I'm usually too close to the joke I'm making to find it funny, or too busy trying to top an audience joke to let it slay me. There was nothing I could do here. I just had to read out the bloody number again. And after that, who knows? Again and again and again; I might be handing out that number to each audience member in turn while they kept passing around the one pen.

I was going to be stuck for the entire evening handing out a plasterer's mobile number, while the show kept floating further and further away.

Eventually, I gathered myself enough to lift the business card for a third time:

'It's 0778 123 . . . Now, do we all have that? Is there anyone else?'

Long pause.

And then a lone voice from the back of the room: 'And they do plastering, right?'

At the end of a two-and-a-half-hour show, after the encore, when any decent, humble man would have finished long ago and gone home, I walked out for one last curtain call. This time I brought my mobile out with me.

Hushing the crowd, I dialled the number on the card. Not Keith's number, of course, but the number for the mysterious M. It went to answer machine:

'Hello,' said I, 'is that M&K ornate plastering?'

There was a huge cheer from the crowd.

'I'm at the City Varieties in the city centre,' I continued, picking at the delicate plasterwork by the side of the stage, which, to be frank, seemed to be showing its age. 'I couldn't help noticing that we have a lot of ornate plastering here that might need replacing.'

More laughter from the crowd.

'You're probably wondering why I chose you for the job . . .' and I paused for the last joke: 'Y'see, I hear you have a van.

'Thank you very much, goodbye, safe home, my name's Dara O Briain. Good night.'

When I was writing this book, I found M&K's card and gave them a call.

'Hello?' said a lady's voice.

'Hello, I'm looking for M&K ornate plastering.'

'Ah, I'm afraid that company doesn't exist any more,' said the lady, who turned out to be Hannah, M's wife.

'Oh, I'm sorry.' And there was a pause, and I became sharply aware how weird this jaunty phone call was going to sound if they'd just spent an ugly couple of years in court sorting out a hideous business split. Or worse.

'My name is Dara O Briain. I spoke to K from the stage a couple of years ago and wanted to catch up with him. Do you mind me asking what happened?'

'Well, Keith had an accident when he fell off a ladder and couldn't work. So Michael had to go on without him. Let me see if I can find you Keith's number though . . .'

As she gave me the number, I had the distinct feeling that there might be a good reason why I have never sought out audience members after a show. A snapshot can be good enough. Maybe now I was going to plunge into a grim real-life story of industrial accidents, forced redundancies and depression, and all I would have to offer would be some forced jollity and my comedy improv skills. I couldn't chicken out now though. I rang Keith.

'Oh hello,' he said, in a cheery and surprised voice.

'You don't sound very depressed,' I said. 'I heard you'd had an accident and couldn't work.'

'Yes, but I had insurance, and now I'm lecturing in Plastering at Leeds College of Building.'

He then went on to give a cheery rundown of a hideous accident, involving his leg getting trapped in the rungs of a ladder as it tipped through a window, a tale which included observations such as 'It's not a good sign to see the sole of your own foot looking up at you,' and 'When they put the morphine in, the orderly said, "Here comes the good stuff," and he wasn't wrong.' It was the most enjoyable chat I've had in ages. Then I remembered why I'd called him.

'Did you ever get any work as a result of me giving out your number that night?'

'We actually got a lot of calls that night, but I ignored them. I presumed that if they were serious they would call back. One of them did, and we went out to see the place.'

'And then . . .'

'Nah, it was shit, so we just told him we were busy.'

So much for my power to move markets.

'Do you get to many other shows?'

'Oh yeah. We saw one of your colleagues from *Mock the Week*, but we left halfway.'

'Really?' I said, my interest rising. 'Was it rubbish?'

'No, it was really good. It's just that me and the wife were having such a good chat that we decided to leave the show and go back to the pub. Actually, we did that when we went to see Lenny Henry as Othello as well. Great first half, but we were having such a good night the two of us, we thought that was enough and went back to the pub.'

We parted with me vowing to track down more of my audience for a chat, and offering him tickets for my next visit to Leeds. I'm sure he'll take the tickets, but if he doesn't make it past the interval, I'm not sure I'd begrudge him.

Although M&K won't be available to do the job, that plasterwork will look stunning the next time the City Varieties opens its doors. The entire complex is being shut for eighteen months for a £9.2 million refurbishment. The final act to appear before the closure was Ken Dodd, and I got the very last ticket to one of the last shows.

When I arrived at the box office I asked the nice lady what time we'd be finished at.

'Well, we've been told twelve forty-five, but with Ken' – and she leaned in and shrugged – 'who knows?'

I'd rung Peter Sandeman, the manager, to see if there was any chance of meeting Ken before the show. Peter couldn't promise me that Ken would have time but, when I arrived to collect my ticket, he did give me some history of the marathon shows.

'He used to do two shows a night, y'know,' he marvelled. 'He'd do one at five and then another at eight thirty. Of course, we'd get to eight twenty-five and there'd be a queue of five hundred people standing out in the cold and Ken still wouldn't have finished the first show.

'By the time we started the late show, we were in danger of running into overtime for all the bar staff. I had to make a deal with Ken. Just get me to an interval by ten thirty, so I get my staff paid up and out, and then you can go on as long as you want after that. Needless to say, he was delighted with that.'

'What time did it all finish up, then?'

'It was after one.'

So Ken would have been doing the guts of eight hours onstage. It's no wonder that, as he's gotten older, he's put that punishing schedule behind him. I asked Peter how long ago this was.

'It must have been about five years ago maybe?'

Ken would have been in his mid-seventies.

Let me be clear about one thing. I am not a lifelong Ken Dodd fan. I have nothing against the man; it's just that his brand of comedy didn't seem to travel to Ireland when I was growing up, especially in comparison with his contemporaries, like Morecambe and Wise, or Les Dawson. There was something very English about it, it seemed to be all silly wordplay and Union Jack coats and performing children. I have only vague memories of his act. I wasn't attending as an act of homage. I'll be honest and admit that there was a genuine danger of my hating it and, moreover, hating it for five hours. This was comedy from a different generation, after all, and if it was a long evening of pre-enlightenment cracks about stupid Irishmen and shiftless foreigners like an extended working man's club set, then I would be in a great deal of pain. (Physical pain, too, given that I would also be squeezing my capacious modern Gaelic arse into a seat made for a Victorian.)

I didn't think that Ken was going to be Bernard Manning but, to be honest, that was because I didn't know what to expect.

I certainly didn't expect to be wrenched from my dinner to come and meet the man.

'Get over here,' Peter said on the phone. 'Ken knows you're in the audience tonight and would love to meet up before the show.'

I dashed over, praying along the way that I'd eaten enough to get me through the night. When I arrived, Ken was at the end of his soundcheck. He wasn't in his stage clothes yet, but already his hair was standing on end, and his eyes were sparkling with energy.

He greeted me with an exaggerated stage bow.

'Good evening, sir, and what an honour it is to have you here with us,' he said.

I'm not practising false modesty here, but I was genuinely surprised that he had any clue who I was.

'Oh that show you do. *Mock the Week*. Those lads are very witty. But, vicious, the lot of you.'

It turned out that Ken is across all of our work.

'That lad from the North-east, he's very good, if you can understand him, he's very funny, Ross Noble ...'

We wandered backstage so that the audience could be let in. In his dressing room, he explained the complex rationale behind the five-hour shows.

'It's my party. I enjoy it. Why would I stop? When you're at a party and you're enjoying yourself, you don't want it to stop, do you?'

And he gave me a reassuring look.

'If you don't make it to the end, I won't mind.'

When the audience had sat down, I got a chance to check out Ken's demographic. It was certainly older than my crowd, but still with a striking number of young people dotted throughout. I didn't feel like I was intruding. Reassuringly, there was even a gay couple in front of me. If the gays are attending, you're usually safe enough. They have great antennae.

At seven thirty on the dot, the lights went down, the band struck up a fanfare and an offstage voice barked out the announcement:

'Good evening, ladies and gentlemen, and welcome to the Ken Dodd Happiness Show! We hope you're going to have an evening filled with laughter! Now please welcome the Squire of Knotty Ash, Ken Dodd!' And we were off.

I can only give you a sense of the show, of course.

This is partly because these are Ken's jokes, not mine, and he's earned the right to get the laughs off them, not me. But it's also because, in the absence of recording equipment, it's difficult to keep track of that amount of material. I would occasionally race to the bathroom and write down a couple of jewels in a pocket-sized notebook but was aware that if anyone saw me they would naturally presume that I was trying to steal his material. That was a scandal I'd sooner avoid.

Watching Ken Dodd do his full show is like tracking a spaceship as it passes all the landmarks of the comedy universe, travelling further and further into the uncharted depths. In comedy, where you rank in the stratosphere can often be told by how long you're allowed to perform for.

Ten minutes, for example, is the standard length of the open-spot set you'd start your career with. It's also the length of a set in an American club, and of the sets Ken would have done in the variety bills throughout his career. Ten minutes into tonight's show, Ken has taken the acclaim of the crowd, introduced the band and made the first of a great deal of quips about just how long the show is going to be ('How exciting to think that we're all going to spend the next seven and a half hours here.'). He's insulted the age of the crowd ('I thought I was in Out-patients'), the venue and the city of Leeds. He's done gags about Gordon Brown, the credit crunch, Elton John's wedding, dog obedience, an imaginary giraffe; even, at this point, I am going to stop trying to remember the topics, let alone the gags, he's firing them out so fast. He would later tell me that this punch, punch one-liner style came about in the rough-and-tumble bills of the fifties, where crowds were quick to move you along.

'They have a plaque in Glasgow, y'know. It just says, "Des O'Connor fell here."'

At the twenty-minute mark, we were passing the standard time for a set in the UK clubs. By now, Ken was making the first allusions to his well-publicized run-in with the revenue commissioners.

'I hate it when those envelopes appear in the post each morning. Those brown envelopes. You know the ones. With "Inland Revenue" written on them. I got one the other day. It said, "Self-assessment Tax". Self-assessment? I invented that.'

That, my friends, is a brilliant joke. If I ever get accused of tax evasion (Dodd was acquitted, let's not forget), I'm stealing that joke.

By the forty-minute mark, we had passed the standard length of a headline set in the out-of-town (i.e. out of London) clubs. At this stage, I was beginning to see the craft behind the gags as well. A great comic is funny between the jokes. Otherwise any fool could just learn some gags off and have a career. Other comics want to see how you handle the quiet moments; and Ken had some lines of schtick that I would have been proud to use.

'Don't worry, I'll find something you like,' he had told us earlier, midway through yet another quickfire burst. At one point, when a gag had got a smaller response than he thought it deserved, he upbraided the crowd. 'There's a name for what I'm doing here, y'know,' he said to them, proudly. 'It's called ... struggling.'

At the hour mark, we were passing the length of the standard Edinburgh Festival show. The move from forty to sixty is the most difficult in comedy, as the smart money says that audiences only laugh for about fifty minutes un-interrupted, meaning that you have an awkward lull in energy just as you try to wind them up for the finale. Ken sidesteps this with the first of the sing-songs, occasionally serious but usually nonsensical, with the crowd doing animal noises or Elvis or a laughing policeman. And if they mess up their part?

'You only have to remember that little bit. I've got nine hours of material to get through tonight.'

By the ninety-minute mark, we've caught up with the majority of touring shows and DVDs.

It was beginning to look like Ken would reach 12.45 a.m. as promised without even pausing for breath, but at this point he takes a break and invites on one of his support acts, a singer who performs a turn of classic British war-time songs.

I'm not a huge fan of vocalists – as a child I used to loathe it when comedy shows suddenly used to stop and bring on a singer to deliver a standard – but, more than that, from her song choice, you could see that this lady was targeting herself at the older members of the crowd. And you suddenly realized that Ken hadn't been. There had been nothing in the previous hour and a half that had felt dated. But suddenly it was all 'White Cliffs of Dover' and the older folks singing along and, for the first time, I felt out of place. As the nice lady sang 'We'll Meet Again', I began to feel my arse getting very numb for the first time.

Luckily for me, after twenty minutes of songs, Ken came back on and did another hour.

By the end of it, he had matched my record time for the room almost exactly. And, although he won't have realized it, he then underlined his superiority by calling the interval.

During the break, when I wasn't furiously scribbling down some of the gags and taking in food and drink, I quizzed a couple of the younger people around me as to why they had come along.

'It's Ken!' the man behind me said. 'We grew up with him.'

'I first saw him thirty-five years ago,' said another. 'And he only did two and a half hours then.'

We then tried to guess how many of the punters, having sat here for almost three hours, would come back for more. The best guess was about three-quarters, but none of us would have been surprised if it had been as low as half.

When the curtain came up, though, we'd only shed about 10 per cent of the crowd, and given that at least that many were septuagenarians, this was a pretty good return.

The second half resumed with another of Ken's guests. This time it was a magic act, a gloriously surreal magic act, where, without comment, an unending supply of birds was revealed from within empty containers, while the band played popular tunes. At one point, a duck flew off the stage and, with no response from the magician, an audience member felt obliged to retrieve it and place it back on the stage. And all the while the band were playing the theme music to *Hawaii Five-O.*

Later, I would learn that the magician had an ostrich but that it was unavailable that night. I bitterly regret missing the ostrich.

After twenty minutes of bird-revealing, the stage was ceded to Ken and, just to round things off, he did a tight hour and three-quarters.

'You do realize, don't you, that most of your families have reported you missing by now?'

It was midway through this section that I was struck by an absence.

We had been led through a massive catalogue of jokes. I've probably never heard the words 'And the doctor said ...' more often in my life (and I'm married to a doctor). We'd had singalongs and sketches and a magician and Ken doing a ventriloquism act. But in almost five hours there hadn't been a single Irishman joke. Or 'Paki' joke. Or any of the other pre-PC old comedy staples that I had been dreading.

Before the show, Ken had let slip his philosophy on comedy.

'People forget,' he'd said, 'that it should all be about one small three-letter word. Joy.'

It's easy to draw a line between the older generation of comedians and the newer acts by just pointing to 'Three men walk into a bar ...' and 'There were these two black lads ...' and being grateful that those old jokes have been put out to pasture. For the really wonderful comedians, though, it was never just about the jokes.

The great comics create their own world, built on their personal crazy logic. We should just be guests in a universe of their creation. It could be angry, or amiable, or surreal. When you watch a great comedian of any generation, you get to take an all-too-brief holiday in their upside-down world. And it feels like a privilege.

By the end of the show, the 90 per cent of us who'd stayed were cheering Ken over the line.

At the finale, there were more songs, we were all standing, and a snow machine fired up and flares went off. We were all hand-in-hand singing 'Auld Lang Syne' and Ken took his final bow to a standing ovation and, without encore, stepped off the stage.

After the show, he graciously invited me into his dressing room, and we shared a few beers and talked like old showbiz troupers together, swapping war stories and comparing rooms we had played. He told me of variety acts long forgotten ('There was a lady contortionist, Eva May Wong, I don't know what she was wearing, a bikini or something, but there was a lot of Chinese showing ...') and crazy supports ('The act was three walruses, and they would do impersonations of Hitler ...'). We agreed about the north of England being easier to play than the south, about how the

City Varieties was the best room to play but that the Gaiety Theatre on the Isle of Man was the prettiest. He showed me the notes that his keyboardist had kept of all the new impromptu lines that had appeared that night. I settled into the warm glow of being part of some glorious line stretching back to the music-hall acts of the Victorian age, until I began to get a little dozy and realized that, if I was tiring, the eighty-two-year-old man who had just finished a five-hour stand-up show, might need a break as well.

And, with much bonhomie, and the gift of a tickling stick, I said my goodbyes to Ken Dodd.

On the way out, I checked my notes. The Happiness Show had finished at 12.50 a.m. Even with all the jokes about the length of the show, the old pro had only gone five minutes over.

Chapter 19:
The Final Show (parts 1 and 2)

Tunbridge Wells

Nine months in, a hundred and three shows done and, in mid-November, we reach the final night of the tour. And if the secret purpose was to unearth the English psyche, it's perhaps right that we should end up in Tunbridge Wells.

Tunbridge Wells (properly Royal Tunbridge Wells, of course; that's what it said on the sign as we arrived) is a spa town in Kent about 30 miles south-east of London. It's a small enough town by English standards, but the BBC once described it as the spiritual home of Middle England. It has a Conservative party-dominated council, is 97.5 per cent white and one of the safest places in the UK, with very low levels of violent crime. It has an unemployment rate of about 1 per cent, which is far below the national average. In 2006, the town was listed as the third best place to live in the UK by the Channel 4 programme *The Best and Worst Places to Live*.

It is genteel and well-to-do, arcaded and prosperous; it has been thus for a few hundred years. In 1606, Lord North discovered a mineral-water spring here and persuaded his posh friends to come and take the waters. His doctor suggested that the waters could cure 'the colic, the melancholy and the vapours, that they could make the lean fat and the fat lean'.

Royal visits, including those of Charles II's wife, Catherine of Braganza, who took the waters here in an attempt to cure her infertility, made it into a very fashionable place. Catherine was a great one for popularizing things; she was actually the first to popularize tea drinking here, after the country had spent most of the 1600s drinking coffee.

The London *beau monde* took to Tunbridge Wells passionately; by the eighteenth century, it was the destination of choice for the luminaries of the London Theatre scene, people such as dramatist Colly Cibber and actor David Garrick. They were drawn here by Richard 'Beau' Nash, who was at that time the 'Master of Ceremonies' (essentially the party-master general) for the equally pretty and quack-laden city of Bath. Tunbridge Wells was, in his eyes, a colony of his kingdom in Bath, and he policed it rigorously, especially the wells and the colonnaded Pantiles area, which were strictly divided by class, with only the gentry allowed on the upper walks.

In 1909, King Edward VII granted the town the prefix 'Royal' in recognition of its long association with the royal family (Royal Leamington Spa is the only other town in England granted this honour).

Personally, sticking 'Royal' on the front of something has me racing in the opposite direction, in this case to the smaller and less feted Tonbridge, a few miles away. I've always fought for Tonbridge when I play Tunbridge; they didn't sell muddy waters to dumb royals four hundred years ago and have suffered since, but they shouldn't feel let down in the historical crime stakes. Tonbridge was the location of the largest cash theft in British history, when over £53.1 million was stolen from a Securitas depot there in February 2006. Only half the money has since been recovered.

Even more impressively, the United Kingdom's first speeding fine was handed down by the Tonbridge Petty Sessions court in 1896. The Victorian boy-racer was a Mr Walter Arnold of East Peckham, who had to cough up a one-shilling fine for doing eight miles an hour in a two-mile-an-hour zone. To give some sense of this breakneck pace, Mr Arnold was only caught when a policeman chased him on a bicycle.

So Tonbridge gets to be the poorer (although not much poorer, this is still Kent) and cooler relation; while Tunbridge shoulders the burden of being shorthand for an entire type of Englishness.

This is partly because it has been mentioned as such in many books, plays, films and television programmes, including *The Importance of being Earnest*, *A Room with a View*, and *On Her Majesty's Secret Service*. Perhaps most famous is the final, loaded line of *Lawrence of Arabia*, when Prince Faisal asks the English diplomat Dryden, played by Claude Rains, what he thinks of the new British hegemony over the Middle East. 'On the whole,' says Dryden, 'I wish I'd stayed in Tunbridge Wells.'

The sign-off 'Disgusted of Tunbridge Wells' became a running joke in *Private Eye* and other magazines, used to send up a certain kind of oversensitive, pedantic Middle Englander. The authors of those 'Why, oh why, oh why must the BBC . . .?' letters to *Points of View* which completely overestimate the importance of a minor problem and use it as evidence to back up the firm belief that England is, as ever, in rapid decline. There is now a pretty horrible website – disgustedoftunbridgewells.co.uk – which encourages people to contribute similar letters of complaint. If you want to get a feel for what kind of letters they want, here's a quote from the site: '. . . the curse of Political Correctness probably had a more detrimental effect on our lives than Brussels, New Labour, American foreign policy, immigration and terrorism combined.'

Now, this sounds like my kind of crowd.

Tunbridge Wells Assembly Hall Theatre

 1 owner of a drain-cleaning company
 1 salesman of engineering equipment
 1 unemployed hedge-fund manager

Or not.

The engineering-equipment guy was the most fun, since he sold levelling equipment and we had a long discussion about spirit levels and how difficult it was to create a more high-tech version of something that was working perfectly well, using only a bubble.

If you want to find the minimum area of the surface across any contour, use a bubble. If you want to make a child laugh, use a bubble. Bubbles are nature's little problem-solvers.

I couldn't find out how useful bubbles were in the cleaning of drains, since the man in my crowd owned the drain-cleaning company and therefore didn't do any of the drain-cleaning himself. This makes him more successful, but less useful in the search for funny. This is one of the corollaries of Dara's Second Law again. People are universally interested in jobs they know have to be done but which they couldn't imagine doing themselves. They're also interested in muck and the mysterious internal workings of their own home. This is why tradesmen often have home-owners leaning over their shoulders while they work. It's not to check on their integrity. It's because we've never seen that panel taken off the wall before. That's exciting to us soft-handed types.

What people aren't that interested in is what it's like to run a small business. So bad news for the drain-cleaning boss. More time on the shop floor for him. And next time a comic asks for the best thing he's found down a drain, start with a human arm and work up from there. A telescope, a magic amulet, pet skeletons, the other £26 million in cash from the Tonbridge Securitas robbery – all of these would have been great answers.

The hedge-fund manager would have welcomed some of that cash. It was now mid-November, and the credit crunch was in full swing, but this was the first person of the tour to give the crowd a slap in the face with it. Not that he meant to; it was an honest answer to the question 'What do you do for a living?' In some towns, the answer 'unemployed hedge-fund manager' would have received a cheer. Not in Tunbridge Wells. This was like their pit closures.

The lowest point of the night, however, was The Whale. From very early on in the gig, somebody was making a keening 'wooo' sound from the middle of the room. The first time I noticed it I presumed it was that 'Ooh – get you', slightly shocked noise that some audience members make to demonstrate loudly to the people around them that they think a joke is rude. That noise drives comics up the wall, incidentally. Actual shock will get either silence or a delayed boo. That 'ooh' noise is a fake, a loud, showy reaction that only succeeds in distracting the rest of the crowd. Rather than listen to the jokes, everyone else is going, 'Is this that shocking? It's not, is it? Why is that other person so shocked? Am I a terrible person?' and missing the next, not particularly shocking joke.

Here, it didn't even come after a risqué joke. The first 'wooo' happened after some piece of whimsy about Tonbridge and Tunbridge and just kept going, intermittently popping up and floating around the room. Under stage lights, I could only see the first three rows anyway, and it was impossible to pin down where the noise came from. 'Woooo!' while I was doing the set-up to the joke. 'Wooo!' just after the punchline. 'Woooo!' while we discussed the drain-cleaning properties of bubbles.

'Is there a whale in the room,' I eventually asked, 'or is it just me? You can all hear that, can't you? Or am I like the *Sixth Sense* for whales? Do the ghosts of dead whales in the Tunbridge area want me to settle unfinished business for them?'

After the laughter died down, the 'wooo' noise happened again, and the audience roared.

'Oh, so it isn't just me. So it's a living whale. So . . . who brought Shamu to the gig?'

And we had a great old time discussing how a whale would settle into Tunbridge Wells, whether Tonbridge would then get a whale of their own and how much whale material I could do in the second half. It was a proper piece of off-the-cuff silliness, a fast-evolving private joke between me and Tunbridge Wells, and it got me to the interval in great form.

During the break, Damon knocked on the dressing-room door.

'That went well, didn't it?' I grinned.

'Yeah, well we've just had someone knock on the stage door,' he said sheepishly, 'and they've asked if you could stop picking on the mentally handicapped guy.'

All I remember from the second half was completely ignoring all the noises from the crowd, which was confusing to most of the audience, who didn't know what I did now, and too little too late for the portion of the crowd who had known all along and probably presumed I had too and so thought I was a heartless prick. The show, and the tour, whimpered to an end. If there were any neat conclusions to be drawn, I couldn't think straight to see them, other than not choosing yet another affluent-southern-suburb gig at which to finish the tour.

At the stage door, there were two young lads who had driven over from Bishop's Stortford, almost the opposite side of London, to see the show. I stood chatting as long as I possibly could so that they could at least say, 'Well, he was chatty afterwards. He may have only looked interested in the show when he could use it to pick on a mentally handicapped guy, but he was very friendly afterwards.'

I waved them off and then Damon drove me home.

Dublin Vicar Street (the previous weekend)

1 mobile-phone salesman (I think)
2 people in IT (probably)
3 other people in finance (possibly)
Basically it was a standard night in Dublin apart from . . .
Sean, who played semi-professional football for local
    club Shelbourne

I'd already had the perfect ending to a show; I shouldn't be selfish. Even while the tour was criss-crossing Britain, I was making guerrilla trips over to Dublin, playing my favourite room and picking up extra gigs along the way. Eventually we reached thirty-four shows in the Irish capital, the last of which, a few days before that night in Tunbridge Wells, is the one worth sharing.

Sean was the first person I spoke to, sitting front and centre. He was nineteen, and rightly proud that, amongst the usual collection of smart professionals with suited jobs in banking and telecommunications, he was kicking a ball for a living:

'Are you good at it?' I said.

'Yeah,' he said, but nicely, not brashly.

'If we got you a ball, could you do keepy-uppys all through the finale?'

'Yeah, of course.' He was even more eager about that suggestion.

The show continued, with me making the odd reference to the ball-juggling we'd all be enjoying later: 'Get yourself warmed up there, Sean, we don't want you tearing any hamstrings later,' that sort of thing.

I thought it was a nicely silly joke and hadn't given it any serious consideration until the head bouncer came into the dressing room during the interval.

'Listen, Dara,' he explained. 'We've been looking everywhere for this football.'

'You're kidding me.'

'No, no. It's just very difficult to find anywhere that's open on a Sunday night.'

'Jesus, don't worry about it, it was just a bit of messing around.'

'Well, one of the lads has gone into the flats behind the theatre and is knocking on doors. If we get anything, we can let you know before the encore.'

Now I was getting giddy. If that was the effort being put in, then I should set this up.

'If you get a ball,' I said, 'leave it just behind the curtain.'

I went out for the second half.

'Sorry, Sean, I know you probably thought we were kidding about, but we've scoured the city looking for a ball. It's a Sunday night, though, and there isn't one to be found. No encore appearance tonight.'

Sean seemed a little disappointed, but the audience had clearly just presumed that I was joking the whole time and didn't seem too surprised. We settled into the second half, and I was able to enjoy it, in that demob-happy way you often get on a last night, telling the stories for the final time. I was also able to share the accumulation of all the great audience stories I'd heard throughout the tour: the Solero man in Oxford, the telly psychic getting her comeuppance in Belfast, the Rolls-Royce worker firing chickens into an engine in Bridlington; all these stories, all the way back to the first crime story about the meat cleaver and the carving knife in Warwick University Arts Centre eight months earlier. The show had grown richer and heavier with all this extra material, and tonight I shared it all with the last Dublin crowd. We must have been there for at least an extra half-hour before I wrapped it up with a 'Thank you very much and good night!'

Now, they know I'm coming back for an encore. Everyone comes back for an encore. Comedy crowds won't hang around waiting as long as rock crowds, though, so you usually walk off, disappear behind the curtain, turn on your heel and walk straight out again. It's such a ludicrous ritual that I had taken, by the end of the tour, to not even walking back to the curtain. 'You know what I'm going to do now?' I'd declare to the crowd.

'I'm going to say a big goodbye and then walk all the way to behind that curtain, count to two and then come out again. What do you say we just pretend I've done that, and I'll stay and stop wasting your time.'

On this last night in Dublin, however, I made the walk back, wishing, wishing all the way back. Please let it be there, please let it be there. I was like a child on Christmas morning. And when I got behind the curtain, there it was. Sitting behind the drapes, blue and black, a child's football. Not some regulation ball like a nineteen-year-old semi-professional athlete would be used to, but that soft football you'd give a six-year-old so he wouldn't hurt his toes kicking it on the beach. I hardly had time to wonder what the bouncers had said to some parent on a Sunday night to get their child's ball off them.

I turned around and walked out again, the ball under my arm. When they saw it, the audience roared. Sean was up out of his chair. I walked out slowly and held the ball aloft.

'We have a ball.'

Sean had to be physically restrained from vaulting on to the stage.

'Relax, champ, not just yet.'

I did the usual encore material, which all felt different because I had a football under my arm. I thanked the IT people we'd spoken to, got them a round of applause. I thanked the banking and finance and mobile-telephony people, got them some applause as well. I particularly thanked the venue staff and the bouncers, and told the crowd how we'd got the ball, so they got a massive round of applause. And then I leaned over to Sean.

'You're on.'

Sean was up on the stage in a leap.

'This is the plan,' I announced. 'Sean here will juggle the ball as I make my run from the back of the stage. As I get to the front, Sean will lob it over to me, I catch it with my right, it goes flying into the crowd, huge ovation, we all go home. Right?'

Sean nods.

I walk to the back of the stage.

'Now, don't fuck this up, Sean, we only get one shot to make this work.'

Sean is already playing keepy-uppys and paying me no attention.

'All right, here goes.'

I start to run in slow-mo towards the front of the stage.

Sean is juggling the ball smoothly. As I approach the lip of the stage, I go, 'Seeeaaaannn'. He lifts the ball over to me. But the ball is light; it's going too far and too high. It crosses my chest and begins to drop on to my left side. I have to shift my weight on to my right leg, correct my stance and spin myself round. I connect with the left leg, solidly, but instead of shooting out into the crowd, the ball goes straight up, high into the lighting gantry, where it disappears from sight. Now, a thousand people are staring at the ceiling, as above them the ball must be pinballing around the fittings and scaffold.

We all wait for the reappearance of the ball. There is enough time for me to wonder what we'll do if it gets wedged or trapped and we never see it again. Not just what we'll say to the crowd; but what we'll say to the six-year-old whose ball it is.

An age passes when, suddenly, above row three, the ball emerges. It drops at a stately pace and a woman rises from her chair to meet it and catches it with both hands above her head.

The room erupts again.

A million funny lines jostle in my head, but this isn't the time for any of them. This is a moment that should be left to speak for itself; if you broke this with a gag you'd ruin it.

The woman throws the ball to me.

'Give her a round of applause.' They do.

And, turning to my accomplice. 'And give it up for Sean.' Massive applause.

And as Sean steps off the stage, 'And one last time' – holding it aloft – 'the ball!' A massive explosion of noise.

Then quietly, and finally, 'I've been Dara O Briain. Thank you and good night.'

And I bow and walk off to the best ovation of the tour.

Because sometimes it doesn't matter how great your material is. Sometimes all the time in the world spent honing routines and shaping one-liners and fashioning gags – it doesn't matter. Sometimes they just want to see a man kick a child's ball in the air.

And if that doesn't make any sense to you – well, you had to be there.

Chapter 20:
In Summation

If you've got this far, one thing should have shone through, other than the excellence of the theatres in England and that you should go and see Ken Dodd live sometime.

It's that all these discussions about national character, all the generalizations, the aspirational lists and the averaging out to define the English Everyman; all this is a lot less instructive, and a lot less funny, than just talking to individuals and hearing what stories they have to tell. The entire national-characteristics 'industry' and, with it, the army of columnists, opinion writers and professional nostalgia-peddlers who are their fellow travellers, are missing the point. What is interesting to us is not the similarity, but the difference. It's the unexpected and diverse that piques our interest, much more so than having our own lives reflected back on to us.

If there is such a thing as national characteristics, certainly from where I stand, onstage with a microphone in my hand, it's really only a collection of shared cultural reference points. Let me use that Tayto story to explain. Apologies to the Irish, who have probably heard me tell it a million times. And please don't pay any attention to the word '(Beat)' that crops up a few times. I'll explain why it's there later. So here's the story. And it's all true, by the way:

A number of years ago, I was doing the after-dinner speech at the Irish Grocers Association Christmas dinner. It was a room filled with representatives from all the major brands. There was a Denny's table. A Kilmeaden table. A Yoplait table. (Beat)

I know, I know. Get me and my sexy celebrity life.

Anyway, I did the speech and was mingling with the crowd when a man pushed through to me and introduced himself as Mick, from Tayto crisps. (Beat)

'Hello, Mick,' say I.

'Hello, Dara,' says Mick. 'I hear you're living in London now.'

'I am, Mick,' says I, 'I've been living in London a couple of years now.'

And Mick leans in and says, 'You must miss the Tayto something terrible.' (Beat)

And I looked at his little face and didn't want to disappoint him, so I said, 'Oh, I do, Mick, I do. More than my family. More than my friends. More than the summer sunshine on the Wicklow Mountains ...' (trails off in reverie)

Mick looks at me, and just says, 'Wait there.'

And then he runs out of the hotel ballroom, out through the hotel lobby, into the hotel car park, opens the boot of his car and takes something out, runs back through the hotel car park, runs through the hotel lobby, works his way through the hotel ballroom until he finds me again; and then presents me with a box of forty-eight packets of Tayto cheese and onion crisps. (Beat)

Now, what I may have forgotten to mention was that this was a black-tie event. I was standing in a tux, trying to look like something out of *Ocean's Eleven*, and now I had a giant box of crisps under my arm.

It's difficult to carry off suave, to look all James Bond,

when you're carrying four dozen packets of cheese and onion.

I had to weave my way out of that room, past all the tables, the Denny table, the HB table, the Pat the Baker table (beat) knowing that, as I walked out, the box of crisps under my arm, they were all looking at me going, 'Look at the fat bastard. Had to get a box of crisps for himself. Probably wouldn't have even done the gig if there weren't some crisps for him at the end. They probably had to lure him on to the stage with a trail of Kimberley (beat) and Mikado (beat) . . . C'mon, you fat prick, get up here, there'll be crisps afterwards . . .'

Let's take a quick break from the story.

As you might have guessed, the word '(beat)' indicates where I had to take a pause, but specifically where I had to take a pause because of the audience laughing when I told the story in Ireland, but not in England. Where I've written '(beat)' are the points where an English crowd just didn't recognize that there was a laugh meant to be there. As you can also see, it's usually after an iconic Irish brand name. They aren't ancient old brand names, like some sort of fake nostalgia thing (hey, does everyone remember Spangles?!). They are all current Irish grocery products, whose place in the firmament anyone would recognize.

In England, you can replace them with Walkers and Walls and whatever, and it'll still work.

However, there is no substitution for the line: 'You must miss the Tayto something terrible.'

This line dies in England, kills in Ireland. In Ireland, it has them roaring. And to understand why, you'd have to know about generations of emigration, and Irish communities all over the world, and care packages being sent from home and people smuggling rashers and crisps through US customs when they go to visit their brother in New York. And it isn't enough for me just to tell you that. You have to get that as fast as the joke is being told, and with me that's pretty fast. You just have to know that. You just have to be Irish.

And without getting that line, the story is just about some man in a tux looking embarrassed with a box of crisps under his arm. Which is fine, but as the man from *The Times* correctly pointed out, it's not finale material.

I'll give you the ending of the story now, as only ever told to the Irish:

… But that's not what they were thinking.

As I walked out of that room, the box of Tayto under my arm, past the Barry's Tea table, past the Odlum's Flour table, past the Chef sauce table, they all watched me go past and then, when I had gone, they turned to each other and furiously went, 'Why the fuck didn't we think of that?'

In England this is the story of a man being embarrassed in a tux with a box of crisps. In Ireland, it's the story of the victory of Mick from Tayto over the Irish grocery industry.

(massive applause)

Take it from me, in Dublin, that's finale material. The only thing that'll top that is if you kick a football into the lighting rig.

Sometimes, that's all national identity is: a shared collection of references. I'm from here, I get that joke; you're not, so you don't.

That might explain people who get incensed by immigrant populations who don't assimilate. 'Our identity is under threat!' just means 'I don't get what they're talking about!' I have zero sympathy for anyone who bleats that their 'identity is being attacked'. You have sole responsibility for defining your identity. If you're having a crisis, the presence of a Halal butcher isn't the cause.

That cultural exclusion has certainly been behind all the bad press young people have been getting, each generation in turn, ever since the Scuttlers in Victorian times. 'This culture is alien to me,' scream the middle-aged. 'Young people are out of control!' They're not, of course. They just don't want you joining in their reindeer games. Get over it.

That inter-generational tension is a given in this country, along with the sudden loss of memory when the baton of outrage is passed on to the next batch of reformed, middle-aged good citizens.

It's as much a constant as the fact that, while Britain is a country that gets a lot done, the national debate will always be dominated by that minority of the population who are Romantic, and perennially disappointed, rather than the majority, who are Pragmatic and therefore off actually doing stuff. And that smaller group has made up its mind on certain things and will not be shifted. The NHS is a disaster, Terminal Five doesn't work, all MPs are corrupt, the Olympics will make the place a laughing stock. The BBC, the school system, public order, the multicultural experiment, country life. Everything is in terminal decline, and it doesn't matter how much contradictory evidence you present. Even if a global survey places the country in the top ten places to live worldwide, you're not having any of it.

That might be the great national trait of the English: you will not be told.

Here's a great example of this. There was a report on the *Daily Mail* website once about the health dangers of processed meat, in particular of the kind found in sausages. Researchers had found that more than a certain amount in the diet could lead to a greater risk of certain cancers. It was something like, more than two sausages a week would lead to a 5 per cent rise, I can't recall the exact figures. Now, this being the *Mail*, the headline was 'Sausages Cause Cancer', but the piece certainly had an air of authority to it, as if it had been taken from a peer-reviewed journal after an extensive piece of research. It seemed like a worthwhile piece of dietary advice.

However, underneath the piece was an online poll. It simply said, 'Do you think that sausages cause cancer?', and you could tick yes or no.

I clicked on the results. Eighty per cent had ticked No.

So, directly underneath an article, about an academic study by trained and learned professionals, giving sound evidence-based advice, the readership of the *Daily Mail* had simply disagreed.

Doctors had said sausages cause cancer. The English said no. You simply will not be told.

And I've found a nice, positive reason for this.

You pride yourselves on your sense of humour. Of course, everyone prides themselves on their national sense of humour; same as nobody writes BSOH on a personal ad. But at least you have the theatres and audiences and a massive comedy industry, live and televised, to back this claim up. So, as a country, you like jokes.

And jokes don't really work in a utopia. Jokes need to be

about incompetence, or weakness, or misfortune. A nation that likes to laugh can't really be sitting round at the same time patting itself on the back for the provision of universal healthcare, or their near-comprehensive rail system, or the imminent arrival of a global pageant like the Olympics.

That's why a nation which continues to achieve on a global level can never admit to it. You have to talk your-selves down. You have to demean your achievements. It's the only way you can keep these jokes coming.

There's nothing funny in being about fifth.

As the deadline for this book approached, it was pretty clear that I was going to be desperately late unless I sequestered myself away from family and home comforts. So I booked myself into a serviced apartment in a hotel complex in the Cotswolds. In the Cotswolds Water Park, to be specific, a series of lakes near Cirencester, which attract water skiers and canoeists and people who want to buy New England-style holiday homes on the water. This lakeside idyll is slightly tempered by the fact that these aren't 'real' lakes; they're gravel quarries, mined to build the nearby M4 motorway, but the ground water has risen to fill in the holes, followed by flora and fauna.

A perfect place to sit and write about England's contrived nostalgia for a rural idyll, then.

Each day I would rise late, ruminate, have some lunch, do some writing, make dinner, do more writing and then, by about midnight, start to go mad for some human contact. I would then walk down to the bar in the hotel lobby and have a couple of pints with delegates of the National Association of Funeral Directors, who were having their annual conference in the same hotel at the same time.

There they would tell me about the hot topics in the funeral-direction industry. It was all quite topical stuff: responses to the credit crunch ('Yes, people are still dying, I know what you're saying, but these days, well ... their families now want the smaller limo ...'); attracting young staff to a traditionally family-run business; and the most sensitive way to deal with a swine flu death.

When I could have been drawing inspiration from the landscape and reflecting on my profound conclusions on the question of identity, I was rolling around in the daily minutiae of these people's lives.

There is so much more laughter in the quirky and distinct details of one person's real life than the prosaic averaging out across the whole population. It's why trading in national stereotypes gets so very dull for a comedian. It's clumsy and inaccurate and, worst of all, predictable. And it will never compare to simply turning to an individual and saying, 'You. Who are you? And what do you do?'

So that's what I'm going to start doing again. After all, I can't stay hiding in the world of books for ever. It's time for me to write a new show and start this whole journey again. It's back to the blank page and bottle of wine; back to the little clubs for the preview nights; and back to nervously try- ing out glimmers of ideas and turning them into routines.

And in some random order, it's back to the suburbs, back to the seaside resorts and back to the cities. It'll be town after town after town again, to meet the locals, exchange stories.

I will go to London and Liverpool, Hull and St Helier; to Bristol and Manchester and Yeovil and York, and, in each of them, if I'm in luck, I'll meet another ambassador for England, another happy emissary for my adopted home, and yet another tiny sliver of evidence that actually, you know, you might not be doing that badly here.

Not that you'll believe it.

Acknowledgements

Are you still reading this? Then there's every chance that you were at one of the gigs I haven't even mentioned and you're now wondering why you didn't make the cut. Let me get to that in just a moment. I have a couple of other thanks to do first. For the tour itself, enormous gratitude goes to Joe Norris, Addison Creswell and all the team at Off the Kerb in London, and to Richard Cooke and Eavan Kenny and all the team at the Lisa Richards Agency in Dublin. In particular, humble thanks to Damon, both for his excellent nanny work during the year but also for raising no objections to being included here. This was despite me reducing a year's worth of excellent company down to him buying drinks and telling me to fuck off occasionally. I haven't done him justice.

My thanks also to my editor at Penguin, Katy Follain, who had the difficult task of turning a career-long presentation style based on cursing and saying 'ehhh' a lot into actually, y'know, writing. It's surprising how much waving your arms around on stage replaces the proper use of pronouns, for example.

Thanks as well to Paul Rouse and Sean Kearns, friends of mine in Dublin, who became interested in this project when I mentioned it in a pub after a hurling match we attended and who then, being proper grown-up historians, pointed me towards lots of the most interesting stuff you've just read. They also suggested at least two of the better jokes.

As for those audience members I never got to mention, please rest assured, it was only due to a lack of space. If I had gone into details about wonderful nights in Halifax, Edinburgh, Glasgow, Castlebar, Cork, Peterborough, Bexhill-on-Sea, Derry, Southend, Hull, Reading, Bristol, Plymouth, Chatham and the Isle of Man, well, we'd be here all night. My thanks to all the people who became the heroes in each of those nights, as well as all of those whose inspired contributions are in the book. You made a year on the road pass very quickly.

to repar you technigy

your accounts?

big hole for all my receipts

no great with dates

teach your self

write the manuals for what you do?

2 cego buildin
a inventories of
around it

get a bit of
between

DARA

GE

SHO

HOS

RICHARD EVANS

former

of the
it was
e pro-
poke
where
had

ome
rns
the

or
r
r

VANILLA FUDGE

Bridlington